RETHINKING THIRD WORLD POLITICS

RETHINKING THIRD WORLD POLITICS

edited by James Manor

LONGMAN
London and New York

LONGMAN GROUP UK LIMITED
Longman House, Burnt Mill, Harlow,
Essex CM20 2JE, England
and Associated Companies throughout the world.

Published in the United States of America
by Longman Publishing, New York

© Longman Group UK Limited 1991

First published 1991
Second impression 1992

BRITISH LIBRARY CATALOGUING IN PUBLICATION DATA
Rethinking Third World Politics.
  I. Manor, James
  320.9171

  ISBN 0-582-07459-2
  ISBN 0-582-07458-4 pbk

LIBRARY OF CONGRESS CATALOGING IN PUBLICATION DATA
Rethinking Third World Politics / edited by James Manor.
    p. cm.
  Papers presented at a conference held in Berlin, mid-1989,
sponsored by the German Foundation for International Development.
  Includes bibliographical references and index.
  ISBN 0-582-07459-2 – ISBN 0-582-07458-4
  1. Developing countries – Politics and government. I. Manor,
James. II. Deutsche Stiftung für Internationale Entwicklung.
JF 60.R45 1991   91-11336
320.9172′4 – dc20   CIP

Set in Linotron 202 10/12 Bembo

Produced by Longman Singapore Publishers (Pte) Ltd.
Printed in Singapore

Contents

Contents

Acknowledgements

The editor and contributors to this book owe an immense debt to the German Foundation for International Development, whose generous support was essential to the success of this project. The Foundation brought contributors from Asia, Africa, Latin America and Europe to the Villa Borsig in Berlin for a week in mid-1989. The facilities, hospitality and staff support in Berlin were superb. The provision of simultaneous translation facilities was particularly important since it enabled us to engage in much more detailed and sophisticated discussions than would otherwise have been possible.

The Foundation has also made it possible for us to make this book available to readers in the Third World at an affordable price. Our special thanks go to Dr Henner Papendieck, the programme officer for this project, to Mrs Christine Schultze and other members of the staff in Berlin, and to Professor Hans-R. Hemmer, Director-General of the Foundation.

We are also grateful to the Noel Buxton Trust and the British Council, which assisted in mounting a series of exploratory seminars in London involving German, French and British scholars during the year prior to the Berlin conference. The School of Oriental and African Studies, University of London, and the Institute of Development Studies, University of Sussex, also provided support for these seminars, which were jointly chaired by the editor and Donal B. Cruise O'Brien.

Thanks are also due to Mary Harper for translating the chapters by Jean-François Bayart and Achille Mbembe from the French, to Dr Christopher Harrison and Pat Root at Longman, and to Marguerite Cooke for vigilant assistance in preparing the manuscript for publication.

J.M.
Brighton, 1990

vii

Contributors

Jean-François Bayart, Centre d'Etudes et de Recherches Internationales, Fondation Nationale des Sciences Politiques, Paris

Chai-Anan Samudavanija, Faculty of Political Science, Chulalongkorn University, Bangkok

Christopher Clapham, Department of Politics and International Relations, University of Lancaster

Richard Crook, Department of Politics, University of Glasgow

Donal B. Cruise O'Brien, Department of Political Studies, School of Oriental and African Studies, University of London

Manuel Antonio Garreton, Facultad Latinamericano de Ciencias Sociales, Santiago

Geoffrey Hawthorn, Faculty of Social and Political Sciences, University of Cambridge

Sudipta Kaviraj, Centre for Political Studies, Jawaharlal Nehru University, New Delhi

James Manor, Institute of Development Studies, University of Sussex

Achille Mbembe, Department of History, Columbia University, New York

Jean-François Medard, Centre d'Etude d'Afrique Noire, Université de Bordeaux I

Eberhard Sandschneider, Arbeitsstelle Politik Chinas und Ostasiens, Universität des Saarlandes, Saarbrucken

Rudolf Wagner, Sinologisches Institut, Universität Heidelberg

For Rajni Kothari
and Benjamin I. Schwartz

Introduction

James Manor

The study of Third World politics is in disarray. This is partly the result of the success of researchers who have produced an explosion of empirical work over the last twenty-five years or so. Because so much is known in so many diverse sub-fields, the task of those who would bring coherence to the field and generate broad theoretical insights has become enormously difficult. This problem affects the field of political science generally,[1] but it is especially acute for those seeking to draw together studies of Asia, Africa and Latin America since the cultural and other complexities that arise are so daunting.

Scholarly over-achievement is not, however, the only reason for the disarray. It is more adequately explained by the severe difficulties encountered by the two paradigms or schools of thought which have dominated the study of Third World politics in recent memory.

The first of these – the 'political development' school – yielded plenty of important insights, but it tended to misperceive both present and past realities and future possibilities. It tended, for example, to create models which presumed more equilibrium and fewer contradictions in societies and polities than were actually there. Its expectations that less developed nations might converge on what Geoffrey Hawthorn here describes as 'an even, equable and eventually self-equilibrating modernity' were misplaced. It often emphasised stability at the expense of change and social justice. Many in this school made simplistic contrasts between 'tradition' and 'modernity', and tended to underestimate the diversity among Third World countries, the importance of political economy within nations and of the international economic order.

The second, 'dependency' school also taught us much that was

1

valuable, but it emphasised the importance of economic forces – especially international forces – at the expense both of politics and of the cultural and historical particularities within nations. Its preoccupation with class as an analytical category underplayed the importance of indigenous or hybrid social institutions. It was useful in analysing small countries which depended heavily on the export of one or two primary commodities, but it was less adequate at assessing larger, more complex political economies. It neither anticipated nor explained the rise of newly industrialising countries on the 'periphery' of the international economic system and the re-emergence of liberal political regimes in places like India after the Emergency and Brazil, Uruguay, Argentina and Chile in the 1980s.[2]

The decline of these two paradigms has naturally generated an appetite for a replacement.[3] An editor from a university press that profited greatly from publishing books based on one of the old paradigms recently asked me to 'telephone immediately' if I caught sight of a new paradigm. She will be disappointed by this volume. Our purpose here is not to unveil or even to seek a new paradigm. That may eventually be necessary, but we prefer to set it to one side for the time being.

Even though we draw upon elements of the old paradigms, we are reacting against them because they distorted our understanding of events in Third World polities as much as they advanced it. Both the 'political development' and 'dependency' schools approached political systems in search of structural determinants which in our view were seldom present. In their eagerness to set agendas for Third World regimes, members of the two schools were often distracted from learning what was actually happening within and around those regimes. With their teleological biases, they tended to begin their studies with the script already half-written. The old paradigms were ideologies as much as they were modes of analysis. They tended towards monopolistic claims of truth for their own world-view. We make no such claim and this means that our map of the discipline of politics looks rather different from theirs.

We are not interested here in influencing the countries that we are studying. We do not even intend these studies to advance the cause of democracy in the Third World, even though we all wish it well. We believe that that cause is best served by studies which provide the most sophisticated possible understanding of how things actually work in Third World political systems. Attempts to orient research to any partisan purpose tend to undermine that sort of understanding. We certainly do not seek to set agendas or to prescribe strategies for

Third World governments – because it is inappropriate,[4] and because attempts at prescription also impede attempts to comprehend what is taking place in these countries. Finally, we refrain from studies of public policy, not because we think that they are unimportant or misguided, but because we already face an over-abundance of difficulties in trying to answer a few basic questions.

These are as follows. What has been happening in Third World political institutions and processes in recent years? What has been happening, first in terms of political practice, and second, in the ways that people conceive of and speak about politics? And how do we find out what has been happening? If new, more satisfactory paradigms are to be devised, or – to put it in the more modest terms that we prefer – if we are to develop a better understanding of politics in Asia, Africa and Latin America, then we need clearer answers to these questions.

To address these issues, a meeting of specialists in Third World politics was organised in Berlin in 1989 – specialists from Asia, Africa, Latin America and Europe.[5] We set out to avoid the tendency in some recent studies to seek not only to analyse but also to influence the countries being studied – by, for example, setting agendas for them.[6] Our aim was and is to be provocative rather than definitive. We did not set out to say the last word on Third World politics,[7] but to generate a little renewal and coherence in a field that badly needs both. We did not seek unanimity, but we achieved much more consensus than we expected. We are in broad agreement on the inadequacies of the old paradigms, and on several other things as well.

First, we agree about the need to pay greater attention to change over time – to recent political trajectories, and often to the '*longue durée*', the longer-term historical background. It is insufficient to focus only or mainly on the condition of a political system in one brief phase. This theme is addressed most explicitly by Jean-François Bayart (in Chapter 3), but it is also evident in the concern of many contributors with the transition from the colonial era, through post-colonial consolidations to more recent events. We hear about this from Sudipta Kaviraj, Geoffrey Hawthorn, Richard Crook, Jean-François Medard, and indeed from Christopher Clapham about Ethiopia, a country that largely escaped colonial control. Those studies neither impose nor expect to discover teleological patterns in recent history. They understand what Albert O. Hirschman calls 'that peculiar open-endedness of history that is the despair of the paradigm-obsessed political scientist'.[8]

Consensus on the importance of a sense of history is perhaps not surprising, given the number of participants from Europe where the fields of history and politics intersect far more than in most North American universities. But we were well nigh astonished to discover the extent to which many of us were preoccupied with the theatrical and imaginary dimensions of politics[9] – those fictive elements which do not always remain entirely fictive and insubstantial.

A concern with these things united people studying such contrasting political systems as the People's Republic of China, Cameroon and Togo. The chapters on those cases are grouped together in Part Two of this book, which is devoted to the theatrical and the imaginary, but the theme crops up again elsewhere. (Indeed, each of the three parts of the book contains chapters that could have appeared in one of the others.) For example, Clapham's study of Ethiopia can be read as an analysis of the practical application of one particular form of the imaginary – with the revolutionary regime there using the script of the Russian Revolution in their attempt to forge a new order.

It is of course true that the cultural particularities in so many different settings vary enormously, so that the content of political theatre and imaginings varies markedly from case to case. It is apparent from the chapters by Rudolf Wagner and Achille Mbembe that the symbols and theatrical devices used by the Tiananmen protesters were not at all like the images of witchcraft and devouring used by Cameroonians when they think and speak about politics. But the importance of the theatrical and imaginary dimensions – and of political discourse more broadly, another major concern of our papers – is common to all cultural settings.

They are important in several ways, two of which should be noted. First and perhaps obviously, by analysing these dimensions, we acquire information which would not necessarily emerge from narrowly materialist or institutional studies that focused, say, on political structures or on socio-economic forces' relations with regimes. As Bayart's chapter suggests, this information can be crucial to our understanding not only of political perceptions and behaviour, but also of material forces and relations and of political institutions themselves.

The study of the theatrical and imaginary dimensions of politics can also serve another, less obvious purpose. As Hawthorn and others here indicate, the political dramas that are being enacted and the imaginings that occur in the Third World are often concerned with more than just political authority and economic development. They often entail attempts to shape, define, create or suppress civil society and popular reactions thereto. They can also entail deep, complex cultural conflicts, encounters between world-views and sets of values, struggles to inspire illusions or devotion, and to transform reality. In other words, the scope of politics in Third World settings is usually broader than in the West, and our modes of analysis must accommodate themselves to that reality more effectively than the familiar paradigms have done. Those paradigms, both liberal and Marxist, tended to obscure the highly varied conceptions in the Third World of what politics actually is, and of what it is for. Studies of the theatrical and imaginary dimensions of politics often provide telling insights here.

We were again surprised to see consensus developing round another, related idea – that in Third World societies, cultures and polities, incongruous or contradictory elements tend to coexist uneasily in disequilibrium, in curious hybrids. We refer here, in part, to the incongruities that develop between the rather empty, unreal language used by many Third World regimes – which our French colleagues call *langue de bois* (wooden language) – and the richer, more genuine language that people use (often furtively) to describe politics. But that is only part of the story. We encounter incongruities on several levels – when we study habits of mind, modes of behaviour and constellations of political and social forces. These hybrids change shape from time to time, but they seldom give way to a single enduring synthesis in the way that analysts working in both the Marxist and liberal or Weberian traditions too often expect. In other words, societies and polities seldom if ever undergo thoroughgoing transformations.

This point commanded wide agreement among us. It initially arose in discussions among Africa and Asia specialists in our group, but no sooner had they agreed among themselves that this was a feature of their regions but not of Latin America, than a Chilean participant protested that his region should not be excluded. This theme is most clearly set out here in the chapter by Chai-Anan Samudavanija, but it has echoes throughout much of this book. We see it, for example, in Medard's analysis of the coexistence within the same institution of the logic of bureaucratic efficiency and the logic of patrimonialism – an uneasy, incongruous mixture of elements which has not been resolved in a tidy synthesis.

Incongruous hybrids also crop up in Bayart's chapter – in his references to the diverse array of repertoires (imported and indigenous) available to African politicians – but he carries us well beyond a mere discussion of these. The second half of his chapter challenges us to undertake the excruciatingly difficult task of linking 'the collective work of the production of the state to the subjective interiority' of both leaders and ordinary folk. He invites us, that is, to integrate studies of material forces and processes – such as the ways in which structures of power and inequality are reconstituted over time – with studies of individual and collective perceptions and cultural proclivities. And he asks us, as we do so, to avoid cultural and materialist determinisms, and to be sensitive to the problems of cultural and political historicity. What he proposes is risky and hugely adventurous, but it excited widespread enthusiasm among us.

Finally, we agreed both that politics must not be underestimated, and that it is essential to study it in an interdisciplinary context. There was widespread concern that the field of Third World politics had been hijacked by economists, sociologists and lawyers – the identity of the main hijackers varies according to the countries that we come from and the countries that we study – and that we needed to reassert the importance of politics. Such reassertions occur repeatedly in this volume, perhaps most vividly in Richard Crook's chapter where he argues that the differences in economic performance between Côte d'Ivoire and Ghana are largely explained by variations in state capacity.

We nevertheless recognise that political institutions should not be studied in isolation, that politics is best understood in the round, with an eye to the complex and problematic relations between those institutions and 'the human realities which they supposedly condition and constrain'.[10] Hence the focus, especially in the final part of this book, on state–society relations and (to a lesser degree) political economy.

There is a common tendency implicit in this set of shared concerns – concerns with change over time, the theatrical and imaginary dimensions of politics, the uneasy coexistence of incongruous elements, the need to integrate analyses of material forces with studies of discourse, perceptions and imaginings, and the need for interdisciplinary work. All of these things drive us in the same direction – towards thick description and away from parsimonious models. And yet we are also concerned with the need to look beyond the distinctive details of any single case study, as our preoccupation (evident in many papers) with comparative analysis indicates.

We have two suggestions for resolving the tension between the need for thick description and the need to compare and, where possible, to generalise. First, more complex analytical models are required if we are to make sense of the daunting complexities of that we encounter in Third World polities. This point is echoed, at least implicitly, throughout this book, but Chai-Anan provides the most forthright statement on the issue. He criticises the tendency to conceive of Third World politics in terms of dichotomies, to think in binary terms of just two sets of categories. Examples of this include the juxtaposition of 'modern' and 'traditional' forces, or of 'democratic' and 'non-democratic' political systems. Studies of the relationship between economic and political development also betray this tendency.

Politics in less developed countries is more complicated than that. To come to terms with the complications, Chai-Anan proposes that we use at least three variables, that we think in terms of a three-dimensional state. He fixes upon politicians' preoccupations with three things: security, development and participation. The resulting analytical model is considerably more complex and flexible than those based on dyads. He then uses the model to remind us that most Third World leaders are usually more concerned with security – their own political and personal security, and that of their regimes – than with economic development or participation. This hugely important point is often underplayed or ignored altogether.

Second, and even more crucially, we need to adopt a more detached, eclectic attitude towards paradigms, all paradigms. (Note the distinction between paradigms and models. There are similarities between them, but a paradigm offers a way of looking at reality, at the world which is all-embracing. A model is something more modest and selective – it is a simplified representation of a specific slice of reality which seeks to identify key variables. The Indian Finance Ministry's model of the Indian economy is an example. It is an ideal type which is meant to be tested empirically for its predictive power, on the assumption that it will not necessarily be entirely successful.) A good start in achieving this change of attitude towards paradigms can be made simply by initiating our inquiries in a new way. When we set out to analyse a particular country's politics, instead of imposing the framework of any one paradigm upon it, we can ask ourselves open-ended questions about the country in question.

Hawthorn offers one useful set of such questions in his chapter (and there are of course others). He suggests that we focus on two problems which have been shared by all Third World nations, including the newly industrialising countries. These are first, their need 'rather quickly to construct themselves politically', and second, the need 'to increase their national income'. In much – perhaps most – of the Third World, these two problems are made especially troublesome by the fact that civil societies have not been established. That means that the creation of civil society is yet another 'task for politics, not a precondition of it' – though as Crook, Medard and others here show, the state sometimes seeks to prevent the emergence of civil society. Hawthorn's questions carry us into a wide-ranging analysis in which no single paradigm is likely to suffice. At their best, studies anchored in the old paradigms got close to success in this kind of analysis, but they fell short far more often.

In appealing for a more detached attitude towards paradigms, we are not implying that we regard them as useless in the study of Third World politics or in the social sciences more generally. On the contrary, they are not only helpful but also essential; however, they often prove to be inadequate for the complex tasks that confront us. We do not want that inadequacy to restrain scholars from tackling these complex tasks. And, above all, we are concerned that scholars do not allow themselves to become the prisoners of paradigms. If we cleave too closely to one or another paradigm – and it matters little which one – it tends to impede us more than it helps us. We are arguing for a more sceptical attitude towards paradigms, which should play a more modest role in analyses of Third World politics. We are appealing for what Hirschman calls a different 'cognitive style'.

One aspect of this new attitude merits special attention. If we pay a little more attention to history – to recent political trajectories and to longer-term patterns of change – it conditions us to make, in Hirschman's words, 'a little more allowance for the unexpected'.[11] We cannot help noticing the frequency with which studies that rely heavily on a single approach are overtaken by events. In a recent paper on China, Benjamin Schwartz recalls how the totalitarian model which once loomed large in the literature on that country was undermined first by the hundred flowers experiment (1956–7) and then, more decisively, by the radical changes in economic policy after 1978. That latter change impelled scholars towards the 'political development' paradigm which did not suffer from the emphasis on stasis that marked the totalitarian model. But some people seized so firmly upon the new paradigm that they took to arguing – teleologi-cally once again – that modernisation and rational development in China were 'irreversible'. Soon enough, however, this view also appeared dated when the initial economic boom in China stalled in the mid-1980s and, more vividly, when party leaders returned to their coercive ways at and after Tiananmen.

Schwartz's point – which is also ours – is that it makes more sense to treat any mode of analysis as an ideal type which can help us to understand limited periods in a nation's history, or certain aspects of patterns of change, but which has limitations.[12] We should be suspicious of paradigms' claims to possess predictive power, lest we be surprised by unexpected turns of events. We should also be wary of paradigms' tendencies to favour particular outcomes, lest we be drawn into wishful thinking.[13] We should be as interested in how individual cases depart from ideal types, and therefore betray important particularities about such cases, as in their conformity to them. We need to be more eclectic, more willing to borrow from various paradigms and to trust our own empirical investigations.

This means not only that students of Third World politics are still 'waiting for a text' (to use Hawthorn's phrase, which he deploys in an appropriately ironic sense) that will unlock the mysteries of these polities, but also that no single text or paradigm is likely to suffice. If we proceed on that expectation, we shall find it easier to assign paradigms the comparatively modest role which they deserve, as aids to understanding whose limitations bear watching. We shall not be restrained from seeking out the particularities, complexities and incongruities of individual cases. We shall be able to engage in the thick description which is essential to an understanding of these systems, and yet by using various familiar approaches, we shall learn things and be comprehensible to scholars who study other cases. As Schwartz puts it, in our search for an analytical framework, we should think in terms of 'an unfolding and unresolved drama rather than of all-encompassing . . . "deep theories" with their claims to provide totalistic, predictive knowledge'.[14] This means, of course, that we shall have to live with a little less certitude than we are used to, but we shall be better able to understand.

NOTES

1. J. Manor, 'Where Now for American Political Science?', *Times Higher Education Supplement* (29 April 1983).
2. On the decline of these paradigms, see for example T. Smith, 'Requiem or New Agenda for Third World Studies', *World Politics* (July 1985).
3. The failure of one school of thought to generate a replacement should be noted. Some economists looked to the neo-liberal paradigm for the study of economic systems, which gained influence just as the 'political development' and 'dependency' schools were encountering difficulties.

(See the work of economists such as Anne O. Krueger, Bela Balassa, Deepak Lal and P. T. Bauer.) But analysts of Third World politics have shown scarcely a flicker of interest in this body of ideas. This is partly because the neo-liberal economists, like the earlier and more optimistic generation of development economists against whom they are reacting, lack a theory of the state. See for example H. Shapiro and L. Taylor, 'The State and Industrial Strategy', *World Development* (1990) pp. 861–78. Indeed, the neo-liberals either dismiss politics as a topic worthy of serious discussion, or they offer an exceedingly simplistic view of it. See J. Manor, 'Politics and the Neo-Liberals', in C. Colclough and J. Manor (eds) *Imperfect Markets or Imperfect States?* (Oxford, 1991). That latter paper also assesses the work of the as yet small number of political scientists using the 'rational choice' approach in the study of Third World politics. We should not associate them too closely with the neo-liberal economists.

4. Albert O. Hirschman suggests a link between the appetite for paradigms and this penchant for agenda-setting. Writing of the former, he says that 'in so far as the social sciences in the United States are concerned, an important role has no doubt been played by the desperate need, on the part of the hegemonic power, for short-cuts to the understanding of multifarious reality that must be coped with and controlled and therefore be understood at once'. But he adds that 'revolutionaries experience the same compulsion'. A. O. Hirschman, 'The Search for Paradigms as a Hindrance to Understanding', in his *A Bias for Hope: Essays on Development and Latin America* (New Haven, Conn., and London, 1971) p. 342.

5. Participants came from Britain, France, Germany, the Soviet Union, China, Thailand, Bangladesh, India, Cameroon, and Chile. They were drawn from a range of methodological traditions, schools of thought and sub-fields within Third World political studies. I am grateful to all of the participants for comments which have helped to shape this introduction. They were Jean-François Bayart, Chai-Anan Samudavan-ija, Christopher Clapham, Richard Crook, Donal B. Cruise O'Brien, Hartmut Elsenhans, Manuel Antonio Garreton, Geoffrey Hawthorn, Sudipta Kaviraj, Talukder Maniruzzaman, Achille Mbembe, Jean-François Medard, Henner Papendieck, Pei Min Xin, Eberhard Sand-schneider, Alexei Vasiliev and Rudolf Wagner.

6. See, for example, S. P. Huntington's 'The Goals of Development' in M. Weiner and S. P. Huntington (eds) *Understanding Political Development* (Boston, Mass., 1987) pp. 3–32.
    Some recent North American studies of politics have tended to approach the subject in something like the way that it is addressed in the present volume. But it is perhaps not accidental that the most interesting such volume was assembled by an interdisciplinary team that contained *no* political scientists. See C. Bright and S. Harding (eds) *Statemaking and Social Movements: Essays in History and Theory* (Ann Arbor, Mich., 1984).

7. We should acknowledge a certain ambivalence about two words that appear in the very title of this book: 'Third World'. One of our contributors, Jean-François Bayart, is mightily impatient with this form

of words and there are good reasons for sharing his view. The extraordinary events in Eastern Europe and the Soviet Union in 1989 and 1990 imply that there is no longer a 'Second World'. More crucially, the term 'Third World' masks enormous historical, cultural, social and political variations. Since one of our main concerns in this collections is the need to pay closer attention to these variations, we obviously do not intend this term to serve as an analytical concept. Indeed, as Sudipta Kaviraj shrewdly observes in his chapter, the term points to the absence of certain kinds of development, and it is exceedingly difficult to theorise about a negative. It is also reasonable to argue that the newly industrialising countries of East and South-east Asia – two of which, Taiwan and South Korea, are examined in Chapter 12 of this book – should no longer be considered part of the 'Third World'.

We nevertheless retain the term, mainly because it provides a convenient form of short hand, but also because the countries to which it refers still have much in common. This is most apparent here from Geoffrey Hawthorn's argument that all of these states face certain common and immensely important problems. His views on this are summarised elsewhere in the introduction.

8. Hirschman, 'The Search . . .', p. 356.
9. It is worth noting the differences between these two terms. The theatrical dimension is the result of initiatives undertaken by political actors – in or out of power – while the imaginary dimension mainly refers to the construction which is put on politics in the popular mind.

   The study of these things is hardly a recent innovation. See the comments on political theatre in W. Bagehot (R. H. S. Crossman, ed.) *The English Constitution* (Glasgow, 1963).
10. B. I. Schwartz, 'A Brief Defense of Political and Intellectual History . . . with Particular Reference to Non-Western Cultures', *Daedalus* (Winter, 1971) p. 98.
11. Hirschman, 'The Search . . .', p. 354.
12. B.I. Schwartz, 'On the New Turn in China', *Dissent* (Fall, 1989) pp. 448–54.
13. Hirschman, 'The Search . . .', pp. 352–4.
14. Schwartz, 'On the New Turn . . .', p. 454.

PART ONE

Conceptualising Third World Politics

CHAPTER ONE
The Three-Dimensional State
Chai-Anan Samudavanija

After nearly three decades of searching for general theories of political development, most Western and Western-influenced scholars still have not abandoned their preoccupation with studying the causal relationships between democracy and socio-economic development, thus maintaining the fundamental assumption that political development is essentially a two-dimensional phenomenon. This is evident, for example, in a recent major work on democracy in developing countries, where one of the editors, a prominent political scientist, wrote in his introduction to the volume:

> Generations of theory have grappled with the relationships between democracy and both the level and the process of socio-economic development. The evidence from our ten cases cannot settle the spirited theoretical controversies that remain with us. Nevertheless, some important insights do emerge. The most obvious of these is the simple static observation that democracy is not incompatible with a low level of development.[1]

This preoccupation reflects a certain poverty of ideas in Western political science. This in turn is rooted in its epistemology, which is essentially based on Aristotelian concept of politics, and rendered more permanent by the influence of the positivist behavioural scientists of the 1960s, who incorporated structural-functionalism into the study of comparative politics.

'The *polis* is by *physis*', wrote Aristotle in his *Politics*. The concept of physis implies the whole process of growth and the concept of being 'grown' as well as the beginning of growing. The whole organised political community (both the centre and periphery) is capable of growing, and can also be decaying, declining, degenerating.

15

The Aristotelian concept of 'Dynamic Nature' leads to the attempt to classify and typologise societies and political systems. Hence political development and modernisation theories, as Lucian Pye correctly observes, have generally been heuristic theories; the focus has been to spell out concepts and identify factors and processes so as better to guide empirical work. By providing preliminary bases for classification and typology-building, the theories set the stage for case-studies with comparative dimensions.[2]

This in turn has three major consequences. One is the tendency to conceive political development in terms of two general dichotomies, that is 'modern' versus 'traditional' societies, and 'democratic' versus 'non-democratic' political systems. The second is the predisposition to analyse political development in terms of *qualitative* changes in values, structures and functions of given political systems, where new values, structures and functions are seen to replace existing ones. The third is the notion that the process of qualitative change is characterised by conflict, whereby opposing forces, for example tradition and modernity, interact in a dialectical mode of thesis, anti-thesis and synthesis.

The modernisationist theorists, both the structural-functional and political cultural schools, have been similarly caught up in this 'Aristotelian trap'. Political culture theorists have been criticised as being culturally deterministic as well as psychologically reductionist. It has also been pointed out that their theory suffers from a lack of dynamism since studies of political culture have failed to deal with the dialectical forces of change. More importantly, their concept of change is inextricably linked with incrementalism and gradualism which carries the political system to its natural end, to the ideal civic culture.[3]

Studies of political culture in the past three decades have relied heavily on analyses of the political socialisation process. The problem is that the mainstream of research focuses almost exclusively on the development of children's political attitudes in stable democratic societies while adult experiences are treated as only marginally significant.

In his recent paper Gabriel Almond argued that the cultural determinism approach is a distortion of his and other theories of political culture and democracy. Political culture has never been viewed by this school as a uniform, monolithic and unchanging phenomenon, but rather as a 'plastic' phenomenon that is open to evolution and change over time. 'Political culture affects political and government structure and performance – constrains it, but surely does not determine it'.[4] This observation is confirmed by the empirical evidence from a recent comparative study of democracy in twenty-six developing countries. This study demonstrates that the political culture of a country, while it may affect the character and viability of democracy, is itself shaped by the contemporary political, economic and social structures, as well as by the historical and cultural inheritance of the past. In other words, the political culture may be as much a consequence of the political system as a cause of it.[5]

Perhaps the criticism of cultural determinism stemmed not from the charge that the political culture theory lacks dynamism but rather from its preoccupation with only one direction of change, that is along more democratic lines. While it is widely accepted that democracy is the least evil form of government, and democratic institutions are better than others that might be established, one may fail to understand the nature and dynamics of change in developing nations if 'core component' of democratic culture is rigidly used as a *single* frame of reference.

The main problem of political development theories is the tendency to conceive political development in terms of two general dichotomies; 'modern' versus 'traditional' societies, and 'democratic' versus 'non-democratic' political systems. There is also the predisposition to analyse political development in terms of qualitative change in values, structures and functions of given political systems, where new values, structures and functions are seen to replace existing ones. Any study of state elites and mass political culture in non-developing nations must first confront this epistemological issue.

In a recent study of the experience of nine states in Asia and the Pacific (China, Indonesia, Japan, Malaysia, Philippines, Singapore, South Korea, Taiwan and Thailand), it was recognised that neither the classical Marxist approach nor the liberal structural-functional theory which lay behind much of the modernisationist approach was adequate in understanding the dynamism of changes in that region. The study views the state as relatively autonomous, and focuses its attention on the relationships between the state and society in the allocation and exercise of power. Although this study veered away from conventional approaches, it still suffers from the traditional tendency to make a typology of regimes based on Aristotelian concepts modified by Dahl. Hence the nine states in Asia and the Pacific are categorised into

1 Leninist states representing essentially a monopoly of power by the state or party as master of the state

2 democratic states representing a regime in which the officers of the state are selected by society by contestation in a free environment
3 the authoritarian, semi-authoritarian and semi-democratic states representing varying degrees in between of the state's influence over society or society's influence over the state.[6]

This study has also tried to establish a paradigm of political trends based on the above-mentioned model illustrated below in Figure 1.[7]

Figure 1 Paradigm of Political Trends

Direction	Extent	Reformist	Transformationist
Liberalising		Consultation	Democratization
Conservatising		Cooptation	Authoritarianization

Although this typology has incorporated a paradigm of political trends to reduce the mechanical nature of the model, it nevertheless neglects the *arena* or policy areas in which the state and society interact. The extent to which each regime performs its tasks may be a combination of both reformist and transformationist means, and it is debatable whether a liberalising direction is pursued in *all* policy areas. In other words, while China, the Soviet Union, Vietnam, Kampuchea, and Laos have shown some liberalising trends in economic activities (the development dimension), party leaders in these countries are less keen to pursue the same approach in other policy areas (security and political participation).

The paradigm rooted in Aristotelian epistemology is inappropriate for studying Asian political systems. For in these systems the relationship between state and society is more complex and multidimensional than in Western ones. And liberal democratic values, structures and functions – if they exist at all – constitute only *one dimension of state–society relations*. Furthermore, in Asian societies, change largely involves adjustment and coexistence between opposing forces, rather than conflict playing itself out through an objective dialectical process. Or to put it another way, in Asian societies, political cultures, structures, functions and processes are mixed.

The relationship between state and society in developing nations is a three-dimensional one, namely security (*S*), development (*D*) and participation (*P*), and the resultant political processes involve interactions among these three dimensions. Here 'democracy' is not a form of political system or a type of regime *à la* Aristotle, but a dimension of state–society relations which are in flux, adjusting to or coexisting and interacting with other dimensions of the state–society relationship.

The dominance of one dimension over the others is due to four major variables related to the state: ideological domination, institutionalisation of structure, the capacity to control and utilise resources, and the adaptive capacity (or the capacity to escape the surrounding societal forces).

Hence, instead of using the Aristotelian concept of political change and development which views changes in terms of societal forces opposing and replacing one another in a progressive unilinear direction, the three-dimensional state model argues that Third World states encompass within themselves many apparently *contradictory* characteristics and structures, for example those of development and underdevelopment, democracy and authoritarianism civilian and military rule, *at the same time*. These contradictory characteristics of Third World political systems are a reflection of their economic and social structures and the different modes of production – feudal capitalist and even socialist – that coexist within Third World societies. At the political level such structures and characteristics struggle against each other, but most of the time, they also come to terms with each other and continue to coexist in uneasy harmony.

Figure 2 (p. 20) shows major characteristics of the Three-Dimensional State coexisting, interacting without any single dimension or mode being capable of completely replacing the other. The result is not a synthesis which exists in one form (democracy, authoritarianism), but an evolving admixture with three dimensions coexisting.

Because there is no single enduring synthesis, it is impossible to speak of a political *system* and *politics* as an authoritative allocation of values in society. It is also difficult to apply concepts of legitimacy and consensus in such a complex situation, as in the cases of Burma and Kampuchea, since there are not only competing 'primordial' loyalties (ethnic, cultural) but also highly complicated ideological values, operating structures, modes of operations and relationships which each group has with the public. The unsettled conflict in Kampuchea is a classic example of a situation in which the Eastonian concept of politics became analytically 'dysfunctional'.

The Three-Dimensional State model recognises a long-standing fact: that a regime, no matter what type of power distribution it has, must pursue at least three goals in order to maintain its power.

Figure 2   The Three-Dimensional State: Major Characteristics

Characteristics	Security Dimension	Participation Dimension	Development Dimension
Dominant values	Unity, stability, order, discipline, honour, valour	Equality, liberty, freedom, justice, participation	Modernity, progress, wealth, stability, continuity, efficiency
Operating structures	Military, police, para-military	Participant political institutions	Bureaucracy, public enterprises, the private sector
Modes of operations	Unified operations command, hierarchical, authoritative	Contestation, bargaining, peaceful mutual adjustment, decentralized	Synoptic, centralized planning, technocratic, managerial
Relationships with the public	Closed, mobilisation, cooptative, suppressive	Open, voluntary, participatory	Dualistic (semi-open), cooptative

It is this relatively all-encompassing legitimacy formula that forces rulers of Third World states to express concern for two other dimensions of the political system – development and participation – that have gained increasing importance during the twentieth century in the world at large, and in the last four decades in the decolonised parts of the globe in particular. The rulers' interest in these two dimensions of the political system is principally based on their recognition that they cannot achieve a degree of legitimacy in the eyes of their subjects (which would allow them to sustain themselves in power without excessive use of force) unless their preoccupation with security is tempered by their concern for the economic development of the people over whom they rule or, alternatively, their commitment to enlarge their popular base of support by providing increasing avenues for the participation of the citizenry in the political life of the country and in the choice of its rulers. Better still, if they are able simultaneously to appear committed to both developmental and participatory values, in addition to their commitment to the security of the state, their legitimacy among their countries' populations is usually greatly enhanced.

This emphasis on development and participation in addition to security and state-building immensely complicates the task of Third World leaders for, as a result, the demands upon them have increased three-fold as compared to the demands on the rulers of the early period of the absolutist state in Europe (for that is the comparable stage of development in terms of state-building that most Third World states are at today). Those European rulers could single-mindedly pursue their goal of state-building without being bothered about escalating demands for political participation and economic redistribution. While the generation of national wealth was one of their major goals as well, this was pursued for the sake of augmenting the power of the absolutist state and, therefore, was an instrument of state-building and was accompanied by a strategy for the centralisation of control over economic resources. It was not perceived by the rulers of the absolutist state as a part of a welfare ideology that was essential to their legitimacy formula.

Today the demonstration effect produced by the existence of the representative and welfare state in most parts of the industrialised world on the populations of the Third World states makes it imperative that Third World leaders swear by the values of development and participation if they are to achieve the minimum legitimacy necessary for them to carry out the work of governing their societies without the use of excessive and brutal force. The different ways in which they do this provide the variations on what can be called the SDP state, where *S* stands for security, *D* for development and *P* for participation. Theoretically these variations can range from SDP, where security is the paramount value, followed by development and participation in that order, to PDS where participation is the paramount value, followed by development and security in that order. The possible variations lying in between are, once again theoretically, SPD, DSP, DPS and PSD.

However, most post-colonial and most South-east Asian regimes are likely to assign the highest value to security among the three objectives mentioned above. But in some cases and for limited periods participation – in the case of the Philippines just after the overthrow of Marcos – can temporarily reach the top of a particular government's political agenda. Such an ordering of priorities usually does not last very long and the insecurities of post-colonial state structures as well as of their regimes soon reassert themselves to make security the prime consideration once again. This happened in the Philippines once the euphoria generated by the 'People Power' revolution had declined. This means that for all practical purposes, there are only two types of states and regimes that we need to be concerned with in our analysis: the SDP state, where development takes precedence over participation, and the SPD state, where participation takes precedence over development. In both cases security remains the foremost objective of the governments concerned.

Nevertheless, even when in normal times security is accorded pride of place in governmental agendas around the Third World, including in South-east Asia, there are two characteristics that distinguish one polity from another and one regime from the next. The first of these is the ordering of the development and participation priorities. In most Third World countries development (at least as measured by GNP) takes precedence over participation. But there are enough Third World polities – like India and, currently, the Philippines and Argentina – where this equation between development and participation is reversed and maintained for a long enough period for the analyst to conclude that they form a sub-category of Third World polities in their own right.

The second distinguished characteristic is the difference in the weightage accorded to security in relation to the other two objectives. Crudely put, this difference could vary from the order of ten to one (or more) to two to one (or less) between security and the next most important objective on the regime's agenda. This difference in the relative weightage of objectives is, in fact, of greater importance in determining the character of a state and of its leadership than the ordering of developmental and participatory priorities *vis-à-vis* each other. This conclusion emerges from the simple consideration that the development–participation relationship, however important in its own right as an analytical problem, is in the case of the overwhelming number of Third World states basically a relationship between two secondary objectives. However, the relative importance of security on the one hand, and development and participation on the other, involves the relationship between a regime's primary and secondary objectives.[8]

Each of these three objectives always influences the character and direction of the other two. It is, therefore, important to keep in mind the nature of contradictions in Third World polities and societies which are always in disequilibrium. Events tend to proceed not in a unilinear direction, but in a gyric manner. The principal object of politics, I believe, is a ceaseless effort to create an equilibrium which is at best conditional and short term in nature.

NOTES

1. L. Diamond, 'Introduction: Persistence, Erosion, Breakdown and Renewal', in L. Diamond, S. M. Lipset and J. J. Linz (eds) *Democracy in Developing Countries* (Boulder, Colo., 1988).
2. L. W. Pye, *Asian Power and Politics: The Cultural Dimensions of Authority* (Cambridge, Mass., 1985) p. 10.
3. See discussion in R. H. Chilcote, *Theories of Comparative Politics: The Search for a Paradigm* (Boulder, Colo., 1981) pp. 234–5.
4. G. Almond, 'The Study of Political Culture', unpublished paper (1987).
5. Diamond, Lipset and Linz (eds) *Democracy in Developing Countries*.
6. S. Ichimura and J. W. Morley, 'The Anomalies of the Asia-Pacific Experience', unpublished paper (November 1988) p. 44.
7. *Ibid.*, p. 45.
8. For further details on this three-dimensional model, see M. Ayoob and Chai-Anan Samudavanija (eds) *Leadership Perceptions and National Security: The South-east Asian Experience* (Singapore, 1988).

CHAPTER TWO
'Waiting for a Text?': Comparing Third World Politics[1]

Geoffrey Hawthorn

There is some doubt now about the comparative study of politics in the Third World. Neither of the two once-favoured paradigms, one insisting on an eventually self-equilibrating 'political development' in the course of what used to be called 'modernisation', the other on the disequilibrating 'dependence' of Third World politics on extra-national economic constraints, has succeeded in capturing all or even much of what we want to capture: what is distinctive about these politics, what the similarities and differences are between them, and how and why they do or do not change. The first of these two models, which came down from the eighteenth-century Scots' view of social evolution through Durkheim to North American function-alism, worked with too blandly, and as it has turned out, too optimistically liberal a *telos*. It also supposed, even if by default, that political 'development' was a largely internal matter. The second, a mixture of (also mainly North American) Marxism and Latin American populism (prompted by the thinking in the Economic Commission for Latin America) did not; indeed, it put most of its emphasis on the constraining and distorting effects of the Third World's economic dependence on the First. In its more radical extensions it also gestured at a future in one or another, perhaps even an autarkic, kind of 'socialism'; but that too has proved impractical. And no new view has replaced these two. Third World politics continue to escape our conceptual net.[2]

One reason for this is clear in what I have already said. Our sense at the beginning of the 1990s of how politics has gone in the newer nations in Africa and Asia in the past thirty or forty years, and also, of the variety and rate of change in the same period in Latin America, is more than a little disillusioned; as so often when illusions fade, it is

24

also more refined.[3] Indeed, it may now be unwise to try to see Third World politics as a single subject at all, suggesting one set of questions and open to one set of answers. Yet, as Manor remarks in his introduction to this book, most of these countries still have a sufficient number of problems in common to justify at least an attempt at what he calls 'renewal and integration' in Third World political studies, a renewal, however, which must take their particularities more seriously than many comparativists have done. I do not attempt anything so grand here as a 'renewal and integration' of the subject. But from the observation that most of these countries do have problems in common it may be possible to say something about their politics which is general and interesting and at the same time respects their idiosyncrasies and increasing variety.

TWO COMMON PROBLEMS

If we accept that many Third World nations are new and that all are *ex hypothesi* 'late developers' in Gerschenkron's sense of the term;[4] if we accept, that is to say, that most of them have had rather quickly to construct themselves politically, that they have all but recently come to the (itself modern) project of trying to increase their national income, and that in some (if not complete) contrast to the now 'developed' countries, they have almost all tried to do so deliberately, through what is loosely called 'the state'; then it is clear that they have almost all faced two common problems.

The first of these is political. Those aspiring to rule these countries have had first and fast and in unpropitious conditions to establish a claim to political authority. (This has not everywhere been necessary. It has been possible in one or two places for such people to deploy pure power and use it simply to cow their subjects and rob them. But this disposition, in the Duvaliers' Haiti, for instance, or in Ngeuma's Equatorial Guinea, has been the exception rather than the rule.)[5] To make a claim to authority, the putative leaders have had to claim an identity for the political space, the territory, over which they hoped to exercise it; to claim an identity for the subjects in that space; and to suggest a plausible connection between those subjects and themselves. The first two claims have had to be particular, to a particular set of people in a particular place; the third has had to be more general, more 'universal', a claim to acceptable rules of rule.

The only conceptual and practical possibility for making all three is now the nation. Indeed 'the democratic-constitutional state', which Habermas thinks 'emerged from the French Revolution', may be 'the only identity formation that [can] unite [the] two moments of the universal and the particular without coercion'.[6] Whatever the real or imagined inheritance of 1789 (a recognisable nationalism in fact predates it), the post–Second World War, post-imperialist world is certainly a world of nominally independent nation states. In it, political legitimacy has in every sense to be an intra- and inter-*national* legitimacy. Its defence, therefore, its ideology, has had to be a nationalism, best glossed with a claim to political authority with more general, what are now usually called 'democratic', rules.[7] The claim to a nation has usually built upon pre-existing sentiments of ethnicity and language and religion. In the modern (as in the early modern) world, such sentiments have often been activated, as Gellner and others before him have argued, by the social corrosions and dislocations of economic development; sometimes by simple oppression; in a few places, by internal and even external war. The printed word and other means of mass communication have been used on increasingly literate populations to fashion the sentiments into what Anderson calls 'imaginary communities'. Intellectuals, as Smith and Kedourie and others have written, have been among the more important agents of this. But whatever the causes, whatever the means, and whatever the agents – and in most places they have been a mixture of all of these – the impulse has self-evidently been political. That is why the resulting ideologies have been framed as nationalisms, and not as some other sort of identity.[8]

The appeal for a common national identity in the modern Third World has commonly been to a common political struggle; the argument for that identity, from a real or imagined pre-history, or failing that, from a theory; the means to the identity, a party. And each, again, has taken a particular form. The political struggle has most often been against a demeaning and exploitative external rule. This was so in Spanish America at the end of the eighteenth century and the beginning of the nineteenth, and in much of Africa and South and South-east Asia, where the rule was also alien, in the twentieth century. But it may have been and may continue to be against some more abstract but equally strongly felt force. ('Dependency' may never have been a sufficient *explanation* of any state of affairs in the Third World. But in Latin America in particular, although not only there, it has often been fiercely felt, something which while itself requiring an explanation, has been and in places continues to be consequential in politics. Consider the feelings that were aroused in the 1980s by high levels of external debt.) The argument for the common identity may have been from a real pre-history, as in Iran and Korea, or from a more imaginary one, as in Mexico and Ethiopia and parts of sub-Saharan Africa, or from a scripturally ordained *telos*, as in Israel. Where one or another kind of history has not been available, the argument has had by default to be made from theory, from a mélange of early modern European republicanisms, for instance, as it was in Venezuela, or from a nineteenth-century European positivism, as it was (in part) in Brazil, or from some hazy *négritude*, or, in historically impoverished and otherwise poorly defined places, from an imported anti-imperialist socialism – or even, as in Qaddafi's Libya (perhaps to avoid what Mao once called 'eight-legged essays on foreign models'), from some more or less elaborate 'third doctrine'. The party which has forged and often forced the identity may have been, and may continue to be, a party in a more or less recognisably late-nineteenth- and twentieth-century Western sense, as in Israel's Likud, for example, or Venezuela's Accion Democratica, or, India's Congress, or, in a more inclusive sense, in Mexico's PRI. Or it may have been a 'party' in name only, a gloss on all but naked factional claim, as in Sekou Touré's PDG in Guinea or Syngman Rhee's Liberal Party in the Republic of Korea. Or with or without the gloss of a party name, it may simply have been the military. But whatever the particularities, the political project has almost always been to define and then to occupy as much of what Fossaert has called the 'social space' as possible, and to defend that occupation with a general claim,[9] as the Gramscians might say, it has been to establish a 'hegemony'.

The second of the two problems faced by the later developers has been that of 'development' itself; it has been economic. It has been a commonplace in conventional liberal understandings of politics, especially in those understandings which led to so much misunderstanding of the Third World from the old models of 'political development', to suppose that the start of politics is separate interests and its end, the liberty to pursue them. The conventional supposition was that liberty is to be understood in what Constant called a modern rather than an ancient sense, as the independence of the individual within the community rather than the independence of the community itself; and that modern liberty and the interests which drive it depend upon free commerce. The inference has been that a modern politics, a proper politics for moderns, follows from and cannot precede an already functioning civil society.[10] Like others who argued in this way in the eighteenth century and into much of the nineteenth,

27

Constant himself was convinced that 'commerce supplies . . . needs' and 'satisfies . . . desires, without the intervention of the authorities'.[11] But whatever the truth of this for early modern Europe (and that was exaggerated), this has not been so for the late developers. As Gerschenkron saw, the later these have been in starting their development, the more they have used public power and authority to develop commerce and industry and trade and the conditions, including the financial conditions, for each. (Commerce, Constant thought, 'is an attempt to conquer, by mutual agreement, what one can no longer hope to obtain through violence'.[12] But in the Third World, commerce and industry and their conditions have themselves often been created by what can be seen as the violence of the state.)

This is why and how the two problems facing Third World countries, the political and the economic, are connected. It is also why almost all these countries display a combination of characters which has been so perplexing, at the very least paradoxical, to Western observers: the combination, as one might describe it, of an incipiently modern economy and (behind the curtain of modern constitutions) an archaic politics; the coexistence of the economics of separate interests and a politics which looks more like that of ancient liberty. (As Hirschman put it, in deliberate recollection of the language of eighteenth-century political economy, these countries have shown themselves to have passions as well as interests.)[13]

It is also why the politics of so many Third World countries have been and continue to be so unsteady. For there is an inherent tension in the two projects. One party will usually try to occupy all the social space in order to engineer some growth; indeed, in the inchoate conditions of post-colonialism, it will often have had actually first to define that space and perhaps even to populate it. It has not often (has it anywhere?) been possible to rely on pre-existing interests in pre-existing institutions in an established civil society. In order to generate growth, it will have had to direct resources to some regions, sectors or enterprises rather than others, and accordingly, to choose, exclude and inevitably disappoint. In some cases, there will have been little or no opposition to these early interventions; in others, there will have been. But as the growth in the favoured parts gets going, opposition from each quarter is likely to grow. Those who are not benefiting will become increasingly resentful of those who are; and those who are (who will themselves come to form distinct interests, between workers and employers for instance) will want more freedom from state control. It is in circumstances such as these, which have been the rule rather than the exception in Third World countries, that one notices the disposition of some states, as Bayart describes it, to 'administer society, even against itself' to fashion it 'according to the explicit, ideal canons of modernity'.[14]

This explains why the liberal paradigms, extrapolated from the imagined facts of Western experience and suggesting an even, equable and eventually self-equilibrating modernity, do not capture the facts of the present Third World; why the more statist of Marxist models, suggesting directive states with an interest merely in accumulation and investment, capture only one side of these facts. It is also why of the European theorists who are still read, perhaps only Max Weber, railing against what was in essence a pre-modern polity running a modern economy and in so doing, creating hostages to future political fortune, now makes sense for these places. But even Weber, although he did describe such a state of affairs for his own late-developing Germany and contemporary Russia, thought it both undesirable and anomalous and unlikely to last.[15] It is no wonder, as Ibrahim Idalo put it eighteen months after the death of Sekou Touré, that 'we' – that is to say, politicians in Third World countries as much as their students – 'are waiting for a text'.

THREE COMMON PRESUMPTIONS

The two problems which I have suggested that all Third World countries have had to face, one political, the other economic, and the tensions and even contradictions that arise in trying to solve them, are common to the Third World. They are what distinguishes it, politically, from the First. (They serve less clearly to distinguish it from the Second, but that is not surprising; with one or two exceptions, like Czechoslovakia, this consists of late developers too.) The problems and their consequences have been as evident, I would suggest, if not to the same degree, in Cuba as in Tanzania, in Venezuela as in Taiwan, in India as in Kenya, in China as in Chile. But as this wide and more or less randomly selected set of instances suggests, to describe them in such a way serves at best to start one off on a new analytical tack. It is not sufficient to explain why each problem has been faced in one way in one place and in another way in another. For no one place, let alone for all, analytically or prescriptively, is it a 'text'.

But it does perhaps make one thing clear. One cannot simply

extrapolate from conventional understandings of politics in the First (and perhaps also the Second) worlds to the Third. This is so for at least three reasons. In the first place, civil societies have not been established in many parts of the Third World. They have been a task for politics, not a pre-existing condition of it. (It is of course mistaken to suppose that First World politics can simply be understood as more the consequence than the cause of the societies in which they occur. But that has been supposed in most liberal and Marxist accounts.)

Second, there is not perhaps anywhere in the Third World a reasonably clear and consistent difference of the kind that many have claimed to see in the First World (if not the Second) between states and regimes. States, Cardoso has suggested, consist in those 'basic alliances', those 'basic "pacts of domination"', which exist 'among social classes or fractions of dominant classes' and 'the norms which guarantee their dominance over the subordinate strata'. They are what Marx had in mind when he described the bourgeois state as the executive committee of the bourgeoisie. Regimes, by contrast, 'are the formal rules that link the main political institutions (legislature to the executive, executive to the judiciary, and party system to them all), as well as the issue of the political nature of the ties between citizens and their rulers (democratic, oligarchic, totalitarian, or whatever)'.[16]

This is certainly an advance on the two pre-existing paradigms, on political 'modernisation' (which tended to be innocent of the state), and on what might be called 'statist Marxism' (which tended to reduce more distinctly political variation). In a few Third World countries, states have indeed outlasted the regimes which purport to direct them. (This is arguably the case, for instance, in Pakistan, and in Malaysia.) In many more, however, states have changed with regimes. (Despite what Cardoso says, this seems to me to be so in much of Latin America.) And in many, the two have been and remain all but indistinguishable. (Consider most of sub-Saharan Africa.) Moreover, and in this respect like the two pre-existing paradigms for the analysis of Third World politics, Cardoso's suggestion presumes that politics is only about political authority and economic direction. It neglects the ways in which and the extent to which – as other chapters in this book, especially those of Bayart and Cruise O'Brien, show – 'states' in newer nations and the 'politics' which the present (not least when the more ordinary affairs of state are not going well) are theatres in which wider dramas are enacted.

Cardoso's distinction, which he devised for southern Latin America in the years of authoritarianism in the later 1960s and 1970s, and the way in which he makes it, both seem more applicable, in so far as they are now applicable anywhere, to politics in the established states of the First World than to those in the Third. But the bounds of the political are themselves changing in the First World (and in the Second), and in so doing, are undermining what agreed understanding there has recently been even there. Initially, political ambitions in Europe were, one might say, 'absolute', directed not only to the day-to-day management of trade, justice and war, but also to 'ultimate' ends, to the moral and spiritual well-being of subjects. They were at least in principle devoted to developing what Pizzorno describes as 'the capacity to induce devotion, self-sacrifice, long-term commitment' and 'hopes or illusions of transforming reality'. That, for instance, was the grand project of the ancient constitutions, and of the early modern humanism which revived it; the assumption was that it was in politics that men became fully human. Politics in the modern sense, the sense that Constant had in mind when he contrasted ancient and modern liberty, was in reaction to this. It consisted in attempts to separate Church from state and to restrict the scope of state action to more minimally essential matters.[17]

But the actual size and scope of states continued to extend. And now in the West, or so Maier and Pizzorno (and others, like Habermas) suggest, but now without the Church, there is a reassertion once again of the politics of ultimate ends. As Pizzorno again says, it is true that 'the re-appropriation is more radical for those weak nations that fight to overcome their disadvantages'. It also 'meets less resistance when a weak civil society is unable to propose alternative identifications to satisfy the need for long-term certainties'. Similarly groups, classes or movements, when they are weak, need explicitly and forcefully to propose long-term ends, to overcome their weakness.[18] That is why such a politics is still more common in the Third World than in the First. But what is interesting about the First is that such a politics is now appearing there also; the lines of the political are being redrawn and in being redrawn, extended. Civil society, one might say, is intruding again, is inviting the state to do so, and is thereby once again blurring the lines between the political and the non-political, between civil societies, states and regimes. Political arguments in the West since the later 1960s have no longer only been about economic growth and distribution, the administration of justice and protection against external attack. They have also and increasingly been about the fuller qualities of life for this and succeeding generations. What students of politics since the Second World War once took as 'normal' and deployed to assess the 'developing' politics of the 'developing' nations, that is to say, our own relatively minimal politics in the twenty years or so since the mid-1940s, now seems exceptional.[19]

What is emerging from these changes is a view of politics as having to do with more than the merely economic, including the material aspects of social security, health and education; a corresponding impatience with existing presumptions about the scope of executive, legislative and even judicial power, which some now wish to see extended and which others, particularly those on the radical right, wish to see reduced (even as these people have also tried to re-moralise public life); and a reformulation of the distinction between the public and the private itself.[20] In an ironic twist on the old presumptions of 'development', the First and Second Worlds are in these respects coming to meet the Third.

If what I have said so far is correct, it is clear that any answer to the question of how, now, to think about Third World politics which presupposes what the scope of all politics is – especially if it supposes that this scope is fairly minimal; which makes a sharp distinction between states and regimes and between both of these and civil society; and which stipulates what the 'normal' functions of each and the 'normal' relations between each are – will at best be outdated and at worst get things quite wrong. In the First World and certainly in the Third (and it seems also now in the Second), all these presumptions are now in practice and so in theory open; more open, indeed, than they have been for at least fifty years. What one has to do is to return to the two common problems that I outlined at the start. For these, for the Third World, are the only two safe generalities there are.[21]

The political project in most Third World countries is in short to pursue two sets of overriding but also often mutually self-defeating ends. The politics is usually framed in a language of democratic constitutionalism which creates a set of nominally common (and indeed putatively 'universal') institutional rules with which to pursue these ends. But it also enshrines a set of political ideas and practices, more idiosyncratic and various than either the common ends or the constitutional rules, with which the ends are pursued and with which the institutions in the constitutions are actually made to work. If this is right, it follows that to grasp the politics of any particular Third World country, and thereby to make illuminating comparisons between two or more of them, is to understand how those in power in each country (and those who seek it) have formulated their ambition to increase revenues and improve production and distribution and capture the social space; how they (or their predecessors) have framed constitutions and formed institutions to realise these ends; how, imaginatively and practically, they have actually used them; and what difficulties they have met in so doing.[22]

FOUR CASES

Consider as examples from each of the three 'Southern' continents, Brazil, India, South Korea, and Zaïre.[23] Each is evidently very different, in many ways, from the others. But each, in the conventional late-twentieth-century sense, is a late developer: Brazil, one might say, from 1930 (when the federal army put Vargas's defeated Liberal Alliance into power, broke the collusion of the old oligarchs and started a new direction in economic ambition that has lasted to the present); India from 1950 (when the first Five-Year Plan was drafted); South Korea from at least 1961 (when the new Third Republic decided to implement the Five-Year Plan which had been drafted earlier that year by the brief and ill-starred Second); and Zaïre from 1965 (at the end of the civil war which had divided the country since independence in 1960). Each country has instituted nominally democratic (although in Zaïre's case, incomplete) constitutions. And each has had a 'party' or a succession of parties which have attempted to capture and command as much of the social space as possible, and where these parties have not succeeded, to make it as difficult as possible for others to do so.

Since all four countries started to 'develop' in what we may agree to be the modern sense of the term, these parties have sought power often to form and always exclusively to continue to occupy the space they thereby created.[24] The differences between the four lie in how those in power have used it in order both to manage the development and to realise their political occupation of the widening and increasingly turbulent space that development creates. As I suggested at the end of the previous section, the variations have not very surprisingly turned on what might be described as structural factors, on the different economic, social and political histories of each place; on cultural differences, on the sentiments and beliefs, including beliefs about what politics is and is for, which persist from that history; and on different degrees of political skill.

In Brazil since 1930, there has been a succession of ruling parties. It was initially Vargas's Liberal Alliance, which Vargas hardened (or was forced to harden) into the more authoritarian *Estado Novo* in 1937–45; which was interrupted by the right (including army officers who disagreed with what they read as Vargas's *peronista* inclination to the workers) in 1945–50; which was continued under another name by Vargas himself from 1950 until his suicide in 1954, and from 1955 to 1959 by Kubitschek; was interrupted again by the right for just one year; was resumed by Goulart between 1961 and 1964; was interrupted again, this time in openly military rule, in 1964–85; and has been revived, albeit precariously, once again.[25]

In India since 1947, by contrast, in South Korea since 1961, and in Zaïre since 1965, one such party has more or less endured, although in each, in a different way and to a different degree. In India, the party has been Congress, interrupted only between 1977 and 1980, and again in 1989. In South Korea, it was first the Korean Central Intelligence Agency, then (formed, financed, staffed and for several years controlled by that agency) the Democratic National Party, and after Park's assassination in 1979 and another military coup in 1980, the cynically named Democratic Justice Party (which notwithstanding yet another new constitution, on the face of it the most liberal South Korea had yet had, ruled until 1987 with a set of edicts promulgated by a state legislative council). In Zaïre, after two years in which Mobutu consolidated his personal power, it has been his more personal Popular Movement for the Revolution (MPR).

In Brazil, the difficulty for all parties has been both regional and economic, and more generally ideological. The political coup in 1930 was made against an oligarchy of prosperous coffee growers in the centre and south of the country. It was made by the federal army in the name of a centralising power which accordingly outlawed provincial militias and attempted to engineer industrialisation. (At the start, when the politics of Brazil were largely the politics of São Paulo, it was a coup made by one group of *paulistas* against another; but this time, for control of the whole country.) However, the landowners, especially in the centre and the north, have never been made completely to relinquish their power (which continues in the composition of the present post-military Senate and in the persistent difficulty since 1985 of passing any effective legislation on agrarian reform, which all except the landowners themselves agree is an obstacle to improved productivity and justice in the countryside). Moreover, the modernisers have created an increasingly large skilled and semi-skilled working class, especially in São Paulo and Rio, which they have from time to time (as in the Vargas years and again between 1961 and 1964) attempted to incorporate in a politics of 'populism' and at other times (as under the military after 1964) attempted to exclude. The result has been a social split cutting at least three ways, exacerbated by intense snobberies and even hatreds (although never hatreds so intense as those in Chile and Argentina), in which more or less democratic constitutions have been written and rewritten, in which oscillation has persisted, and in which compromise has rarely been acceptable and always fragile and short-lived. Not only have there been continuing divisions between those who aspire to rule; there has not even been agreement on the rules of rule.[26]

India is an even larger and more heterogeneous country with a very stratified society in which communal divisions were not all removed by partition in 1947. One might expect it politically to have shown some of the features of Brazil. But with the exception of the years of Emergency Rule in 1975–7, which Mrs Gandhi began by rounding up the lawyers in the capital, two years in which it did for a moment seem plausible to some to draw dark comparisons between what was being done in Delhi and Brasilia, it has not. There are at least two explanations for this, each compatible with the other. The first draws attention to the extraordinary complexity, both social and cultural, of India, to what Manor calls the 'multi-vocality' of local society (and the nature of British rule, which did little to reduce it) and to the resultant inclination, quite foreign to Brazil, South Korea or Zaïre, to compromise and stand-off. If there was not a pre-existing civil society in the modern sense, that is to say, an established division of interdependent interests in a recognisably modern economy, there were long-settled ways of life and long-established patterns of cooperation or, at least, of mutual accommodation.[27] The second explanation, which presumes the first and extends it, emphasises the political bargain that the largely urban and middle-class Congress Party made with landlords in the late 1930s and cemented at independence, in which, in return for the crucial rural vote, and notwithstanding its stated commitment to structural reforms to raise agricultural production and redress inequalities in the countryside, the party agreed not to disturb the rural status quo (including the level of agricultural taxation). The resulting collusion was precarious, since the landlords realised that they could extract a higher and higher price for the exchange; but it has been reinforced, so the argument runs, by a distinct but compatible collusion between what Bardhan has suggested are not two but three dominant interests in India, of agricultural owners, industrialists, and the public bureaucrats; a collusion against the poor and structural change.[28] Rule has from time to time been contested, but the rules of rule have been generally agreed.

If there is anything in either of these interpretations, and I believe that there is, then they can together explain what has always seemed difficult to explain, which is why 'the world's largest democracy' has managed to sustain itself as it has: how the ruling party, although never having managed to affect the reforms it said that it wanted to, has (at least until the late 1980s) remained the ruling party, how it has been able to allow a degree of negotiation, and how it has only rarely had to resort to pre-emptive political exclusions of the kind that have been so usual in the other three countries.[29]

Political exclusion, often with violence, has been the rule in South Korea. But this has not been for Brazilian reasons, or for what I will explain as Zaïrean ones; but in this respect only since the way in which it has done so is very different) more like India, one party has since 1961 managed to retain control. Its wish to do so has its origins in the Japanese defeat and surrender in 1945. The southern two-thirds of the Korean peninsula was occupied by the United States to receive that surrender and resist the Soviet Union. Some in the State Department pursued a plan for trusteeship for the whole country, by which both the United States and the Soviet Union (and in some variants of the proposal, other powers also) would supervise the government until such time as Koreans were thought able to govern themselves. But the United States military government in Seoul was at once faced with the spontaneous organisation of 'people's committees' under the general direction of a left-wing Korean People's Republic. (This republic had been encouraged by the departing Japanese in the belief that the Soviet Union would occupy the whole peninsula and, faced with such an inheritance, would be less punitive to the departing regime; the KPR was declared immediately before the Americans arrived.) The Americans, unlike their Soviet counterparts in Pyongyang, found these committees unacceptable (the reason or excuse was that, pending trusteeship, no one group could be favoured), and came in part by design and in part by default to support Koreans who opposed them from the right.[30]

The result was the not wholly intended First Republic of Korea in Seoul in 1948, a nominally democratic but in fact corrupt, conservative and indeed authoritarian regime which the Americans themselves were not displeased to see defeated in popular demonstrations in the capital in 1960. A more properly democratic experiment, the Second Republic, was soon overtaken by an army coup which had been planned before the First ended, and from this point, in 1961, one single (if intensely factionalised) party was in control. This continued the hostility to the left, but unlike the party (in effect the one man, Syngman Rhee) who had run the First, it accepted Japanese financial assistance, took advantage of the Americans' need for logistic support for Vietnam, and set about the planned economic development of the country. Unlike the factions in the Brazilian military and the civilian middle class which have been dedicated to such development there, however, this new party did not have to contend with conservative landowners. Nor did it initially have to worry, as did Brazilians, about a politically activated working class. It was able to use the fear of the Democratic People's Republic in the north (and indeed the fact that the two countries were still officially at war) to suppress any left-wing activity. And although it came under pressure in 1986 and 1987 both from its own *chaebols*, the large corporations which it had itself created, and from the United States, as well as from students to observe constitutional properties; and although it did so, subsequently dismantling much of its repressive apparatus; it was and has continued to be able to take advantage of its remarkable economic success, and in the absence of unity and a clear alternative policy in the opposition, to retain control.[31]

Despite their differences, Brazil, India and South Korea have all managed to maintain themselves as political societies. Indeed, in each, even in Brazil, the central state has extended the range and nature of its authority. This has not been so in Zaïre. One group there has indeed managed to retain power, but it has been able to do so not only by exclusion but also by effectively abandoning the pretension to establish authority and promote economic development throughout the national territory. As so often in sub-Saharan Africa, but perhaps nowhere more than in what was the Belgian Congo, the initial conditions were not favourable. From 1908 Brussels instituted a Société Générale to exploit the mineral deposits in the south, forced peasants to produce food on pain of imprisonment, and until the 1950s, ignored the wider welfare of the native population. Here and there, the Catholic Church's *mission civilisatrice* had done a little for elementary education, but at independence in 1960, there was still not one trained native doctor, engineer or lawyer. The new Congo was precipitated into independence with virtually no resources for rule, and with poorly articulated programmes of what to do with such rule, one from Lumumba's centrally inclined party, one from Kasa-vubu's more federalist one, and one, a little later, from Tshombe's claim for a separate Katanga in the south. At the end of a prolonged civil war, in part a war simply between different contenders for power, in part a war about control of the abundant deposits of copper and other minerals in the south (and a war which was exacerbated by international involvements), Mobutu, who controlled the army, took power, and has retained it ever since.

This power, however, has become increasingly personal and limited. After an avowedly 'exceptional' regime between 1965 and 1970, Mobutu did fashion a new constitution; he created a party, the MPR, which by 1974 had become as he put it 'the sole institution', 'the nation politically organised'; he made a few feeble attempts to generate a national ideology; and he instituted a few measures, in industry (which were more or less disastrous) and in agriculture (which were largely ineffective) to improve production. But the reach of his state was always at best fitful, and at the edges of the vast territory, negligible. Zaïre suffered heavily from the fall in the international price of copper, on which it had continued to rely, in 1974–5; and by the early 1980s, it had virtually ceased to exist as a macro-economic entity at all.[32] Civil society in Zaïre has increasingly disengaged from the state, to which it offers no resistance; and the regime is now largely devoted to sustaining its monopoly over the symbols of central power around the capital and in the south. Mobutu tried (how hard, is debatable) to solve the two problems presented to all new nations, and failed. He is maintained now only by the fact that many of his own actions have by now destroyed or effectively diverted internal opposition, by his enormous personal fortune (which together with what remains of Zaïre's state revenue pays for a foreign palace guard), and because it suits most international interests that for the moment at least (although changes in the politics of southern Africa may change this) he should be.

These, sketchily put, are the most obvious differences between the four countries. And they are clearly considerable. But they are all intelligible within the same frame. Those aspiring to power in each of the four have faced the two problems that I outlined at the beginning, the political problem of occupying (and often first defining) the 'social space' and of then legitimising that occupation, and the economic problem of engineering some economic development. They have all deployed the rhetoric of nationalism, although interestingly enough, given its other problems, only Brazil has been able to do so without difficulty. (Congress solved a large part of its national problem by agreeing to the partition of India in 1947 and to a redrawing of some state boundaries on linguistic lines in 1956, but some of the pre-existing divisions remain. Zaïre went to civil war between 1960 and 1965 over its integrity, and has now effectively abandoned any concerted attempt internally to sustain that integrity. The leaders of South Korea have until recently been blessed in this respect by the fact that Syngman Rhee refused to sign the armistice with the North at the end of the war in 1953, with the result that the South still remains nominally at war and has been able to justify many of its actions accordingly, even though the majority of South Koreans, even if they prefer a quiet life, aspire to reunification.)[33] Moreover, the ruling parties in all four countries (even Mobutu's) have used the apparatus of constitutional democracy to try to legitimise their actual practices, although only the Indians have continued work with the constitution with which they began.[34] In each of these ways, in what they have attempted to do, in the way in which they have each attempted to do it, and in their relative kinds and degrees of success, they are comparable.

But why, in the terms that I have set out, has their success been so varied? There are perhaps four sorts of reasons.[35] The first, as I have suggested, is 'structural'. In their attempts to effect political authority and economic development, those who have aspired to power in each country have in different ways and to different degrees been constrained or enabled by pre-existing distributions of economic and political interest: more constrained than enabled in Brazil and also Zaïre, where the disproportionate and easily realisable wealth of the south had established a separate interest; more enabled than constrained in South Korea, where civil society was suppressed under the Japanese and divided after their defeat; initially constrained in India (certainly if one takes Nehru's original ambitions for the mass of the population there) but turned, by skill and just sufficient economic growth in both industry and agriculture, to what has hitherto proved to be an advantageous coalition.

The second reason for the different kinds and degrees of success in the four countries in realising the first, more political, of the two projects I have described is economic. This is perhaps most evident in South Korea, where it is arguable that Park and Chun could not have maintained the regimes they did for so long without it. It is clear also by contrast in Zaïre, where, if there had been the kind of economic preconditions that obtained before independence in somewhere like Côte d'Ivoire (where a native planter class had established itself) and none of the distortions introduced by the disproportionate resources of the south, the ruling party might have been able more effectively to sustain its authority over the whole territory. Brazil and India, however, present a different contrast, and qualify the importance of growth. Brazil's economic success, especially in the 1950s and again, for a while, after the military coup in 1964, was considerable; yet it has done little to resolve (some might say that it has even done something to exacerbate) the persistent inability to agree about the rules of rule. India's economic growth, on the other hand, although not negligible, has been sluggish, and yet this seems not too adversely to have affected the power of the Congress Party and the propensity to compromise which has marked that power. The qualification is indeed a complex one. If growth occurs, and (as in India) does not create new interests to threaten the party which engineered it, it can sustain that party. But, as I have already said, if it does create new interests (or, as in Brazil, if it reinforces some pre-existing interests at the expense of others), it can have the opposite effect, or at least (as again in Brazil) pre-empt compromise.[36]

Third, pre-existing conceptions of what politics is and is for have themselves enabled or disabled what compromise might be possible. Brazilians of both right and left, in so far as this distinction there makes sense, have continued to deploy the old Iberian rhetoric of an absolute honour with which to justify themselves and to castigate and exclude (and at moments, although never as extensively as in Argentina or Chile, even to torture and to kill) their opponents. As recent attempts to control the state budget have made clear, they have also continued to suppose that the state in part exists to provide patronage. Together, these presumptions pre-empt any easy acceptance of a politics to serve the wider public. Koreans, although they act in an entirely different tradition, have tended to share these two presumptions. The Third and Fourth Republics were, as we in the West would see it, financially and politically corrupt, and those in opposition to the regime were more often than not regarded as traitors. Moreover, these regimes perpetuated the ancient disposition in the peninsula to an intensely factional conciliar rule, hostile to all compromise, took advantage of the equally ancient dictum that the governing council is always right and the people always wrong, and persistently resisted an extension of powers. Although there is an evident cultural difference between the two, it does not do much to explain the political differences. They lie more in the structural contrast between the two societies, in the fact that contenders for power in Brazil have always had to face entrenched opposition, whereas (with the exception of the students and for a moment in 1987, the large corporations) those in South Korea since 1948 have not.

In Zaïre, by contrast, the ruling group, effectively the ruling person, has continued to take it for granted that public office is not so much about principles and serving a public as a route to wealth for oneself and one's own. (Mobutu's personal fortune is commonly estimated to be about the same as Zaïre's national debt.) Like other African leaders (Mobutu is remarkable only in his excesses, and in the size and potential wealth of the area over which, in name, he rules), he has cared little for the general welfare of his public; his is an extreme instance of Bayart's *'politique du ventre'*.[37] Only in India was there a pre-existing conception (extended after independence to the national level) of such a politics, and of the accommodations necessary to maintain it. Only Indians (if one accepts Manor's case) came to independent rule with a conception of the point and scope of politics which more closely (although even there far from exactly) coincided with what in the West has been taken to be political 'modernity', and partly by conviction but more by necessity, have managed to sustain it.

Finally, and independently of social and economic conditions and even of political tradition (although not entirely so), there is, as in any politics, anywhere, variable political skill. As I hinted at the end of the second section, such skill becomes more rather than less important as 'development' proceeds. There is a tension, a contradiction even, not only between the two projects themselves, but also, if they succeed, in their success. If a party succeeds in capturing the social space and in generating economic development within it, it is going to create the conditions for its own opposition and even defeat. It will create a civil society, with all the various and often conflicting interests that such a society itself creates. What a Vargas managed to do in Brazil in the 1930s and even the early 1950s, therefore, or a Park in South Korea in the 1960s and early 1970s, or a Nehru in India in the 1950s, a Sarney or a Roh or a Gandhi, indeed anyone, will find difficult to continue in the 1980s and 1990s. There is in this respect a structural reason for expecting the politics of a 'developing' country to be more rather than less unstable as development proceeds.[38]

But structures, of course, at best (or at worst) constrain opportunities; they rarely determine what is made of them. Even allowing for the increasingly less favourable conditions, there were differences between the political skills of Vargas and his protégé Goulart (and also between Neves, who was elected to the presidency in 1985 but then died before he could take office, and Sarney, the elected vice-president, who succeeded him), between Nehru and his daughter, and between Mobutu and someone like Rawlings in Ghana, which to some degree explain the political difficulties that these countries have more recently experienced. Conversely, there is a considerable difference of skill between Chun, the president of South Korea in the first years of the Fifth Republic, and his successor Roh (as there has been between Alfonsín and Menem in Argentina, or between Lusinchi and Pérez in Venezuela). In South Korea in 1987 (as in Argentina or Venezuela in 1988 and 1989), it was by no means assured that the problems which had accumulated under the previous regime would so readily be addressed.

To grasp the politics of any one Third World country and thereby to make illuminating comparisons between the politics of several is to understand how those in power (and those who seek it) have framed the common ambition to capture and define the social and political space and economically to develop; how they (or their predecessors) have framed constitutions and formed institutions to realise these ends; and the ways in which, imaginatively and practically, these and other more or less institutionalised institutions have actually been used. As I said at the start of this chapter, this is much less than a 'renewal and integration' of the subject. It throws what is at best a coarse conceptual net over the matter, and will not satisfy those who are still waiting for a text. It consists simply in standing back and reflecting on what it is that almost all the leaders of almost all new nations have wished to do; taking seriously the instruments of political 'modernity', rhetorical and real, with which they have tried to do it; noticing that these instruments are much more flexible and less fixed in the 'modern' itself, in the politics of the West (and the industrial East), than they once appeared to be; and remembering that politics everywhere, and *a fortiori* in the Third World, is a matter of local invention as much as international imitation.[39] Nevertheless, although there is not and is not likely to be, in the Third World or anywhere else, any marked convergence on a common conception of what power is for and what rule consists in, to see what the two Third World projects are, and to understand the kinds of predicaments which those who try to realise them can produce, is to understand more, and to understand more on these people's own terms, than if one persists with the increasingly anachronistic abstractions of older social theories.[40]

NOTES

1. I am grateful to John Dunn, David Lehmann, James Manor, Emma Rothschild and John Thompson for comments on the first and even

vaguer version of this chapter, and for what I learnt at the conference in Berlin in 1989, at which I presented that version.

2.   The literature on political 'modernisation' or 'development', and on the various interpretations of the international political economy and its effects, is too familiar to cite again. But those who know the first will notice some similarity between my characterisation of the problems posed to all Third World countries and S. P. Huntington's in his *Political Order in Changing Societies* (New Haven, Conn., 1968). See also his 'The Change to Change: Modernization, Development and Politics', *Comparative Politics* (Jan. 1965) pp. 283–322 and 'Will More Countries Become Democratic?' *Political Science Quarterly* (July 1984) pp. 193–218. For ideological as well as analytical reasons, Huntington's analysis has been underrated. But there are at least two differences between us: I suggest that one should be more sensitive to the different conceptions of what politics consists in different places, and accordingly, less bullish in one's recommendations (which are anyway, here, no part of my concern) as to what any Third World party should try to do (see also my remark in the last clause of the chapter, and on Huntington's right-wing Leninism and its influence; also note 8). On the more recent fashion for thinking about Third World politics from a more deliberately statist point of view, which is only hinted at in Huntington's book, see the reviews by S. Krasner, 'Approaches to the State: Alternative Conceptions and Historical Dynamics', *Comparative Politics* (Jan. 1984), pp. 223–46 and T. Skocpol, 'Bringing the State Back In', in P. B. Evans, D. Reuschemeyer and T. Skocpol (eds) *Bringing the State Back In* (Cambridge, 1985) pp. 3–37.

3.   Compare A. O. Hirschman's retrospective reflections on earlier economic hopes for the Third World: 'The Rise and Decline of Development Economics', in *Essays in Trespassing: Economics to Politics and Beyond* (Cambridge, 1981) pp. 1–33.

4.   A. Gerschenkron, 'Economic Backwardness in Historical Perspective', in *Economic Backwardness in Historical Perspective* (Cambridge, Mass., 1962) pp. 5–30.

5.   On the latter, M. Liniger-Goumaz, *De la Guinée-Equatoriale Nguémiste: Eléments pour le Dossier de l'Afro-Fascisme* (Geneva, 1983).

6.   J. Habermas, F. Lawrence (trans.) *The Philosophical Discourse of Modernity: Twelve Lectures* (Cambridge, 1987) pp. 365–6.

7.   J. M. Dunn, 'We are All Democrats Today', in his *Western Political Theory in the Face of the Future* (Cambridge, 1978) p. 1.

8.   E. Gellner, *Nations and Nationalism* (Oxford, 1983); B. Anderson, *Imagined Communities: Reflections on the Origin and Spread of Nationalism* (London, 1983); A. Smith, *The Ethnic Origins of Nations* (Oxford, 1986); E. Kedourie, 'Introduction', in Kedourie (ed.) *Nationalism in Asia and Africa* (London, 1972) pp. 1–152. On early modern Europe, see J. A. Armstrong, *Nations before Nationalism* (Chapel Hill, NC, 1982) and on England, France, Germany and Russia, a forthcoming book by Liah Greenfeld (from whose conversation I have learnt much about the subject and how to think about it). An interesting variant on nationalist ideologies is that developed by the Shi'ite *ulama* for the present regime in Iran. This may at first sight seem to be more universal in its claims,

less narrowly nationalist, than others; and in its use of sacred texts with an import for all believers everywhere, it is. It has nevertheless been deployed with impressive ingenuity (Iran in the 1980s has had intellectuals in politics) to justify a particular rule for a particular place: see S. A. Arjomand, *The Turban for the Crown: The Islamic Revolution in Iran* (New York, 1988). Iranians are, however, unusual in not having a secular democratic constitution. Those supporting the Shah before 1978 had been attracted by Huntington's arguments (as had those behind Park Chung Hee in South Korea and Costa e Silva in Brazil in the late 1960s). Abrahamian reports that Iranians returning from graduate courses in politics in the United States in the first half of the 1970s used Huntington's book to legitimise the new and unequivocally authoritarian Rastakhiz Party which the Shah had founded in March 1975, and were in this respect if no other ironically at one with the ex-Tudeh Party members working with a more ordinarily (that is to say left-wing) Leninist model: E. Abrahamian, *Iran between Two Revolutions* (Princeton, NJ, 1982) p. 441.

9 R. Fossaert, *La Société: Les États* (Paris, 1981) vol. 5, p. 184, quoted by J.-F. Bayart, 'Civil Society in Africa', in P. Chabal (ed.) *Political Domination in Africa: Reflections on the Limits of Power* (Cambridge, 1986) p. 112. But the image is not only academic: in its campaign against the Brazilian military government's ARENA party in 1974, the MDB defined its strategy as 'the occupation of all available political space' – M.H. Moreira Alves, *State and Opposition in Military Brazil* (Austin, Tex., 1985) p. 144.

10. B. Constant, 'The Liberty of the Ancients Compared with that of the Moderns' [1819], in B. Fontana (ed.) *Benjamin Constant: Political Writings* (Cambridge, 1988) pp. 309–28.

11. *Ibid.*, p. 315.

12. *Ibid.*, p. 313.

13. Hirschman, 'The Rise and Decline', p. 24. As Hirschman has elsewhere explained, the widespread eighteenth-century hope, echoed by Constant at the beginning of the nineteenth, was that the destructively passionate politics of ancient liberty would be replaced by a more peaceful and prudent politics of material interest: *The Passions and the Interests: Political Arguments for Capitalism before its Triumph* (Princeton, NJ, 1977). On Adam Smith's particularly interesting and influential arguments, see I. Hont and M. Ignatieff, 'Needs and Justice in *The Wealth of Nations*: An Introductory Essay', in Hont and Ignatieff (eds) *Wealth and Virtue: The Shaping of Political Economy in the Scottish Enlightenment* (Cambridge, 1983) pp. 1–44. To the extent that those aspiring to rule in most Third World countries have had the economic ambition as well as the political, it makes sense to talk about these politics as 'the politics of development', although development, as I hope I make clear, is by no means all that these politics have been about.

14. Bayart, 'Civil Society in Africa', p. 122.

15. 'Economic Policy and the National Interest in Imperial Germany' [1985] and 'The Prospects for Liberal Democracy in Tsarist Russia' [1960], in W. G. Runciman (ed.) *Max Weber: Selections in Translation*, E. Matthews (trans.) (Cambridge, 1978) pp. 263–8, 269–84. I would not wish to

suggest that attempts to grasp the politics of Third World countries in a Marxist frame are always mistaken. Not only do some of the protagonists themselves work within such a frame, which requires one to take it seriously, but also it is compatible with the kind of analysis I suggest here – see for instance J. Dunkerley's illuminating *Power in the Isthmus: A Political History of Modern Central America* (London, 1988). My question, which I do not have the space to answer here, would be whether Marxism adds anything to such an analysis.

16. F. H. Cardoso, 'On the Characterisation of Authoritarian Regimes in Latin America', in D. Collier (ed.) *The New Authoritarianism in Latin America* (Princeton, NJ, 1979) pp. 38–40.

17. C. S. Maier, 'Introduction', A Pizzorno, 'Politics Unbound', in Maier (ed.) *Changing Boundaries of the Political: Essays on the Evolving Balance between the State and Society, Public and Private in Europe* (Cambridge, 1987) pp. 1–24, 27–62. The reassertion in the Renaissance of what was taken to be classical republicanism can in this respect be seen as a reaction. Three late instances of it in the West were Rousseau's attempt to rescue an ancient virtue in the face of the unheroic corrosions of commerce, Marx's ingenious and dramatic transference of the seat of virtue from the upper classes to the lower, and the call to militant heroism, from which neither conservatives, nor liberals, nor indeed Marx himself, were immune, in colonial conquest. One of the most vigorous and telling arguments against revived republican humanism was Adam Smith's; there is an excellent account in I. Hont and M. Ignatieff, 'Needs and Justice . . .'.

18. Pizzorno, 'Politics Unbound', p. 56. I gloss Pizzorno's account; not all the points in the paragraph are his.

19. Maier, 'Introduction', p. 21.

20. The most elaborate and extreme and impressive defence of such a view (from what may roughly be described as the left) is R. Mangabeira Unger's *Social Theory, its Situation and its Task: A Critical Introduction to 'Politics'* and *False Necessity, Anti-Necessitarian Social Theory in the Service of Radical Democracy: Part I of 'Politics'* (Cambridge, 1987). There is a collection of more and less favourable comments on this remarkable work in *Northwestern University Law Review* (1987). In this context, it is interesting that it was devised in the experience of Unger's native Brazil in the 1960s and 1970s as a programme for all three Worlds: *Social Theory*, pp. 67–79, especially p. 79. In the second volume of his *Theory of Communicative Action*, Habermas suggests that there are limits to the extent to which the 'new social movements' can reappropriate the increasingly rationalised and intrusive modern state (in the First World; he never mentions the Third); there is a clear account in S. K. White, *The Recent Work of Jürgen Habermas: Reason, Justice and Modernity* (Cambridge, 1988) pp. 90 ff.

21. But one should not simply abandon the distinction between states and regimes. For there is the fact of the language (the near 'universal' fact of the near 'universal' language) of democratic constitutionalism with which almost all modern states have attempted formally to constitute themselves. It is regimes which initiate constitutions and which work them (more or less) as they are intended to be worked. It is also regimes which

(more or less frequently) change them. But the constitutions are the constitutions of states which are (more or less sincerely) expected to continue from regime to regime and to bind them all. As my parentheses suggest, and as anyone who is familiar with Third World politics will know, the distinction is in many places observed more in principle than in practice. But the fact that constitutions, for the state, are so persistently at issue between those contending for power in Third World countries makes it clear that in this respect at least the distinction between state and regime, although clouded by actual practice, is (and not least for just this reason) important in trying to understand what political disputes in these countries are about. In this respect at least, if also, in many places, only in this respect, the distinction between state and regime is a fact of political life.

22. I put all this (here and in most of what I say in the next section) as though the understanding has to be an understanding of internal politics, but this is only to simplify. The 'dependency' theorists were right to insist that Third World nations are in the more ordinary sense of the word exceptionally dependent on the (far from completely systematic) international economic and political 'system', and that this dependence affects their opportunities and constraints and often also their ambitions. With the abandonment almost everywhere of socialism in the 1980s (only Cuba and North Korea now stand out) and the connected fact, for many Third World economies, of increasingly severe international financial constraints, this is now perhaps true of more nations than before. For a good discussion of the range and nature of external influences on national politics in a set of Third World countries, see Whitehead's essay on the international influences on the 'democratisation' of regimes in Latin America in the 1980s in G. O'Donnell, P. C. Schmitter and L. Whitehead (eds) *Transitions from Authoritarian Rule: Prospects for Democracy* (Baltimore, Md, 1986).

23. I choose Brazil, India and the Republic of Korea because I have been familiar with each for some time. I am less directly familiar with any regime in sub-Saharan Africa, but have been impressed by Bayart's 'Civil Society in Africa' and by the intrinsic fascination and comparative interest of the extraordinary case of Zaïre as described by C. Young and T. Turner, *The Rise and Decline of the Zaïrean State* (Madison, Wis., 1985), P. M. Boyle, 'A view from Zaïre', *World Politics* (Jan. 1988) pp. 269–86, and J.-C. Willame, 'Political Succession in Zaïre, or Back to Machiavelli', *Journal of Modern African Studies* (March 1988) pp. 37–49. I have excluded socialist states from my examples, because they present additional complications. But there is no reason to think that they cannot be looked at in the same way. See, for instance, and despite his disavowal of comparative analysis, Dunkerley, *Power in the Isthmus*, especially the conclusion.

24. It is incidentally interesting how important the communists' model of the 'vanguard party' has been in India, South Korea and Zaïre. The importance of the Soviet model to Nehru, and his determination to rule as directly as he could from Delhi, are well known. Less familiar, perhaps, is the all but acknowledged dependence of the political architect of the Third Republic in Korea, Jim Jong Pil, on the model of the

Democratic People's Republic in the north. Mobutu instituted a programme of 'radicalisation' after a visit to China and North Korea in 1974. It would not be true to say that at no point in the modern political history of India, South Korea or Brazil (if not of Zaïre) has there been political competition at the ballot box. There has been, intermittently, in all three, although with few exceptions (in Brazil in the elections in 1950, 1955, 1961 and 1974 – although one must remember that illiterates, about 44 per cent of the adult population in 1974, did not have the vote there, in India in the elections in 1977 and 1980, in Korea in 1960), the competitions have been in one way or another, to a greater or lesser extent, uneven and constrained.

25. The best account of the years to the later 1970s is P. Flynn, *Brazil: A Political Analysis* (London, 1978). Moreira Alves, *State and Opposition in Military Brazil*, is excellent on government and opposition during the years of military rule, 1964–85.

26. The contrast is not only with the other countries I have mentioned here. Within Latin America, it is also I think suggestively with Colombia, where in the twenty years after 1958 (more precariously since) 120 or so political families in Bogotá managed to recover political control after *la violencia* and General Rojas's short-lived attempt to create a mass movement outside all parties in what they glossed as a statesmanlike agreement nominally to divide power between the two old political parties. There is a full account in J. Hartlyn, *The Politics of Coalition Rule in Colombia* (Cambridge, 1988). The Colombians could not agree on the rules of the game. (The country has paid a price in economic development, however, and that caused one of the problems that the coalition was facing by the early 1980s. The rural infrastructure was so undeveloped that it was more profitable to refine and market cocaine hydrochloride than corn. Decent roads would perhaps have done much to keep civil society in Colombia more civil.) On how Brazilians, by contrast, have not been able to agree on the rules of rule, see the revealing political ethnography of the elite there in 1971–2 by P. McDonough, *Power and Ideology in Brazil* (Princeton, NJ, 1981). McDonough found that there was most agreement between these people on 'moral' issues (Catholicism is not politically so important in Brazil as in some parts of Spanish America), some agreement on economic policy, least on the ground rules of rule itself.

27. J. Manor, 'How and Why Liberal and Representative Politics Emerged in India', *Political Studies* (March 1990) pp. 20–38. This paragraph greatly simplifies Manor's account.

28. P. Bardhan, *The Political Economy of Development in India* (Oxford, 1984). How the deal between Congress and the landlords as it existed to the late 1960s actually worked is well described by A. Carter, *Elite Politics in Rural India: Political Stratification and Alliances in Western Maharastra* (Cambridge, 1974); the way in which it has broken down and driven Congress to resort more to overt repression is described by P. R. Brass (with particular reference to the northern state of Uttar Pradesh) in 'National Power and Local Politics in India: A Twenty-Year Perspective', *Modern Asian Studies* 18 (1984) pp. 89–118 and (with reference to the Punjab) in 'The Punjab Crisis and the Unity of India', in A. Kohli

(ed.) *India's Democracy: An Analysis of Changing State–Society Relations* (Princeton, NJ, 1988). In the south and east, a long-standing hostility to the power from the north, together with more immediate anxieties about the Hindi nationalists in the Janata coalition in 1975–80, have complicated the pattern that Carter describes, which was always more clearly prevalent in the north and west. On the differences between the north and the south, see for instance F. Frankel, 'Middle Classes and Castes in India's Politics: Prospects for Political Accommodation', in Kohli, *India's Democracy*.

29. If it had, as Manor says, its success would have been much less assured. The single best account of this dilemma in the first thirty years of Congress rule is F. R. Frankel, *India's Political Economy 1947–77: The Gradual Revolution* (Princeton, NJ, 1978).

30. The most detailed account of these years, excellent on the Koreans' politics, cruder and more contentious on the Americans' policy towards them, is B. Cumings, *The Origins of the Korean War: Liberation and the Emergence of Separate Regimes* (Princeton, NJ, 1981). American policy both in Washington and in Seoul from 1945 to 1950 is more sympathetically analysed by J. I. Matray, *The Reluctant Crusade* (Honolulu, 1985).

31. The increasing political pressure on the Fifth Republic in 1986–7 was caused by the fact that the president, Chun Doo Hwan, had committed himself to stepping down by February 1988. The only history of Korea in English that goes beyond 1960 (it runs to 1981) is A.C. Nahm, *Korea: Tradition and Transformation, A History of the Korean People* (Seoul and Elizabeth, NJ, 1988). A useful and more critical set of essays (with a brief but perceptive one by G. Henderson, who was the best writer in English on modern South Korean politics) is J. Sullivan and R. Foss (eds) *Two Koreas – One Future?* (Lanham, Md, 1987) Park's motto could well have been A. Przeworski's nice phrase: 'future legitimation requires present accumulation' – *Capitalism and Social Democracy* (Cambridge, 1985) p. 165.

32. When a delegation from the IMF eventually arrived in Kinshasa to try to salvage the economy, they could find no authoritative accounts. They had eventually to do the necessary paperwork themselves.

33. One of the many evident simplifications of this account is that the battle in Brazil (within the military itself, for instance, between 1964 and 1985) has been between self-described 'nationalist' and 'internationalists', although there is more to be said about the ways in which the internationalists have deployed their argument to seek foreign (and especially United States) support for what are their own national ends. Korea is unusual among developing nations in having a long tradition of cultural, now national, identity. The division of the country since 1945, complete by 1948, has saddened ordinary Koreans, but in both Seoul and Pyongyang has ironically enabled their rulers to make claims for legitimacy which they would otherwise have had to make, perhaps – given the pre-existing unity of the country – with more difficulty, in more orthodox ways.

34. A further and distinct but related similarity is that the parties in these four countries and in others in the Third World have had to face the fact that to make their initial claim to authority, they have had to try to

appeal to as large a number of people as possible; but that to secure it, and to prepare for power, they have had to organise themselves at the centre. This is a dilemma which faces all parties everywhere, but none so much as those on the left and those which, on the left or not, seek to occupy as much of the 'social space' as they can. (It was especially evident for the Indonesian Communist Party before 1965: see R. Mortimer, *Indonesian Communism after Sukarno: Ideology and Politics, 1959–1965* [Ithaca, NY, 1974]). It was famously raised by Michels after his experience as an Italian delegate to the German SPD and has recently been discussed by A. Panebianco, *Political Parties: Organisation and Power*, M. Silver (trans.) (Cambridge, 1988). Panebianco believes that the 'elite-professional' parties that emerge in this way from 'mass-bureaucratic' ones are inherently unstable. This instability has allowed the redefining of politics in the industrial democracies that is discussed by Maier and Pizzorno.

35. Again, I exclude external factors. Another essay would be necessary to show that where there is high debt and an at least in part weak economy, where political authority has depended on public spending, and where there has been and continues to be a fierce debate about the relative merits of a 'national' and an 'international' path to 'development' (as in Brazil), external factors will exacerbate instability; that where there is high debt but the other conditions are absent, and where there is a continuing comparative advantage in the international economy, difficulties (as in South Korea in 1979–81) will be at best temporary; and that where there is low debt, and where political authority has not depended on high levels of public spending (as in India until the mid-1980s), there will also be fewer problems. Such an essay would also have to explain how more directly political pressures (arguably weaker now on most parts of the Third World than in the 1950s and 1960s) do and do not affect the capacities of parties to sustain their internal authority. (In this respect, Zaïre is the most conspicuous case. Most commentators agree that were it not for the interest of Western powers in having a large ally immediately north of southern Africa in the 1970s and 1980s, Mobutu's regime would have long since collapsed. As Willame argues ('Political succession'), the longer this has gone on, the more difficult have Mobutu's internal opponents found it to maintain and organise themselves, thereby providing an additional, internal reason for supposing that he will be able to continue in power for some years to come.)

36. Perhaps the most dramatic recent instance of fast growth creating new interests which cannot be accommodated in the pre-existing state of affairs is that caused in Colombia by the refining and export of cocaine.

37. *L'Etat en Afrique: La Politique du Ventre* (Paris, 1989).

38. These difficulties perhaps go some way towards explaining why the more purely theatrical aspects of Third World politics have in many places become more rather than less evident as time goes by. They may be all that the less fortunate or competent rulers have left with which to maintain the appearance of rule.

39. More exactly, the political constitutions tend to be imitative, but the ways in which they are used tend not to be. It is more generally striking

to a Northern observer of Southern politics how uncurious those in the South are about each other, although not about the North.

40. Or in J. Elster's sensible distinction (*Nuts and Bolts for the Social Sciences* [Cambridge, 1989]), there may be more to be gained from looking at the 'mechanisms' which, given certain interests, operate in certain situations, than in trying to devise more general 'theories'.

CHAPTER THREE

Finishing with the Idea of the Third World: The Concept of the Political Trajectory*

Jean-François Bayart

Academic analysis of societies of the 'south' has long been divided between the conflicting theories of 'modernisation' and 'dependency'. Paradoxically these opposing schools of thought also share a common belief: that of external factors being the major influence behind political change in Africa, Latin America and Asia since the global expansion of Western imperialism. It is of little essential importance that one theory emphasises the rise of 'modernisation' to the detriment of 'tradition', whereas the other concentrates on an undifferentiated 'periphery' which is in a dependent relationship working to the advantage of the 'centre'. As the emphasis has been put upon an explanation based upon external factors, the unity and specificity of the economic and political problems faced by these three continents has been postulated. This has given rise to the invention of the fantasy of the 'Third World' and to the theory of the radical extraneity of the modern state based on the model of Western bureaucracy. This alienation is then held responsible for most of the problems associated with political underdevelopment.

Quite surprisingly, the third trend, that of historical sociology, which has been experiencing a revival since the 1960s, and focuses on the analysis of certain Asian political structures (India, China, Japan, the Ottoman Empire) without taking any account of sub-Saharan Africa and Latin America, has not broken away from the aforementioned perspective, despite expectations that it might. Take for example Perry Anderson's hesitations when he attempts to evaluate the influences of 'external dynamics' and 'internal dynamics' in the development of the absolute state in Eastern Europe and Japan. Other

---

* Translated from the French by Mary Harper.

examples are the exaggerated attention given to the 'world system' by Immanuel Wallerstein, and the assertions of Bertrand Badie and Pierre Birnbaum that the state in Africa and Asia is 'a purely imported product'.[1]

The concepts which we continue to use when attempting to analyse the so-called Third World – starting with the disastrous notion of 'development' – the debates which have dominated the last decades, and the economic policies of the Bretton Woods' multilateral institutions, show that the West remains deeply reliant upon a fantasy inherited from the colonial period, and, in all likelihood, from an even older philosophical tradition.[2]

POLITICAL 'HISTORICITY' IN AFRICA AND ASIA

During this period of 'Euromania', it is perhaps more important than ever before to abandon this theoretical provincialism, and to acknowledge the historical irreducibility, as well as the great political diversity, of the 'Third World'. The development of the international economic system since the mid-1970s – especially the recurring oil crises and the 'unleashing'of the Asian 'dragons' – has demolished the significance of the underdevelopment category by showing how these countries have many different destinies. Moreover, there are now an appreciable number of studies which put the impact of Western imperialist expansion into perspective as well as revealing the distinct historical foundations of modern states.

Perhaps the theory of extraneity mistakes the exceptions for the rule. The state in Africa, and even more so in Asia, should not be considered *a priori* as a simple product of the colonial period. Many political systems existed in these two continents before Western colonisation: particularly in China, Korea, Japan, Vietnam, Cambodia, Siam, Afghanistan, Ethiopia, Egypt, Madagascar (and many others), and also, although it is less well known, in the Maghreb states, and, in a more subtle way, in India, where the state heritage from the Moghul period is not insignificant.[3] When the colonialists effectively acted as a demiurge, such as by building Iraq, Syria and Jordan from the ruins of the Ottoman Empire, or by creating most of the sub-Saharan African states (with the exception of Lesotho, Swaziland, Rwanda and Burundi), they did not do so *ex nihilo*; and colonial creations were also subject to multiple acts of reappropriation by indigenous social groups.[4] Therefore, these states, which are reputed to be artificial, rest in reality upon their own social foundations; they neither lack 'structural roots in society', nor do they resemble 'balloons in the sky', a term which Goran Hyden employs in reference to sub-Saharan Africa.[5] The vigorous desire of indigenous populations to appropriate the whole of what Nigerians call the 'national cake' suggests that territorial boundaries are not considered to be entirely arbitrary; their unity is usually claimed, even when this leads to problems and plays a role in civil wars, such as those in Chad, Uganda and the Sudan.

It must finally be added that the state boundaries demarcated by the colonialists have continued to be a part of larger historical and geographical areas which, as if by magic, have continued to play an active role, and have resurfaced even though the European colonialists claimed to have put an end to them. In this way, the Maghreb has reclaimed the *Drang nach Suden* which was previously prevented by the French colonial administration, although Arabic and Indian networks were being established in British East Africa. In more general terms, these historical fields of intra-continental and intercontinental interaction have contributed to the distinct historicity of societies in Africa and Asia; diminishing the usefulness of the over-arching binary distinctions between East and West, and North and South. Despite forty years of revolutionary disturbances, the overseas diaspora has safeguarded continental China from being integrated into the Asian totality, to the point of having a decisive influence on its 'opening up' during the 1980s; in a similar vein, the numerous and often contradictory dynamics of Islam have given rise to a world-wide integration, which owes little to the hegemony of the northern hemisphere unless it undermines them from within.

Now that the theory of extraneity is no longer valid, the modern state in Africa and Asia needs to be analysed in light of what Fernand Braudel has called the *'longue durée'* or even the *'très longue durée'*. All too often, political analysis restricts itself, at worst to the 'short period, in terms of individuals' (David Easton's period of 'authorities'), or better, to 'the recitative of the circumstance, the cycle, the intercycle' (the period of 'regimes' or systems, always according to the Eastonian sense of the word, but also in the Brazilian sense: *o sistema*). Political analysis has therefore neglected the *longue durée* perspective, even though this was entirely avoidable: as Braudel reminds us, 'political history is not necessarily factual history, nor is it condemned to be'. Perry Anderson's concept of the historical trajectory, which insists upon the distinct historicity of the many ways in which states develop, in opposition to the weak ahistorical

53

comparativism underlying the notion of the Third World, allows modern politics to be placed in the context of these layers of slow-moving history, of 'this profundity, this semi-immobility [around which] everything gravitates'.[6]

METHODOLOGY

At this stage of the argument, certain methodological points must be clarified. First, the recourse to history (or to anthropology) should not lead to the underestimation of the role of social change and political innovations during the last century. It is certainly worthwhile to analyse the development of the state from a post-Hegelian and post-Marxist point of view – to understand that, through politics, the individual is a product of society, according to a perspective which holds the support of a fairly wide consensus today.[7] In this context, the Braudelian idea of the 'prisons of the *longue durée*' is too restrictive.[8] It would be more meaningful to speak of 'probation' – more from the morphological point of view or from that of the technology of politics, than from the perspectives of its philosophy or socio-economic basis. The serious ruptures caused by Western colonisation of Africa and Asia should not be underestimated under the pretext of avoiding the dependency 'vulgate'. For example, the introduction of modern transport systems, fire-arms and computers to sub-Saharan Africa has permitted not only a change in the size of political area, but also, more prosaically, a dramatic intensification of social control; never before have dominant groups had such effective means of surveying, constraining and dissuading subordinate groups. Therefore, the idea of the 'trajectory' means only that these undeniable ruptures, which can, in some respects, be compared from one society to another, take on their critical significance as a result of their own distinct histories.

Second, comparing these distinctive histories, under the form of trajectories, should not lead to the renunciation of all attempts of comparative analysis, as does Richard Bendix (who believes comparison shows up the radical diversity of each case) or Perry Anderson (who believes that history is a series of differentiated progressions, as unique in their origins as in their destinies).[9] The historical trajectories of politics can be analysed in terms of their heterogeneity, not so that they be submerged under a universalist label (the Third World; the question of development; the post-colonial state; authoritarianism, democracy or totalitarianism), but to establish the foundations of an interpretative analysis of contemporary forms of power, to lead to common problematisations of their genealogies, and to bring together attempts that have been made to decode them.[10]

Third, a trajectory does not have to be considered as an evolutionary or teleological concept (although Perry Anderson could not escape from this notion), nor should we assume its totality or coherence at the risk of oversimplifying the terms of comparison, as does John Armstrong when he organises his study of ethnicity and nationalism in the areas of the Mediterranean basin around the bi-polar model of the nomadic (Arab) and the sedentary (Jewish). Other examples of oversimplification are Raphael Draï's opposition of the Hebrews' invention of liberty and responsibility to the Egyptians' Pharaoic model, and Bertrand Badie's model of 'the two states', the Christian and the Muslim.[11] A political trajectory is nothing but an ideal type, whereas any given historical society is characterised by its lack of achievement and incomplete integration, by the subtle interplay of the 'Full' and the 'Empty' so dear to Chinese artists in the past.[12]

Finally, it is especially important to stress that the historical trajectory of a state does not solely follow an inherent logic, as Barrington Moore seems to believe.[13] Instead, it is situated at the intersection of 'internal dynamics' and 'external dynamics'.[14] The classical theory of the extraneity of the state in Africa and Asia (especially in the dependency model) does nothing but exaggerate a very old problem, in relation to which the particularity of the Third World is far from clear. Edmund Leach's excellent analysis of the Kachin of Burma has been widely corroborated by other examples, both Asian and African: traditional societies were also 'systems' – to such an extent that S.J. Tambiah refers to a 'galactic political arena' in reference to South and South-east Asia – and their relationships with the exterior also played a role in their genesis.[15] The development of the nation-state in Western Europe was often based on competition (the Franco-British rivalry provides an archetypal example), and this was frequently incorporated into trans-national movements which transcended the state.[16] The recognition of the distinct historicity of the modern state in Africa and Asia has been made possible by the location of the many 'external dynamics' which have contributed to its development. Rather than insisting that analysts restrict themselves to monographies of particular trajectories abandoning their international contexts, it is suggested that simplistic and univocal interpretations such as those of 'dependency' and 'modernisation' be dispensed with.

THE CONTINUITY OF 'CIVILISATIONS'

On the basis of these premises, three ways of reconstructing the historicity of the modern state in Africa and Asia in terms of the *longue durée* can be considered. Even though it is the most impressionistic and, without doubt, the most problematic from a methodological point of view, the first way is interesting, perhaps because it is based on a collaboration of the diverse disciplines which make up the social sciences. This method consists of examining the evolution of 'civilisations' defined by Fernand Braudel as 'realities of the long inexhaustible past'. The historian sets out with the hypothesis of fundamental continuity: 'civilisations survive political, social, economic, and even ideological upheavals, which they otherwise control by insidious or even powerful means'.[17] Thus the significance of the colonial or paracolonial caesura is immediately put into perspective. This caesura is substituted by the identification of the trajectory of a 'civilisation', which is made up of 'borrowings' and 'refusals' in a given historical and cultural period; and, which is of the greatest interest to the political scientist, the tracing of its development through the centuries up to the modern period. If this approach is to be realistic in practice, and if teleological traps are to be avoided (as much as they possibly can be), it has to invert itself and adopt a regressive approach; it should examine the structures of the *longue durée* which underpin present civilisations, and more particularly, forms of power and exploitation.

It is therefore proposed that the post-colonial state south of the Sahara is seen as a new incarnation of a multisecular trajectory which is characterised by – along with other features of 'civilisation' such as the oral tradition, limited development of productive forces, extensive agriculture and animal husbandry without private land ownership, and weak social and cultural polarisation – low rates of economic accumulation and political centralisation, which are based more on the control of resources gained from dependence on the exterior, than from intensive exploitation of the dominated populations.[18] Now, as before, Africa exports its factors of production in their raw state – its work-force, primary products and capital – and those who administer this unequal relationship with the international economic system obtain from it the resources of their domestic domination. A century of colonisation and decolonisation has doubtless changed the level and nature of this system. But the continuation of this system whereby contemporary political institutions gain their resources externally while under-exploiting the interior makes sense in comparison with the productivist trajectory of South-east Asia, for example. And the 'declassification' of Africa in the international scene, which has been taking place over the last few years,[19] must be related more to its historical background than to the disembodied political economy of 'development', even though there has been a change in the sub-continent's orientation such as the intensification of the social relations of production due to the pressure of the population explosion.

SCENARIOS OF INEQUALITY

The second method of apprehending the historicity of the modern state in Asia and Africa is, *nolens volens*, more Marxist than Braudelian in inspiration. It detaches itself from the structural links – Perry Anderson's 'concatenations' – whereby social inequalities are generated from one historical trajectory to another, and places the emphasis on their particularities: 'And yet, after having accentuated the fundamental parallels between European and Japanese feudalism as regards the internal articulation of their modes of production, the enormous difference between their trajectories remains to be considered', notes the historian of the absolute state.[20] This approach identifies regional or national scenarios for the construction of the state – for example scenarios of conservative modernisation, of social revolution, of the reciprocal assimilation of elites – and in this way introduces a precise mode of comparison.[21] It calls into question the classical categories upon which the ahistorical comparative method of the 1960s and 1970s such as dependency and modernisation theory are founded.

The idea that the notion of 'class society' is universally applicable does not stand up to the scrupulous examination of what Georges Balandier proposes to call the 'systems of inequality and domination' in Africa and Asia.[22] It is not that this concept totally ignores social classes (for example some outstanding works of historical sociology have established, along the lines of E. P. Thompson's pioneering works, the existence of a working class in some sub-Saharan African countries, despite their low levels of industrialisation), but that class relations are not of paramount importance for the explanation of most social relations which structure these systems of inequality and domination.[23]

The social groups involved in the invention of politics in Africa and Asia have their own historicity, which should prevent them from being assimilated too hastily into categories evolving from Western experiences of inequality, even when they do qualify for the category of 'social class'. Thus the working class in sub-Saharan Africa is run through with divisions from traditional societies, especially the cleavages between elders and juniors or between nobles and inferiors.[24] In India, the category of 'princes', originating to a significant extent from the colonial period, should not be seen as aristocratic or feudal, any more than the category of 'traditional chief' in sub-Saharan Africa should be.[25] The notion of the bourgeoisie, employed *ad nauseum* to identify the emergent dominant class in Third World countries, is also inappropriate. This is due to the absence of the 'plurisecular' experience of conflict and also of an alliance and compromise with a real feudal aristocracy, from which the bourgeoisie emerged in the West before securing its dominance.

In other words, the 'class struggle' was first based on class structure before becoming a struggle between classes.[26] To whatever degree the economies of the 'South' have experienced capitalist 'internationalisation', it cannot be presupposed that the emerging systems of inequality and domination will match those known in the West and Eastern Europe. Their constitutional base is different although the nature of this difference must be delimited with great care. The specific nature of the dominant class in post-colonial sub-Saharan Africa does not lie in the 'straddling' between positions of power and positions of accumulation, as has often been said (after all, the Ancien Regime in France did not operate any differently, and Africa does not hold a monopoly on 'corruption'), but in the profitable nature of these 'straddling' procedures, where, in South-east Asia, a productive conception of a prebendal economy prevails. Equally the nomenclature of communist and socialist regimes in China, Vietnam, Algeria and Syria refer to diverse lines of concatenation, and cannot possibly be assimilated to the historical experience of inequality in the Soviet Union.

Nor must there be over-linear, evolutionist or teleological notions of the trajectories of social inequality. The old forms can subordinate the new ones – such as the caste system in India which spread over a wider territorial area due to 'modernisation' – and new forms can rapidly be reabsorbed, as in the case of the Yoruba 'peasantry' in Nigeria, who, after the oil boom, abandoned cocoa production to invest in the tertiary and informal sectors in the towns.[27]

Finally, and most importantly, delimitation of the scenarios of inequality will remain highly approximate as long as they do not include cultural representations through which social groups are assembled. In spite of what Marxist economic determinism may say, social classes, or more generally, social categories, are also communities of morals, ideals and values.[28] This is one reason why it is indispensable to use the third method of envisaging the historicity of politics in Asia and Africa, which involves the identification of the cultural logic underlying configurations of power.

CULTURAL CONFIGURATIONS OF POLITICS

According to Louis Dumont, the caste system in India is based on politics' subordinated autonomy to that of religion, and on the separation of the hierarchical status from that of power. The caste system is an expression of inequality which cannot be reduced to social stratification, and it belongs specifically to Indian culture. Contrary to what certain semantic analogies suggest, the caste system has not been transplanted into neighbouring countries: in Indo-China and Indonesia, the king was not dispossessed of his religious prerogatives and the supremacy of the priest was not established.[29] The characterisation of inequality comes from the particular configuration of the political arena. It is possible to be even more precise by noting that inequality cannot be dissociated from symbolic representations of purity and impurity. In other words, the social foundations of the state cannot be analysed without simultaneously taking the cultural construction of politics into account: it is not only due to the absence of feudalism that the concept of the bourgeoisie is inappropriate for the dominant groups in sub-Saharan Africa, but also because these groups adhere to an ethos of munificence which does not have many of Max Weber's 'affinities' with the 'spirit of capitalism'. The identification of specific political configurations in Africa and Asia rapidly leads one to examine their genesis, such as Bertrand Badie's model whereby he opposes a Western European trajectory to an Islamic trajectory of the state.[30]

From this point of view, the notion of concatenation, which was first used apropos of the linking and articulation of heterogenous modes of production, is of equal validity for what Michel Foucault would call the 'archaeology' of politics in Africa and Asia.[31] It can show how the Indian Republic inherited both colonial and Moghul traces, as well as how two constitutive elements of the Indian social configuration – the subordination of political autonomy to religious autonomy, and the caste system – have, paradoxically, sometimes reinforced the democratic parliamentary system.[32] At the heart of the sub-Saharan state the influence of a 'triple history' can be seen – the pre-colonial, the colonial and the post-colonial – which 'had a concurrent effect':[33] Mobutu's personality cult extends Pierre Mulele's Marxist millenarianism of the 1964–5 rebellions, the charismatic figure of Patrice Lumumba, the syncretic movements of independent churches from the colonial period and the prophetic movements of the more distant past.

It is particularly important to have a generative understanding of specific political configurations from one Third World society to another, because this avoids erroneously universalist interpretations of such societies. The well-known distinction between 'state' and 'civil society' was also made on the basis of the historical experience of Western Europe. As this distinction is already being contested within this particular context, it meets with even more serious objections when it is applied to political trajectories in Africa and Asia, in spite of the new 'vulgate' which has been all the rage since the mid-1970s (which included an over-hasty reading of some of my writings even though I defend myself against this!), and also in spite of the empirical appearances of the post-colonial era.[34]

As a general rule, the modern state has tended to be defined in opposition to society, due to an authoritarian conception of politics and 'development' inherited from the colonial period, and fairly close to Lumière's philosophy of the *Policeystaat*: and society has not hesitated to make its 'revenge' on the state, by bypassing it, wrecking it economically with the burgeoning 'informal sector', acting as a parasite on its sociability and its clientele, by defining itself in relation to economic, political or cultural systems which transcend the state, by submerging the state with its spectacular claims and mobilisations such as in China, South Korea, Afghanistan, Iran, Turkey and Algeria.[35] Of course, there are exceptions to this general rule of the Third World's post-colonial destiny. Without doubt, the greatest exception is that of India, which, as Rajni Kothari emphasises, is 'deviant' (even if, deep down, Nehru was inclined to modernise the country 'from above', more so perhaps than Gandhi wished, and if, conversely, Patel's strategy of indirect centralisation was partly based on Sir Ahmadu Bello's project in Nigeria, for example).[36] But on the whole, this binomial of modernising authoritarianism/societal resistance typifies reasonably well the vicious circle in which the Third World is trapped, and which is presently seeking to crush the growing claims for democracy, and the interventionism of the multilateral institutions of Bretton Woods.

Despite appearances, this binomial does not gain anything from being conceptualised within the framework of the distinction between 'state and civil society'. Instead of being 'an historic and political universal which could be used to analyse all concrete systems', this theory is nothing but 'a method of schematization belonging to one particular technology of government'[37] (that of the West), *except that* (and this is the root of all the difficulties) this 'particular technology of government' was exported into non-Western countries, took root there, and penetrated their imaginary conception of politics. In view of the appalling crises facing his country, Abdou Diouf, president of the Republic of Senegal, deduced the need for a 'redefinition of the relations between the state and civil society',[38] even if this was only to cajole France and the United States by proving Senegal's 'liberalism' and commitment to the 'market economy'. Over and above this mirror-like effect between the West and the Third World, the state/civil society dichotomy obliterates what should really attract our attention: the deep history which underlies the present, the buried layers of the *longue durée*.

It is illuminating in this respect to compare the cases of Turkey and Iran. At the end of the 1970s each of the two countries experienced 'society's revenge' against authoritarian modernisation: in Iran, the Islamic revolution swept away the Shah's regime and, in Turkey, the union of the tension of the extreme right and the terrorism of the extreme left literally imploded the post-Kemalist system, whose stability had already been shaken by the rural area's electoral procrastination since 1950. The two events were so similar in certain respects that many observers feared that the Islamic revolution would be extended to Anatolia, but the respective evolutions of politics in the two countries reveal very different historical configurations.

The Ottoman Empire was originally a patrimonial system whose economic ascendancy, in the absence of feudal structures, prevented the formation of a genuine, juridically constituted civil society. It presented itself as a political whole, headed by the Padishah who had to reach a compromise with the religious authority of the *ulema* and the autonomy of the *millet*. The political whole was governed less by coercion than by patronage, enabled by the resources of the guilds and the brotherhoods. It was only with Western colonisation of the empire and the emergence of a market society that the 'bifurcation' of state and society came about: as I. Sunar writes, 'it is no longer the state as society, but the state against society'.[39] This contradiction continued to dominate in the twentieth century, such as in the People's Republican Party which, if one agrees with the perspective

61

some Turkish authors have on Tocquevillian literature,[40] lies, in many respects, in a direct relationship with the authoritarian reformism of the Tanzimat. This contradiction resulted in the institution of a fiercely secular state which crushed the power of the *ulema* and the brotherhoods.

The case of Iran is different, although one can find certain elements of this contradiction between modernising authoritarianism and societal dynamics. Historically the central power of the Safavide asserted itself – even more decidedly than in the Ottoman Empire, where the role of the bureaucracy and the army prevailed – with the help of the Shiite *ulema* who were called upon by the Arab World to codify into a monotheistic religion the somewhat heterodox faith of the Turkish tribes who had installed Shah Ismael on the throne. And, also more completely than in the Ottoman Empire, these Shiite *ulema* acquired financial and economic power without giving any real compensation to their Sunni peers. After the fall of the Safavides, they even formed (from their establishment in Iraq) a relationship of exteriority with the political power, which was in some respects closer to the model of Roman Christianity than to Byzantine and Russian Caesaro-Papism or to the Ottoman model of *Develt-Baba* (Father-State).

After acquiring this autonomy, the Shiite *ulema* have dedicated themselves to conserving it throughout the twentieth century, even though this meant joining a nationalistic constitutional revolution from 1905 to 1911, and then leading the Islamic revolution of 1979, the better to defend themselves against Western secularisation threatened by European expansionism from the end of the nineteenth century, and the civilising mania of the Pahlavi. The nature of the problem was then inverted under Khomeni as the direct exercise of authority was entrusted to the *faquih*. This was a truly revolutionary innovation, but a short-lived one: the *velayate faquih* did not survive the disgrace of Ayatollah Montazeri – the only ozma who accepted this innovation – and the death of the imam.[41] Despite this, from the Ottoman-Turkish trajectory to the Iranian trajectory, the classical *din/dawla* (religion/state) distinction continues. *To some extent*, this is similar to the Western binomial of state/civil society, but it does not have the same meaning due to the lack of similar historical experiences. Under these conditions, Iranian Islamism does not foreshadow the regime that will emerge once the slow process of the reappropriation of Turkish republican institutions, which has been going on since the election of 1950, is completed.

It can be generally concluded that concepts based on Western experiences of the state cannot substitute entirely for indigenous concepts of politics without having a negative effect. This is not to say that a strictly emic approach should be adopted, which would replace an imperial scientific provincialism with a series of country-specific scientific provincialisms: the need for common 'problematisations' is not in question. But if the trap of specious comparisons is to be avoided, the cultural logic which gives form to the configurations of power historically situated in Africa and Asia must be restored.

The Egyptian Islamists' critique of the modern Islamic state as a *jahiliyya*, the debate about the margins of autonomy of the *hokumat* (the state apparatus) in relation to the doctors of holy law which divides the Afghan resistance, and China's 'plurisecular' oscillation between a *fengtian* concept of government which is community-based, egalitarian, anti-mercantile and anti-bureaucratic, and a *junxian* model which is bureaucratic, centralised, tolerant of the rise of the private sector and social inequality, need to be properly understood since they are in danger of being seriously misunderstood. Well before the 1989 crisis, Yves Chevrier revealed the limits of Deng Xiaoping's modernisation drive, and showed that the transition from a Maoist *fengtian* to the reformist *junxian* did not represent or even foreshadow a real advance for 'civil society'.[42] The 'developers' belief in the urgency of the 'privatisation' of African economies postulates the existence of a public sector whose development has been impeded by the straddling process; by feigning ignorance that the privatisation of the state renders the privatisation of the economy quite superfluous, they bypass an obstacle that otherwise impedes the continent's 'take-off' more seriously, that is the richness of the ethos of munificence and the culture of extraversion as ideologies for the profits gained from dependency under which the dominant groups have lived for several centuries.

BEYOND CULTURALIST EXPLANATIONS: DISCURSIVE GENRES OF POLITICS

Understanding the cultural historicity of Africa and Asia conditions the understanding of their political historicity. Once again, methodology must be refined if one does not want to fall into the rut of culturalism, or to attribute imaginary explanatory virtues to African, Arab, Indian or Chinese 'traditions', when we know that they have been 'invented'[43] and that they are polysemic.

We propose to identify several political categories which give form to politics in a given historical field, such as the sub-Saharan post-colonial state; although the list is not exhaustive, examples of such categories are: the French Jacobin state model, the British system of government, Soviet, North Korean or Chinese models, American federalism; Islamic, Protestant or Catholic categories; indigenous categories of royal or lineage power, the world of the invisible, prophecy, and so on. Each of these categories constitutes what we have chosen to call (borrowing from linguist Mikhaïl Bakhtin) a 'discursive genre' of politics, in the sense of a 'relatively stable type of expression' created by a 'sphere of language use', for example, of a religious, economic or diplomatic nature.[44]

Due to its historical nature, this stability of expressions is entirely relative. In particular, the continuation of certain signifiers does not necessarily presupppose that of the signified: the Egyptian Islamists' concept of the *jahiliyya*, and Sadat's assassin's reading of Ibn Tai-miyya, refer to the political realities of the twentieth century, which are radically new, and could not have been imagined some centuries or even decades ago. Even more importantly, the 'discursive genres' of politics do not have univocal significations within them; they are subject to contradictory interpretations, and, once again, the debates at the heart of Islam supply perhaps the best example of this. Finally, the discursive genres are not necessarily mutually incompatible. Authors mix them freely, and attribute this peculiar label (which belongs to all situations of cultural hybridation) to political systems in Africa and Asia, such as Congolese leaders who mix Marxist–Leninist jargon, the fetishistic practices of the invisible world, and the glamour of the big labels of French, Italian and Japanese *haute couture*.

Against this shimmering backcloth – that is the globalisation of the market of cultural representations, which brought about the incredible success of Michael Jackson, the vogue of kung-fu films, and the lively activities of international sects of diverse religious origins, and which Salman Rushdie reconstructs for our pleasure in his famous *Satanic Verses* – the particular relations between the indigenous and the external from which political arenas are organised, develop from one society to another. In many respects, Pierre Bourdieu's notion of the 'legitimate problematic' sums up this procedure of the discursive unification of political space, provided that its original monism is acknowledged.[45] Once again, these 'fields of the politically thinkable', whose construction brings about social domination, are heterogenous and partially reversible. An error of current analysis is to emphasise only one of the discursive genres that make up these political fields,

thus adopting an unduly reductive approach for the political identification of societies. For example a number of observers have typified
sub-Saharan socialist systems only according to their Marxist-Leninist
characteristics, failing to notice that the category of the invisible,
which is also very active, confines these systems in fixed places and
moments in the struggle for power. Another error is the exaggeration
of the dominant groups' contribution to the production of these
'legitimate problematics' and the playing down of the role of the
subordinated in political innovation; in reality, contemporary cultures
of the state are created by all social actors, including those from
'below', even if their contribution does not necessarily contradict that
of the powerful.[46]

Neither the structure of inequality, the quest for hegemony nor the
legitimate problematic of politics have any meaning unless they are
interpreted in terms of the expressions of all social actors. Michel
Foucault defines power along these lines as an 'action upon actions':

> It is a set of actions upon possible actions: this set of actions operates
> upon the field of possibilities where the behaviour of acting subjects is
> situated: it incites, it misleads, it diverts, it facilitates, it renders more
> difficult, it widens or it limits, it makes more or less possible, and at the
> limit, it constrains or completely prevents; but it is always a way of
> acting upon an acting subject or subjects, as much as they act or are likely
> to act.

Analysis then moves towards the understanding of this mode of
'governmentality' as a 'way of governing the actions of individuals or
groups': 'to govern . . . is to structure other people's possible field of
action'.[47] In this way, the multiple cultural logics inherent in the sub-
Saharan post-colonial state seem to comply, or at least to compromise
with, the dominant element which Cameroonians call the 'politics of
the belly'. This is an idiom which stretches from the shores of the
Indian Ocean to those of the Atlantic and the Sahara. 'Corruption' in
itself has nothing about it that is specifically African. As we have
already seen, the particularity of the sub-continent, in terms of its
civilisation, lies in the correlation between the common practice of
straddling between positions of power and those of enrichment, and
the perpetuation of an economy of profit, or of predation, whereas
South-east Asia, for example, links most prebends to the birth of a
productive economy. In relation to the structure of inequality, this
corruption is due to the recent nature, and often the incompleteness,
of social polarisation, political centralisation, private appropriation of
the means of production, and the formation of social classes. And, in
relation to political characteristics, this corruption is rooted in the

moral representation of civic *homo africanus*, via the manducatory symbols and beliefs it puts into question (see Achille Mbembe's Chapter 8 in this volume).

Of course this idiom of the belly does not only belong to Africa. In the seventeenth century the Tuscans said their proveditor 'ate' everything he could lay his hands on.[48] The Spanish have a proverb similar to the well-known Cameroonian saying – 'the goat eats there where it is tethered'. In *The Oak and the Calf*, Solzhenitsyn writes that members of the *nomenklatura* 'gnaw'. This goes as far as Jacques Chirac in France who, according to *Le Canard enchaîné*, complained that the 'reformers' of his party did not have the 'recognition of the belly'. Meanwhile, in Africa, the theme of 'eating' refers to two original and closely linked cultural characteristics: that of munificence which gives a political quality to physical corpulence, and, especially, that of the invisible which is made up of the nocturnal world of the ancestors, dreams, divination, magic and witches. When Africans declare that their leaders 'eat' them, as a way of saying that they exploit them economically with exorbitant levies, this assertion takes on a disturbing connotation which haunts them from childhood and does not cease to obsess them until death: that is the spectre of an attack by witchcraft which creates prosperity for the aggressor and failure, sickness and unhappiness for the victim.

This world vision is not a residual tradition that will sooner or later be eradicated by 'development'. It exists right at the heart of the continent's modernity. Personal, familial, social and political relations exist implicitly in representations of the invisible. Also, the slave trade was once seen as a particular form of witchcraft, such as that of the *ekong* in Cameroon. The post-colonial and para-capitalist state, with its inexplicable rise of individuals, its factional struggles, electoral battles, ministerial reshufflements and permanent denunciations continues to participate in the nocturnal dimension. And, as Denise Paulme has found in several folk-tales, those who hold positions of power are represented as child-devouring ogresses.[49]

When the *Cameroon Tribune* caricaturist depicts the famous goat as saying: 'I eat, therefore I am', this gives a very precise idea of the contours of the 'field of the politically thinkable' in post-colonial African societies.[50] According to a character in a well-known Kenyan novel, these societies know only one law: 'You eat somebody or you are eaten.'[51] This does not mean that this governmentality comes from a traditional culture that is impossible to bypass, nor that it removes a growing number of African citizens from the field of criticism. Nor, finally, does this governmentality represent the entirety of the sub-continent's political imagination, which Marc Augé calls 'the ideological'.[52] But this governmentality has hemmed in all strategies and institutions which have worked to create modern Africa, especially the administrations, the nationalist or revolutionary parties, and the Christian churches.[53] And political experiments which have attempted to break away from this have suffered for a long time, or have, in turn, been absorbed by it; the governmentality of the belly has continued to structure their 'possible field of action'.

Analysis of this governmentality leads one to ask questions about the way it 'subjugates' (in Foucault's sense, it predisposes, it inclines) the different discursive genres of politics to the domain of subjectivity:

> In this sense, 'to be subject' is therefore 'to belong to', in other words to behave as both an element of and an actor in a global process whose development defines the current field of possible experiences, inside of which the fact of being subject can only be situated.[54]

By paraphrasing Foucault, when he defines the philosophical profession, we see that the political scientist must question 'his belonging (or, we can add, the belonging of others) to a certain "we", to a "we" that is related to a cultural whole pertaining to his own situation'.[55] In Iran, this is the practice of *hejab*. Farida Adelkhah shows that this practice consists of a subjectivity which is the *hejab-e darun*, the interior *hejab*, manifested by certain qualities and values (modesty, steadfastness, solemnity, spiritual pride, chastity, dignity, seriousness, etc.), before being a vestimentary device. Therefore this vestimentary device cannot be defined simply in terms of a crude sociology of domination. The *hejab* is a positive norm; it is an action whereby Muslim women can make a contribution to the production of revolutionary modernity; and, as it is imposed by the clergy, it is subject to several expressive acts of reappropriation.[56]

There is also the question of the possible links between this subjectivity of the *hejab* and a more general system of expressions which transcend the Islamic problematic. It is important to realise that this cannot be subject to a culturalist interpretation in search of an eternal Iranian spirit which would precede, and put into perspective, the society's commitment to the faith of the Prophet, a little like the way in which the Shah fantasised when he celebrated the 2,535th anniversary of the Persian Empire. On the other hand, it can be asked if, and how, the *hejab-e darun* attests that the government of a society whose cult of the imam, or legitimate dissimulation (*ketman*), for example, is a religious actualisation; and also if, and how, this governmentality of dissimulation forms *stricto sensu* the political field in its expressive categories and in its practices.[57]

It is doubtless risky to try to link the collective work of the production of the state to the subjective interiorty of its actors in this way. However, this does not nullify the value of the results of almost two centuries of social science, as much as crude economism, or even the utilitarian consensus of Marxists or liberals, would lead us to believe, even though it was believed that social sciences had to be confined within these limits. Marx can also be read in terms of the antipodes of Marxism. And the definition of the individual has become one of the major challenges of political struggles over the last few decades. The growth of calls for democracy in countries of the South who had thought it 'progressive' to abstain from this, the dramatic return of religious issues to the political arena, the loss of credibility in the communist model, must all be due, in part, to the contradictions in the materiality of the state. But it is also contested in the name of liberty, faith and will; for example it is because *homo africanus* is trapped in a web of social relations which are simultaneously sensory and affective, that s/he prefers to 'eat' rather than to produce. In conclusion, analysis of African and Asian societies must no longer ignore the multiple procedures whereby states are individually created, and through which the state is a link between fear and hope, suffering and joy, life and death. In this way, the institutions and economies of the Third World should be analysed by way of a genuine questioning of a philosophical order and not by the ideological messianism which underlies this deplorable concept.

NOTES

1. P. Anderson, *L'Etat Absolutiste: Ses Origines et Ses Voies* (Paris, 1978); I. Wallerstein, *The Modern World System: Capitalist Agriculture and the Origins of the European World Economy in the Sixteenth Century* (New York, 1974); B. Badie and P. Birnbaum, *Sociologie de l'Etat* (Paris, 1978) pp. 178 and 181.
2. See for example on the subject of the Orient, M. Rodinson, *La Fascination de l'Islam* (Paris, 1980); E. W. Saïd, *L'Orientalisme: L'Orient créé par l'Occident* (Paris, 1980); A. Grosrichard, *Structures du Sérail: La Fiction du Despotisme Asiatique dans l'Occident Classique* (Paris, 1979); L. Valensi, *Venise et la Sublime Porte: La Naissance du Despote* (Paris, 1987). For a more general perspective, see T. Todorov, *Nous et Les Autres: La Réflexion Française sur la Diversité Humaine* (Paris, 1989).

3. M. Gaborieau, 'Le Leg de la Civilisation Musulmane aux Formations Etatiques du Sous-continent Indien' and M. Camau, 'Politique dans le Passé, Politique Aujourd'hui au Maghreb', *Table Ronde sur les Trajectoires du Politique en Afrique et en Asie, III° Congrès National de l'Association Française de Science Politique* (Bordeaux, 1988).

4. J.-F. Bayart, *L'Etat au Cameroun* (Paris, 1979) and *L'Etat en Afrique: La Politique du Ventre* (Paris, 1989); G. Salamé (ed.) *The Foundations of the Arab State* (London, 1987).

5. G. Hyden, *No Shortcuts to Progress: African Development Management in Perspective* (London, 1983) p. 19.

6. F. Braudel, 'La Longue Durée', in *Ecrits sur l'Histoire* (Paris, 1985) pp. 41–83.

7. See M. Henry, *Marx. T.1: Une Philosophie de la Réalité* (Paris, 1976) p. 109 and the works of G. Balandier, A. Touraine, A. Giddens and P. Veyne.

8. M. Vovelle, *Idéologies et Mentalités* (Paris, 1982) pp. 203 ff.

9. T. Skocpol (ed.) *Vision and Method in Historical Sociology* (Cambridge, 1984).

10. We are using the concepts and formulations of M. Foucault here.

11. J. A. Armstrong, *Nations before Nationalism* (Chapel Hill, NC, 1982); R. Draï, *La Sortie d'Egypte: L'Invention de la Liberté* (Paris, 1986) and *La Traversée du Désert: L'invention de la Responsabilité* (Paris, 1988); B. Badie, *Le Deux Etats: Pouvoir et Société en Occident et en Terre d'Islam* (Paris, 1986).

12. Bayart, *L'Etat en Afrique*.

13. B. Moore, *Les Origines Sociales de la Dictature et de la Démocratie* (Paris, 1969).

14. G. Balandier, *Sens et Puissance* (Paris, 1971).

15. E. R. Leach, *Political Systems of Highland Burma* (London, 1954); G. Balandier, *ibid.*, and *Anthropologie Politique* (Paris, 1967); I. Kopytoff (ed.) *The African Frontier: The Reproduction of Traditional African Societies* (Bloomington, Ind., 1987); J. P. Warnier, *Echanges, Developpement et Hiérarchies dans le Bamenda Pré-colonial (Cameroun)* (Stuttgart, 1985).

16. A. R. Zolberg, 'L'Influence des Facteurs "Externes" sur l'Ordre Politique "Interne"', in M. Grawitz and J. Leca (dir.) *Traité de Science Politique* (Paris, n.d.) pp. 567–98.

17. Braudel, 'La Longue Durée', p. 303.

18. Bayart, *L'Etat en Afrique*.

19. Z. Kaïdi, 'Le Déclassement International de l'Afrique', *Politique Etrangère* (1988) pp. 667–80.

20. P. Anderson, *L'Etat Absolutiste . . .*, vol. ii, pp. 246–7.

21. See for example Bayart, *L'Etat en Afrique* and *L'Etat au Cameroun*.

22. G. Balandier, *Anthropo-logiques* (Paris, 1974).

23. *Ibid.*; A. Giddens, *The Class Structure of Advanced Societies* (London, 1973) p. 132.

24. J.-P. Olivier de Sardan, *Les Sociétés Songhaï-Zarma (Niger-Mali): Chefs, Guerriers, Esclaves, Paysans . . .* (Paris, 1984); M. Samuel, Le Prolétariat Africain Noir en France (Paris, 1978); P. Devauges, *L'Oncle, le Ndoki et l'Entrepreneur: La Petite Entreprise Congolaise à Brazzaville* (Paris, 1977); P. M. Lubeck, *Islam and Urban Labour in Northern Nigeria: The Making of a Muslim Working Class* (Cambridge, 1986).

25. C. Hurtig, *Les Maharajahs et la Politique dans l'Inde Contemporaine* (Paris, 1988); Bayart, *L'Etat en Afrique*.

26. A. Przeworsky, 'Proletariat into a Class: The Process of Class Formation from Karl Kautsky's *The Class Struggle* to Recent Controversies', *Politics and Society* (4, 1977) pp. 343–401.

27. S. Berry, *Fathers Work for Their Sons: Accumulation, Mobility and Class Formation in an Extended Yoruba Community* (Berkeley, Calif., 1985).

28. M. Weber, *Economy and Society* (Berkeley, Calif., 1978) vol. ii, pp. 927–93; E. P. Thompson, *The Making of the English Working Class* (London, 1963).

29. L. Dumont, *Homo Hierarchicus: Le Système des Castes et Ses Implications* (Paris, 1966); C. Geertz, *Bali: Interprétation d'une Culture* (Paris, 1983) p. 59.

30. Badie, *Les deux Etats* . . .

31. M. Foucault, *Les Mots et les Choses: Une Archéologie des Sciences Humaines* (Paris, 1966); *L'Archéologie du Savoir* (Paris, 1969).

32. H. Stern, 'A Propos d'une Coïncidence: Comment Parler de Démocratie dans l'Inde de la Caste?', *Esprit* (Jan. 1985) pp. 7–17; R. Kothari, 'Démocratie et Non-Démocratie en Inde', *ibid.*, pp. 18–30; Dumont, *Homo Hierarchicus* . . ., and *La Civilisation Indienne et Nous* (Paris, 1964).

33. G. Balandier, 'Le Contexte Sociologique de la Vie Politique en Afrique Noire', *Revue Française de Science Politique* (September 1959) pp. 598–609.

34. Badie and Birnbaum, *Sociologie de l'Etat* . . . and G. Lavau, 'A Propos de Trois Livres sur l'Etat', *Revue Française de Science Politique* (April 1980) pp. 396–412.

35. J.-F. Bayart, 'La Revanche des Sociétés Africaines', *Politique Africaine* (September 1983) pp. 95–127 and 'L'Enonciation du Politique', *Revue Française de Science Politique* (June 1985) pp. 343–73.

36. Kothari, 'Démocratie et Non-Démocratie . . .'.

37. M. Foucault, *Résumé des Cours: 1970–1982* (Paris, 1989) p. 113.

38. *Marchés Tropicaux et Méditerranéens* (17 May 1985) p. 1,233.

39. I. Sunar, *State and Society in the Politics of Turkey's Development* (Ankara, 1974).

40. A. Kazancigil and E. Özbudun (eds) *Atatürk, Founder of a Modern State* (London, 1981).

41. N. R. Keddie (ed.) *Scholars, Saints and Sufis: Muslim Religious Institutions since 1500* (Berkeley, Calif., 1972); S. A. Argomand, *The Shadow of God and the Hidden Imam: Religion, Political Order and Societal Change in Shi'ite Iran from the Beginning to 1890* (Chicago, Ill., 1984); M. M. J. Fisher, *Iran: From Religious Dispute to Revolution* (Cambridge, Mass., 1980).

42. Y. Chevirer, 'L'Etat en Chine: Paradoxes et Polarités', *Table Ronde sur les Trajectoires* . . .

43. E. Hobsbawm and T. Ranger (eds) *The Invention of Tradition* (Cambridge, 1983).

44. Mikhaïl Bakhtin, cited in T. Todorov, *Michaïl Bakhtin, le Principe Dialogique, suivi des Ecrits du Cercle de Bakhtin* (Paris, 1981) pp. 90–1 and 127–8.

45. See the critique of Pierre Bourdieu by M. De Certau, *L'Invention du Quotidien: tome 1: Arts de Faire* (Paris, UGE, 1980) pp. 108 ff.

46. Bayart, 'L'Enonciation du Politique . . .' and 'Le Politique par le Bas en

Afrique Noire: Questions de Méthode', *Politique Africaine* (January 1981) pp. 53–82.

47. M. Foucault, 'Le Pouvoir, Comment s'Exerce-t-il?', in H. L. Dreyfus and P. Rabinow, *Michel Foucault; un Parcours Philosophique* (Paris, 1984) pp. 313–14.

48. J.-C. Waquet, *De la Corruption: Morale et Pourvoir à Florence aux XVII et XVIIIe Siècles* (Paris, 1984) p. 26.

49. D. Paulme, *La Mère Dévorante: Essai sur la Morphologie des Contes Africains* (Paris, 1976).

50. *Cameroon Tribune* (Yaoundé) (8–9 May 1988).

51. The character of the prostitute in *Petals of Blood* by James Ngugi, cited by J. Iliffe, *The African Poor: A History* (Cambridge, 1987) p. 249.

52. M. Augé, *Pouvoirs de Vie, Pouvoirs de Mort* (Paris, 1977).

53. Bayart, *L'Etat en Afrique* . . . and 'Les Eglises Chrétiennes et la Politique du Ventre: le Partage du Gateau Ecclésial', *Politique Africaine* (September 1989) pp. 3–26.

54. P. Macherey, 'Pour une Histoire Naturelle des Normes', in *Michel Foucault Philosophe: Rencontre Internationale: Paris, 9, 10, 11 Janvier 1988* (Paris, 1989) pp. 207 ff.

55. *Ibid.*, pp. 209–10.

56. F. Adelkhah, *La Révolution au Féminin: Une Approche Anthropologique de l'Iran Contemporain* (Paris, 1990).

57. M. Henry, *Marx.* . . .

CHAPTER FOUR

On State, Society and Discourse in India

Sudipta Kaviraj

This chapter seeks to place the relation between state and society in India in a broader than usual perspective. It tries to do so in two ways. It tries first to set out the processes of modern Indian politics in terms of a long-term historical understanding, rather than pretend, as is often done, that all the causalities of politics somehow sprang up in 1947. Second, it suggests that the historical argument reveals problems of a theoretical character, and that without dealing with some of these methodological and philosophical issues it is impossible to tackle some of the difficulties faced by empirical explanations. The chapter is divided into four parts. The first makes some preliminary theoretical remarks, the second assesses some of the initiatives or proposals for modernity that the colonial power set in motion, the third tries to analyse what happens to these after independence, and the final part returns to some questions of theory.

It is often said that to use concepts like 'state' and 'society' is not helpful, because of their abstractness and excessive generality. But I think that it is possible to begin at a still more radical starting-point. To analyse the relation between state and society in India, it could be argued, is impossible because they do not exist in India, at least not so securely as to apply these concepts unproblematically to their analysis. This may help us understand something quite fundamental. 'Society' can mean just any set of actually existing social relations, and that is the sense in which it is often used in the social science literature. But it can also mean a specific kind of society, known often as *gesellschaft*. 'State', similarly, can mean either any system of political rule or regime, or a specific, historically indexed style of impersonal governance, and, of course, there is a close historical connection between these ways of seeing the society and the state.[1] A state of this modern kind can exist, some types of social theory would assert, only on condition that it is embedded or surrounded by a 'civil society' of this kind. And it has been argued that one of the major problems for political construction in India is precisely the setting up of a modern state without the presence of a civil society.[2] So the underlying theoretical questions here would be: what are the conditions in which society and state in the generic sense of these words allow themselves to be shaped into states and societies in the second sense; and are these processes such that collective intentionalities, like legislation or con-stitution-making, are able to create them, or are they products of something more glacial, less intentional, more mysterious?

If all societies have 'structures' (in the sense in which structuralists use the term – it can be very different from the self-description of the formal organisation that a society offers), and if states have to obey their logic, and adapt to its compulsions, it becomes necessary to begin the story of the Indian state somewhat earlier than the point at which it is ordinarily done. It becomes necessary to tell the story of modernity as inextricably linked to the story of colonialism. This will, as we shall see, alter the punctuation and the shape of this narrative quite significantly at some points. In order to understand some of the present political difficulties of the Indian state, it is necessary to think in ways that are undetermined by the dominant myths and narrative strategies of nationalist historiography.

But it is important to see that modernisation theories also give rise to a largely parallel illusion in the analysis of social change. It is one of their serious drawbacks to encourage the notion that it is only modernity which has institutions, and it is only modernity which is rational. It is clear that if we work with a thin theory of rationality, then many of the practices condemned as hopelessly traditional (and devoid of any possible rational justification) can be rationally justified, unless the abstract definition of rationalism itself is surreptitiously packed with presuppositions of European enlightenment thinking. Getting people to ground their practices differently is not just dispelling a false consciousness, but a contestation of rationalities differently constructed. Similarly modernity does not build insti-tutions in an empty space. It has to rework the logic of existing structures, which have their own, sometimes surprisingly resilient, justificatory structures. The entry of modernity into the discourses and practices of a society depends, I shall argue, on a gradual, dialogical, discursive undermining of these historically rational grounds. And this cannot happen without extending much greater hermeneutic charity towards the practices we try to destroy. For the

73

first condition for setting up a critical, dialogical relation with them is to identify these beliefs correctly, and to see their structures of justification.

THE STRUCTURE OF TRADITIONAL SOCIETY AND THE SPACE OF THE STATE[3]

Several features of the traditional construction of Indian society must be noted if we are to understand exactly where the state is placed and exactly what it can and cannot do. First, the caste system is significant not only for its great internal complexity, but also the principles on which this complexity is constructed. Unlike pre-modern European societies which seem to have had a symmetrical hierarchy, its internal principle of the organisation of inequality was an *asymmetric* one. By this I mean that if social hierarchy is a complex concept, and it is disaggregated into several different criteria of ranking individuals and groups – say between control over economic assets, political power and ritual status – the rank ordering in India would be asymmetric between the upper caste groups. That is if ritual status ranks groups as ABC, political power might rank as BCA, and control of the economy CBA. Of course caste had a history, and the *jati* system which actually functioned on the ground was quite different from the ideological self-presentation of the *varna* system. But the advantage of seeing this model as presenting a sort of faded but still discernible background ideology of social practices is that it helps account for the relative infrequency of lower-order defiance in Indian history. It makes it cognitively more difficult to identify the structure of dominance because of some dispersal of power among the superordinant groups. Second, by this dispersal, it also imposes a strong necessity of a broad coalition among the upper strata in Indian society.

A second feature is the relation between society and the state. This depended on the way in which the social groups that were given to people's immediate 'natural consciousness' were themselves structured. Since the scale of social action was small, and highly segmented – despite the recent discovery by Cambridge history of much large-scale economic activity which they call, a trifle boldly, the growth of capitalism – this had some interesting consequences for the reach, structure and form of political power. The 'sovereignty' of the state was two-layered. (This is to indulge in something I have been criticising: for one of the major problems of theorising the field of power is precisely the absence of something like what was called sovereignty in modern Europe; yet let us approach the unfamiliar first through the familiar.) Often there existed a distant, formally all-encompassing empire, but actual political suffering was caused on an everyday basis by neighbourhood tyrants. There also were consider-able powers of self-regulation by these communities. (However, calling them in some ways self-regulating does not mean romanticis-ing them into democratic communities, or unchanging ones. Self-regulating communities can also create and maintain hierarchies of the most debasing sort.)

Thus the state, or the upper layers of it, which the colonial and the national regimes saw themselves as historically succeeding, sat in the middle of a peculiar segmentary social arrangement. I shall call this, by a deliberate misuse of a Hegelian metaphor, a circle of circles, each circle formed by a community of a neighbourhood mix of caste, religious denomination and occupation. The state would occupy, to extend the metaphor, a kind of high ground in the middle of this circle of circles. It enjoyed great ceremonial eminence, but in fact it had rather limited powers to interfere with the social segments' internal organisation. Its classical economic relation with these com-munities over which it formally presided would be in terms of tax and rent. And while its rent demands would fluctuate according to its military needs and its ability to despoil, it could not (in its own interest or in the pretended interest of the whole society) restructure the productive or occupational organisation of these social groups. One of our crucial points is that the conceptual language of acting 'on behalf' of the society as a whole was unavailable to this state.

Two implications follow from this. First, the eminence or the spectacular majesty of the state (at least the large state at the imperial centre) was combined with a certain marginality in terms of both time and space. Incursions by this high state were in the most literal sense spectacular – both wondrous to behold and unlikely to happen every day. The large and high state therefore had an ineradicable link with spectacle, pomp and majesty, symbolic rituals, rather than the slovenly and malodorous business of the everyday use of power, a sort of double image which one finds in both the British period and after independence.

But there is another implication of this picture, which has some importance for an understanding of the communal problem in India. I submit, against the grain of nationalist mythology about the common Indian past, that we must see the process of admission of alien groups into Indian society in a slightly altered way. For the standard nationalist picture of what happened, that normally goes under the name of a composite culture, is implicitly a self-congratulatory Hindu idea, celebrating the great readiness of the Hindus (and later also of Muslims) to absorb outsiders, after a few initial battles. In order to make my point, I shall use another theoretical distinction.

Using Toennies's idea of *gemeinschaft*, I should like to suggest that the sense of the community can be of various types. I shall make a distinction here between what I shall call fuzzy and enumerated or counted communities. The traditional sense of community, I suggest, was fuzzy in two senses. It was fuzzy first in the sense that the construction of individual or collective identity depended very heavily on a sense of context. Belonging to varying layers of community was not seen as disreputable or unreasonable. Given different situations, a pre-modern person could have said that his community was either his religious or caste or occupational group, or his village or his region. He might find it difficult to render these varying communities, to all of which he belonged, into some unimpeachable hierarchy, either moral or political. But I do not think that they could be accused of lack of precision in their social concepts. They would have fairly clear ideas about how to deal with unfamiliarity, or likeness and unlikeness, and be able to sort these things out for appropriate moves in social practice. The distinction I am drawing then is not between a precise and an imprecise way of thinking about the social world, but between precisions of different kinds. And of course very different types of social worlds could be constructed out of these different ways of thinking precisely about likeness and difference.

This implies an answer to the question that early nationalists inflicted on themselves: how could such a large entity as India be so easily colonised by the British? The short answer is that the question was wrong. The horizon of belongingness and consequently of conceivable social action was such that there was no India to conquer. Since the British inhabited a different discourse of social science and looked at historical and social reality quite differently, for them there was an externally given object – India – that was the target of their political control and conquest. But the Indian opposition they had to face did not reason through similar concepts. Thus one princely ruler looked on with unruffled equanimity at the undoing of his immediate neighbour, perhaps his immediate predecessor in the British agenda of conquest, and deplored philosophically the changeability of the human condition including those of small princes. Basically the fuzziness of their sense of community meant that it occurred to none of them to ask how many of them there were in the world, and what, if they agreed to bend their energies into a common action, they would be able to wreak upon the world to their common benefit. At one level of course it was a society like any other: people lived in groups, had wars, peace, conflicts, births, deaths and diseases. But the great difference was that they suffered or enjoyed these constituents of their common fates more passively, without any ideas of their magnitudes or numbers.

Another result of this was the manner in which external groups were allowed into this society. Contrary to nationalist ideas and narratives, when new groups with hard, irreducibly different social attributes and markers entered into this society, they did not automatically create a new culture composed of elements of both; more likely, they would be allowed to enter into the circle of circles by forming a circle of their own. Initially this would make the society's general architecture lose its shape a little, but it would generally adjust to their presence. But this circle, of Muslim culture and community, existed not in any open dialogic communication with the rest of society, but as a circle unto itself. It existed in a kind of back-to-back adjacency with the rest – by way of a very peculiar combination of absorption and rejection.

THE PROPOSALS OF COLONIAL MODERNITY

Into such a society – a circle of circles, but each circle relatively unenumerated and incapable of acting as a collective group – colonial power brought a series of basic changes. Ironically such changes could have been brought in only by an external power – external not merely in terms of coming from outside, but also in the sense of using a social conceptualisation that was fundamentally alien to this arrangement. Even the Mughal state could not do it, because it would have accepted eminence at the price of the traditional marginality. It could be done only by a political apparatus which had totally different moral, political and, most significantly, cognitive values.

Curiously, however, British colonial policy did not have a single, unhesitating answer to the question of what to do in this very unfamiliar society. Its political history shows that it went through two policy phases, or at least there were two strategies between which its policies actually oscillated, sometimes to its great advantage. At first, the new colonial apparatus exercised caution, and occupied

77

India by a mix of military power and subtle diplomacy, the high ground in the middle of the circle of circles. This, however, pushed them into contradictions. For whatever their sense of the strangeness of the country and the thinness of colonial presence, the British colonial state represented the great conquering discourse of enlightenment rationalism, entering into India precisely at the moment of its greatest unchecked arrogance. As inheritors and representatives of this discourse, which carried everything before it, this colonial state could hardly adopt for long such a self-denying attitude. As it had restructured everything in Europe – the productive system, the political regimes, the moral and cognitive orders – it would do the same in India, particularly as some empirically inclined theorists of that generation considered the colonies a massive laboratory of utilitarian or other theoretical experiments. Consequently the colonial state could not settle simply for eminence at the cost of its marginality; it began to take initiatives to introduce the logic of modernity into Indian society. But this modernity did not enter into a passive society. Sometimes its initiatives were resisted by pre-existing structural forms. At times, there was a more direct form of collective resistance. Therefore the map of continuity and discontinuity that this state left behind at the time of independence was rather complex, and has to be traced with care.

Most significantly, of course, initiatives for what has come to be known as modernity came to assume an external character. Acceptance of modernity came to be connected, ineradicably, with subjection. This again points to two different problems, one theoretical, the other political. Theoretically, because modernity was externally introduced, it is explanatorily unhelpful to apply the logical format of the 'transition process' to this pattern of change. Such a logical format would be wrong on two counts. First, however subtly, it would imply that what was proposed to be built was something like European capitalism. (And in any case, historians have forcefully argued that what it was to replace was not like feudalism, with or without modificatory adjectives.) But more fundamentally, the logical structure of endogenous change does not apply here. Here transformation agendas attack as an external force. This externality is not something that can be casually mentioned and forgotten. It is inscribed on every move, every object, every proposal, every legislative act, each line of causality. It comes to be marked on the epoch itself. This repetitive emphasis on externality should not be seen as a nationalist initiative that is so well rehearsed in Indian social science. I use it for just the opposite reason – to reject and deconstruct some of the well-known nationalist arguments about Indian history.[4]

Quite apart from the externality of the entire historical proposal of modernity, some of its contents were remarkable. Institutional changes that colonial modernisation sought to introduce into Indian society could be broadly divided into three main types, two of which have been fairly well documented and analysed. Economic reforms, or rather alterations (because these changes usually were unaccompanied by the moral arguments that attend genuine reformist impulses) did not foreshadow a construction of a classical capitalist economy, with its necessary emphasis on extractive and transport sectors. What happened was the creation of a degenerate version of capitalism, what early dependency theorists called the 'development of underdevelopment'. Political changes that accompanied these initiatives were of a very peculiar sort, and have been, in my judgement, often misread. In fact it was clear from the early period of colonial rule that Britain could not, without infringing the fundamental logic of colonialism, introduce forms of political rule current in Europe. However, in order to make the economic part of the social world tractable and amenable to its control, the colonial regime brought in a set of fundamental legal identifications which were new and unprecedented in the Indian context. Although the political institutions of liberalism were not introduced, precisely because the political forms of liberalism were deeply intricated with the system of property rights, the colonial state gradually introduced the complete vocabulary of liberal rights in the economic and social fields. It brought in the idea of a state as an impersonal regime of relations, the idea of an individual subject (which was necessary particularly to introduce the new regime of property and the entire regime of taxes and other obligations), the equality of rights or rightlessness – in which the important thing was the constitution of the political-individual subject, rather than whether he enjoyed democracy of suffered subjection – and finally, a state which (illegitimately under colonialism) pretended to represent the collective interest of the society, and from whose legitimate interference nothing in society was morally immune.

Evidently this entire gamut of conceptual transformations formed a structure. These concepts could not exist and flourish separately, they were preconditionally linked, and formed in their totality a new way of conceiving the political world. The major difference between its introduction in Europe and in India was of course that, while in Europe these were seen by the major part of society as a result of experimentation in controlling and reducing irresponsible power, and therefore as liberating, in India they seemed the reverse. The society had to subject to them, as a result of the irresistible power of the colonial rulers. This array of ideas, when seen in their totality, constituted the invention of a new political world, or a re-cognising of the world, and of the position of the society and the state in their modern versions – society as a large complex of *gesellschaft* organisations, and the state as an impersonal apparatus of public power.

A final point must be made about this picture of colonialism and its intrication with modernity. The colonial structure represented not only a set of new institutions, but also a set of discourses. And the connection between the practices, institutions and discourses could never be underestimated by this generation of colonial rulers, bred on the idea of the strong relation between knowledge and power, and seeing Europe's conquest of India as a consequence of Europe's scientific advance. Clearly the new institutions were operable and intelligible only if worked through the new discourses of society and power. Long inhabitance in this society had taught the colonisers deep differences in the structures of consciousness of this society. Traditional Indian discourse formed a structure, just as rationalist discourses did, and there was no simple incremental transition from one to the other. Since colonial authority could not be legitimised in terms of the constituted common sense of traditional Indian society, the proper course of action was to try to reconstitute this common sense. This is why the question of education, the instrumentality through which the common sense of a society was created, was of such central concern to British colonial authority.

In this field, the British followed what could be called a Gramscian line. Their strategy seemed to be that if a leading section of Indian society could be made to reconstitute their common sense, through the channels of encouragement, emulation, pressure, control, the rest of the society could also be expected to picture society similarly, at least in the fullness of time. Of course this operation went out of their control, and in time produced results which must have completely surprised them, and even their political successors. But it is interesting to see how these went. First, of course, the British colonial apparatus undertook an enormous and unprecedented enumeration of everything in Indian society. Thus, this imposed on social action a completely different picture of what the social world was really like. From fuzzy communities people had to get used to the strains of living in enumerated ones – with very different consolations and highly abstract threats. Nationalists soon began to turn this counting to good use, and often began to comfort themselves with the eventual power of such overwhelming numbers, particularly when their movement seemed to be in decline. Colonial authorities themselves would try, at a later stage, to turn this counting against them by enumerating the Muslims against Hindus. This showed one implication of living in a society that was enumerated; it was not just a secular nation which could name itself in this way. If disgruntled, other communities, based on other, different principles, could emerge in this way. Whether they did so or not depended to a large extent on the cultural reproduction of the national community. These communities, as Benedict Anderson has argued forcefully,[5] have nothing objective about them. If not given grounds for continuing to imagine themselves in a particular way, they might rapidly decline and dissolve.

At another level too the initiatives of the colonial state were unsuccessful, or at least came up against peculiar limits. The British had expected to alter the self-evidential view of the social world not only of the new elite, but also of the common people through their cultural initiatives. The new elite, it was expected, would carry this new alphabet of social reasoning into the lower orders in a sort of Gramscian relay of ideology. But the structure of traditional culture reflected the same segmentation as its social structure, and so it was not so easy to identify the site of such a common sense which could be replaced with a new one. But the cultural space of Indian society was also divided in a different way, between the high and the subaltern cultures. It is wrong to believe, as conventional sociology and cultural theory does, that the difference shown by dominant and lower-order ideas are merely 'failures' to copy correctly, that the lower-order versions of the epics for instance would merely be badly thought out versions of high literature. More often, as the work of subaltern historians seem to show, they are different stories, in terms of structure, escaping censorship and punishment by keeping a tenuous formal semblance of identity. Structural readings of popular stagings of the *ramlila* would often be significantly different from that of the great epic. Illiteracy implies not just the 'lack' or 'absence' of the high discourse, but the presence of a very different one whose rules, codes, emphases and ironies are entirely different. And just as the intricacies of the upper discourse are not gathered by the lower, the intricacies, and inflections of the lower discourse are also unavailable to the literate and higher culture. The culture of the lower orders, therefore, has potent means of not learning, insulating out the cultural instruction coming from the top. It is not surprising that the noisy political discourse of a garrulous, ambitious, self-regarding new middle class would not by itself be able to enter into the confidentiality of the discourse of the lower orders and reorder their alphabet. It failed to create a single circle of publicity for political ideas, as the British and the Indian elite had expected. This resulted in my judgement in the most significant cultural fact of modern Indian political life. There were two ways of dividing Indian society – in terms of discourses and in terms of political ideology – and the two divisions would be asymmetric.

This will become clearer if we relate this to the history of Indian nationalism. How does this relate to the spread of nationalist ideology? Does drawing this distinction do something to the major distinctions or nationalist politics, or does it make us displace in some way our analysis of the national state?

The introduction of this new discourse – limited, imperfect, thin as it was – also produced other unintended consequences. The modern elite in Indian society of course began to inhabit this new social conceptual world with relative ease. But very soon they turned the political point of this discourse against colonial authority itself, earning (not entirely unjustifiably) notoriety for their ingratitude. They came to have internal dissatisfactions, which arose out of figuring the political world out in the modernist-rationalist way. Indian nationalism, at least the form in which it came to be enshrined in the Congress, was primarily a product of this discourse, a complex of dissatisfactions worked out by the modernist rationalistic elite. It is necessary to analyse the internal logic of this body of ideas more carefully.

THE SYLLOGISTIC STRUCTURE OF NATIONALISM

The first item in this ideology was of course the double complaint about the economics of colonialism. Contrary to the justificatory argument given in favour of imperialism, it seemed to impoverish the colony to enrich the metropolis. Politically the rationalist conception of the world strongly emphasised autonomy and self-determination, and it was inconsistent to promote the autonomy of the individual and discourage it for collective entities like the nation. This was particularly so because a connection between the economic and political arguments of this rationalist liberalism seemed natural and politically inviting. To the early nationalist elite this connexion was so clear as to be put into a nearly syllogistic form.

1 The proposal of rationalistic modernity was rationally acceptable, and indeed deeply desirable. It was rational to wish to live in a civilisation structured according to rationalist principles. And the picture of this civilisation was one that emerged in Europe. The new elite looked covetously at that part of European history.

2 Originally colonialism may have seemed an ally in this process, through its support for social reform. But as its logic unfolded, colonialism seemed to be a more complex and sinister process, incompatible with its declared ideology. Instead of helping, it hindered politico-economic development in the direction of capitalism, liberalism, modernity. Instead of creating a world-wide commonwealth of societies moving in parallel, if somewhat unequal motion, towards this rationalist, liberal modernity, it exploited colonies and made it difficult for them to embark on this path.

3 The rationalist argument itself suggested a different course. Liberal democracy, based on individual and collective self-determination was rationally the best form of government. Collective self-determination implied a movement to end colonial rule in India, to take national destiny into 'our own' hands. Once colonialism was removed, all these ideals could be realised. The political form would naturally be some sort of universal suffrage democracy, and what this sovereign state would try to achieve would be of course what had already been accomplished in the west, in other words a re-enactment. Although startling in some ways, this shows how strong the relations are between the positions advocated by earlier nationalists like Naoroji,[6] and later, far more radical ones like Nehru, if seen in terms not of political ideology but of the discourse about history. Of course, the differences are fundamental and obvious: Naoroji expected the colonial power to accomplish this re-enactment (or did he? Was he really pretending to be trapped inside their ideology in order to stretch it to its limits, bring it to a crisis, and reveal itself?). Nehru had no such illusions. Re-enactment for Naoroji would have meant the happy replication in India of the desirable society of nineteenth-century *laissez faire* capitalism of England – liberal, property-oriented, unequal. By Nehru's time what was to be re-enacted had altered in several ways. The ideal model itself had been restructured by the internal critiques of Western political reason, through socialism, to issue in a more redistributivist model of democracy. But a re-enactment it remained. The historical task for the movement of Indian nationalism, led by its modernist middle class, was not to invent an ideal

adequate to the structure, pressure or logic of Indian history, that is the structure and discursive possibilities of their own society and history. It was to follow tasks, models, ideals and historical paths that were universal, but enacted earlier only in Europe, through discourses that were equally universal.

This point should be made with some care. Nothing is simpler than a sort of anachronistic criticism of nationalist leaders, accusing them of not seeing things that were revealed only by later history. As nationalists they were intensely conscious of the peculiarity and specificity of their own history. What they made appears to be not a political but a cognitive mistake, along with their generation of social scientists. They acted on an uncomplex and overrationalistic theory of social change. First of all, they considered all 'forward' transformations irreversible, because they assumed that given the basic rationality of all men, there could be no two opinions about their progressiveness. It will be seen that the picture I have drawn is similar to the one offered in recent years by observers like Kothari, Nandy and Madan.[7]

This kind of theory is unlikely to be valid or universally popular, but it could create difficulties in a different direction, in the internal compatibility of principles. If much of Indian society did not agree with a single rationality or its single, dominant construction, given an adult suffrage democracy, it could lead to paradoxes. Democracy works, alas, on a sociological theory of truth. It allows to members of the largest number the right to act upon the political world, assuming that their beliefs about how it was were the true ones. And they can go on building the political world for the relevant period of the 'truthfulness' of their views. This brings us to the elite–mass relation in the last phase of the nationalist movement, because after freedom that would be written as the state–society relation. The elite's view of the truth of the political world would become the state's view – though there are various serious internal limits to this, because a state as vast as modern India's is deeply stratified, and the lower elements of the bureaucracy would hardly share the rationality of the elites at the commanding heights. There could be subtle and subterranean resistance from some layers of society. For although the masses in times of great political movements follow their elites, they do not surrender the confidentiality of their political world. From the analytical point of view, however, it may be difficult to produce maps of these ideas or plot their cognitive terrain, because unlike the ideas of the elite and the state which are constantly broadcast, propagated, repeated, theirs are less structured. But precisely for that reason they might be excellent as defensive weapons.

The colonial period saw the appearance of two types of divisions in Indian society: the discursive division between those who made the world they inhabited intelligible via modernist discourse and those who did not. This division ran decisively between the Indian elite and the lower orders. On top of it, however, nationalism put in place a political division between colonialism and the Indian nation. I consider Gandhi's discourse or rather his discursive position to be of crucial importance. This is not because he created a discourse of inexhaustible originality, as some argue; but his kind of discourse managed to bridge the gulf between the two sides, and keep the values, objectives and conceptions of the world of the two sides intelligible to each other.

The Indian national movement did not produce an inevitable Nehruvian result. The way in which Nehru was able to shape the ideals of the Indian state after independence was partly a result of some fortuitous circumstances. No logic of the previous movements, no wave made it necessary for the Nehruvian elite to come to power, but there was something deeper which went in favour of this modernist dominance at the time of independence. He enjoyed a silent but subtle and massively significant cultural approval of the modern elite. Members of this class, dispersed thinly but crucially throughout the governmental and modern sectors, approved spontaneously the assumption of power by a rationalist 'philosopher king' – though some of them knew that he might incline towards a statist radicalism common in the 1940s and 1950s. However, this did not represent a serious discontinuity at the level of discourse. Entrepreneurial groups and politicians favouring the propertied classes knew that they would have differences with Nehru, on socialism, the state sector, redistribution, foreign policy, land reforms, the state's power to take away property, and so on. But these were comprehensible differences, differences of political ideology among those who inhabited the same social discourse. Political disagreement is of course a form of successful communication.

A paradox of mobilisation made this early period of political construction in India relatively easy. If the divergent types of political discourse, with what they considered to be politically rational, their incommensurable ideals, had simultaneously found utterance in Indian political life, it might have been exceedingly difficult to carry on institutional formation. But the backwash of mobilisation of the national movement ensured an implicit trust of the masses in the initiatives of their leaders. Thus these various conflicting discourses were not brought immediately into dialogue on equal terms. During the nationalist struggle there had occasionally been distinct initiatives from the lower orders when political space was opened up within the national movement. But recent historical research has also shown how quickly the main Congress leadership was able to shut off such space, or bring their movements under control. Thus the support that the Congress leadership received was not of the kind that the bourgeoisie in classical bourgeois revolutions of the West created for themselves, by reconstituting through a process of prior cultural movement a hegemony and directive pre-eminence for themselves. Ordinary people were mobilised in the Indian national movement in tremendous numbers, but not by creating hegemony of this kind. At the same time, as the failure of the communist moves towards insurgency indicated, the subaltern groups were not ready to break with the bourgeois nationalist leadership, and prepared to take large world-constructing actions on their own.

This led to several consequences. First, of course, the setting up of political institutions passed off relatively peacefully; the Constituent Assembly, though strangely unrepresentative, still represented a sufficient consensus of the organised groups to bring off a constitution which was not seriously contested. At the same time, internal realignments within the Congress led to serious political decisions. The systematic exodus of the socialist left from the Congress weakened Nehru considerably inside the party that he formally commanded, but the death of Patel also left his own personal eminence uncontested. He was therefore free to pursue a set of policies for which his party colleagues were not wholly enthusiastic. The construction he placed on secularism for instance was clearly resented by a section of Congress leaders. His drive for redistributive policies of land reforms met with serious, if undeclared hostility from his own party's lower-level leadership. Most Congress leaders were more lukewarm than Nehru about developing friendly relations with the Soviet Union. Few understood in a clear theoretical form the logic of the massive heavy industrialisation drive that he pursued through the second Five-Year Plan. This shows in a sense a miraculous contingency of some of the central segments of the fairly impressive institutional structure that Congress under Nehru built up. But precisely because of his relative isolation within his own party, Nehru undertook another initative which has seemed over the long run to overshadow other parts of his institutional strategy.

Nehru began to create a base, an alternative apparatus in the bureaucracy. Planning, on a large scale from 1956 onwards, made for a great extension of an economic bureaucracy inside government. As the rhetoric of social justice and redistribution increased, this bureaucracy expanded rapidly. This differed from classical European bourgeois revolutions, where capitalism first emerged in initiatives and in institutions within civil society, and the state was later used as an instrument to correct its spontaneous production of inequality. In India there was no developed civil society and many of capitalism's classical initiatives within civil society were undertaken by the state.[8] The most serious consequence of this, of course, was that the state became omnipresent, since it was performing functions left to the institutions of civil society, and it was impossible to abjure transactions with this state. At the same time, it could work only through the techniques of an unreconstructed colonialist bureaucratic style, wholly monological, criminally wasteful, utterly irresponsible and unresponsive to public sensitivity. Its history had made it ill equipped to be civil or solicitous, or to explain itself. And naturally, its manner rather than its policies was bound to create a scramble. Those after power would want to get into its seats, completely screened as they appeared to be from accountability, and those who could not get into them would become increasingly alienated.

The manner and structure of capitalist growth accentuated such differences. Instead of reducing regional inequalities, capitalism intensified them and tended to concentrate opportunities and resources in centres of political power. The cultural consequences of this process have not been analysed carefully until recently. Over the long term, the strategy of development in India, precisely through its relative successes, has tended to reopen the deep division of discourse in Indian society, between a homogenising elite-speaking English, the Esperanto of the upper orders, and a vast lower-order population looking and speaking with an intense vernacular hostility against some of the consequences of this form of capitalist development.

THE NATURE OF INDIAN NATIONALISM

From this point of view it appears justified to say with Rajni Kothari[9] that the first phase of Indian politics was built on a kind of consensus, but he seems to have misjudged the nature of the consensus he identified, and its possibilities. It was of course an elite consensus, which passed uncontested because of its nearness to the mobilisation of the national movement, and the relation of implicit trust between its leadership and the masses. It was a consensus of discourse, rather than of ideological positions. The institutional pattern that Nehru wished to put in place came up against serious ideological criticism from the left, especially the socialists and the communists. But there *was* still a commonality at a different level: they had very different things to say about the political world, its structure, purposes and ideals, but they shared a common way of arguing about these things. This seemed to create real divisions among them, which was what they primarily saw. But this also created underlying unities among them when looked at from outside of this discourse, which is what must have impressed the other classes and groups in Indian society. The constitutional frame that was adopted, though it was exhaustingly detailed (and therefore a lawyers' constitution rather than a citizens'), still was silent and vague on various questions. And although the ideological conflicts in the Constituent Assembly went in favour of a more conservative reading of the Congress programme, the Nehru regime took significant steps immediately afterwards to counteract this in actual policy. The Planning Commission, soon to become the actual centre of economic policy-making, remained outside the formal constitutional framework. Initially the federal structure worked through the federalism inside the Congress Party rather than constitutional channels. The regime of rights centred on the individual subject, made legal concessions to minority rights which could be enjoyed only as members of communities, rather than as bourgeois individuals. But despite these underlying problems which took some time to break out into the open, the achievements of the Nehru regime were massive by any standards. True, some of this was fortuitous, and caused by the fortunate overdetermination at the time of freedom. But one can clearly see that given a slightly different turn of events, India could have had a very different set of foundational policies, and these most likely would have been more retrograde.

It is in the economic sphere that Nehru's policies have enjoyed the greatest long-term success, though at the start his government often seemed on the point of being overwhelmed by financial and resource difficulties. By the time he became prime minister, Nehru had moved away from his 'scientific socialist' beliefs, though importantly he would still have characterised his beliefs as scientific. From his point of view, he had moved away from that doctrine because it was not scientific. He had given up that construction of socialism, but he had not given up science. Still his commitment to a British Labour version of social democracy made him interfere with what others would have considered the more 'natural' course of capitalist growth. Indeed, Nehru's certainties were shaped by and shared with the emerging discourses of social theory, soon to be inscribed on the whole world in the form of reformist Keynesian economism in all sectors of public policy. The economic growth of society was predicated on the building of the industrial sector. In this, heavy capital goods industries took precedence and since these could not be built by private capital, this led to the steady growth of a large public sector with strong links to ministerial bureaucracies.[10] In this milieu, it was subtly misleading to speak in the language of the interventionist state, and to transfer, implicitly, a whole set of expectations from the European case because that was a language on which the history of European capitalism was inscribed quite clearly. In Europe, the state did 'intervene' in a society whose basic structures had earlier been formed by civil society, and the existence of a strong civil society made the state act in responsible ways. In India, where there was no prior civil society, one could hardly talk of an interventionist state since many of those institutions were brought into existence by the state. Therefore, in a subtle but significant way, the direction of the descriptive language and justificatory rhetoric was wrong.

Some of the problems of this kind of economic planning have been noted for a long time. Even economists who favour the state sector and its leading role agree that the planning models probably neglected the question of agriculture. Not surprisingly the Nehru regime faced both economic and political difficulties arising out of food shortages during the late 1950s. The theoretical fault in all this was that the regime worked, along with all others thinking about development at the time, irrespective of ideological positions, with a heavily reductive economistic theory of social change. Economic arguments tended to be aggressively ahistorical. Everything else was turned into problems to which economic policies had the solutions. The sequence in which the sectors had emerged, their specific institutional forms, how the historical sequence of their emergence could have affected their institutional logic – such questions were seldom asked. There is a minor irony in this since much of this discussion was analysed by Marxism, and Marxism in its classical form at least is deeply sensitive to sequences and trajectories.

Second, the irresistible bureaucratisation of social life, in the absence of the structures of civil society, created difficulties. But the effects of this politics on the discursive map of Indian society were interesting, and these have not been carefully analysed. The structure of Nehruvian democracy was raised on an anomalous base. It did represent, as some of its admirers put it lyrically, the greatest experiment with democracy in the history of the world, but that was possible partly because the large masses on whom these rights were conferred found them too unfamiliar at first to use them immediately. Planning was aimed not only at the construction of a wide industrial base, but also at the reduction of some of the gross inequalities in incomes. Nehru certainly saw an alleviation of poverty as a condition for genuine democracy, but it depended increasingly on the monologic instruments of the state and its bureaucracy rather than dialogical, movement-like forms. The falling apart of the Gandhian language in Indian politics, which had reduced for a time the hostile unfamiliarity between elite and subaltern political semiotics, contributed to this widening gap, accentuating this ironical divergence between populist government policies and popular consciousness. And the discourse of the elite tended to turn increasingly inwards in two senses. First, the debates were directed at the intelligibility and justifiability in terms of the political stances of the high discourse, leaving the task of formation of a vernacular, popular discourse around these questions to an unmindful educational policy. Second, there was a further tendency in later years to withdraw issues of development from public arenas of discussion and to surrender it to so-called expert groups, creating a sort of elite confidentiality around the vital decisions about politics and society.

It must be acknowledged that Nehru personally was conscious of this withdrawal, and sought to continue to publicise the development debate. But it was not a matter so much of personal predilections of leaders, but a tendency of the structure of development strategy. Indian democracy remained vibrant, with occasional mass movements being able to register their demands on the state, as with the regional autonomy movements of the 1950s, and the food movements some years later. So the enormous extension of the state was not coercive, but remained external. The elite around Nehru were sensitive about retaining democratic forms and pursuing, within what they considered to be reasonable limits, the reformist aspirations of the state. But they did not see the problem of its externality. In retrospect, its basic failure seems to have been the nearly total neglect of the question of the cultural reproduction of society. It did not try deliberately to create or reconstitute popular common sense about the political world, taking the new conceptual vocabulary of rights, institutions and impersonal power into the vernacular everyday discourses of rural or small town Indian society. It neglected the creation of a common thicker we-ness (something that was a deeper sense of community than merely the common opposition to the British) and the creation of a single political language for the entire polity.

Thus, unnoticed by the bustling technocracy of the modern sector, the transient links across the political and discursive divide tended to give way. The independent Indian state followed a programme of modernity which was not sought to be grounded in the political vocabulary of the nation, or at least of its major part. As a result, precisely those ideals – of a modern nationalism, industrial modernity, secular state, democracy and minority rights – came in the long run to appear not as institutions won by a common national movement, but as ideals intelligible to and pursued by the modern elite which inherited power from the British. More than that: subtle and interesting things began to happen to this logic of 'modernisation' which have gone unnoticed in the works of its supporters or opponents. Precisely because the state continued to expand, precisely because it went in a frenetic search of alibis to control ever larger areas of social life, it had to find its personnel, especially at lower levels, from groups who did not inhabit the modernist discourse. Thus it is wrong to believe that the Indian state or its massive bureaucracy is a huge Weberian organisation binding the relaxed, fuzzy, slow-moving society in an iron structure. What has actually been happening is more complex. By overstretching, the state has been forced to recruit personnel from the groups who speak and interpret the world in terms of the other discourse. Since major government policies have their final point of implementation very low down in the bureaucracy, they are reinterpreted beyond recognition.

As a result of its uncontrolled growth, the policies of the state have also lost some of their cohesion. If one does not have a purely romantic view of the Indian past, one can see the direction this reinterpretation of government policies, this utilisation of internal space for lower-level initiative would take. It is not surprising that arguments of social justice are often used as an unanswerable justification for the encouragement of nepotism and corruption. Indeed there is very little corruption in India that is not done for high moral principles. The actual conduct for those in authority has also tended in recent years to slide backwards towards a more historically 'familiar' style or irresponsible power, with the withdrawal of significant decisions, under various excuses, from the arenas of public criticism and responsibility. It must be seen, while debating the effects and justification of modernity, that these trends come straight out of India's glorious past.

However, the point here is not to tell the story of Indian politics, or to present a convincing periodisation. In the accepted ways of standard social science the story has been told many times over. Indeed my point is that despite those familiar narratives of the achievements and failures of Indian democratic institutions, there appears to be another story to be told. This seems to be sketchily glimpsed by many recent observers of Indian politics, but no one seems to know what it is a story of. I am quite clear that this ambiguity is reflected in the curious way I have just presented the problem. I think it can be sorted out in a preliminary way by using the distinction between political ideology and structures of discourse, and acknowledging that the classifications that can be produced by their different criteria look quite different. I should like to look at some of these diagnoses of the recent problems of the Indian state, and move our discussion towards some theoretical conclusions.

POLITICAL DIAGNOSES

One of the punctuations generally observed in Indian politics is the spectacular difference between the Nehru period, which ended in 1964, and the later one. There is a further division: the electoral instability of governments in the period after the fourth general elections in 1967 has since been changed into a more serious and frightening uncertainty about the state form itself. On the one side the political behaviour of party leaders and managers seems to discredit the institutions of democracy; on the other, sometimes popular anger against such political games has assumed a form in which it seems that it might pass into a vote of no confidence on the state form itself.

What has been the historical record of this complex of institutions? This question has been discussed so often that it is only some of its implications which need to be assessed. But we must also keep in view the standard and fairly reasonable defence by Nehru's followers (in ideas, not in party affiliation: indeed, the Congress Party under later leaders has been the main destroyer of the institutional logic that Nehru sought to make safe) that forty years is too short a span for institutions to take root or to adapt themselves to a very different historical milieu. But even in the short term, its achievements are not negligible. Unlike in most other Third World states, a formal democratic constitution was not initially adopted, to be dropped soon after in favour of dictatorial authority. In fact, the way the emergency ended in India showed the great ideological depth of the democratic idea. Mrs Gandhi believed that even the record of the emergency regime had to be electorally justified. Often, however, other achievements of the Nehruvian model are clouded in a discussion either of pure economic growth, in which dictatorial regimes accepting subordinate productive roles in the international capitalist system are shown to be remarkably superior to India's record in growth rates, or of radical theories based on strategic ignorance, which show the distributive advantages of a communist economy. But industrialisation in India, though wasteful in many ways, has a wide base. And the institutional form of the economy has ensured that its political sovereignty has not been renegotiated through extreme economic pressure. All these relative achievements are undeniable, but this shows the present predicament of the Indian state in a curious light. For the state is not threatened by forces from outside. On the contrary, most powers acknowledge its resilience and regional dominance. But it appears threatened from inside. Its difficulties arise not because its performance had been bad, but rather from what its rulers would no doubt consider among its modest achievements. And most remarkably, the institutional forms that the early nationalist leadership created for the benefit and well-being of the common people seem to have come under greater pressure the more common people have entered into the spectacle of party politics.

This then is the basic form of the paradox of democracy in India. It is undoubtedly true that some of Indira Gandhi's electoral moves, and the rhetoric used consistently by all political parties – of popular participation, realisation of rights, eradication of poverty – have led to a greater political articulateness of the ordinary people. To that extent high politics, even in the spectacular arenas, which were earlier preserves of the modernist elite, are coming under pressure from the alphabet of the lower discourse. It seems, however, that the more ordinary people have written their minds into the format of politics, the greater the pressure or threat on democratic structures as generally understood in terms of Western precedents. There seems to be some incompatibility between the institutional logic of democratic forms and the logic of popular mobilisation. The more one part of the democratic ideal is realised the more the other part is undermined. The paradox, to put it in the way in which T.N. Madan has done recently,[11] is that if Indian politics becomes genuinely democratic in the sense of coming into line with what the majority of ordinary Indians would consider reasonable, it will become less democratic in the sense of conforming to the principles of a secular, democratic state acceptable to the early nationalist elite. What seems to have begun in Indian politics is a conflict over intelligibility, a writing of the political world that is more fundamental than traditional ideological disputes. It appears that the difference between the two discourses is reappearing, now that the lower discourse is asserting itself and making itself heard precisely through the opportunities created by the upper one. The way it rewrites the political world might not be liked by the ruling modernist elites, but it is too late to disenfranchise them.

This is an interesting and challenging line of thought, and very different from earlier diagnoses of political difficulties in India. Earlier, social scientists usually began by expressing solidarity with the project of introducing modernity, equating the modernity with a re-enactment of the European drama. (Indeed, there was no Asian drama to stage at all. What occurred in India was merely the Asian premier of the European narrative, luckily with an appropriately cultivated cast.) They expressed irritation or puzzlement at the obduracy with which the society seemed to resist it, and such resistance was generally accounted for through some simple, malignant form of direct political agency – corruption, lack of political will, and so on. The explanation that I am proposing seeks a less agency-oriented answer to the difficulties, and is prepared to be puzzled by deeper questions, and is ready to turn the questions around towards social science itself. From this perspective, the equation is to be arranged not between a rational programme prepared by the elite and carried out by an instrumentally viewed state on the one hand, and a resisting, irrational society, but the other way around. Indian politicians of the Nehru type made a mistake very similar to the one that has now been, a trifle theatrically, traced through the entire history of social science. Western social theory moved from a sort of high orientalism practised by Marx and Weber to a very inadequate theory of modernisation worked out by Parsonian developmentalists, a move often celebrated as from philosophy to science, but in fact from tragedy to farce.

Nothing is more disorienting than when our fundamental taxonomies are turned around and we blink at a world in which things occupy entirely unaccustomed places. This argument tries something like this about development thinking in India. Clearly many Indian social scientists carried on their earlier debates within a world which was firmly held by the solid homogenising taxonomies established by nationalist beliefs. Most political argument was internal to these boundaries. The emergence of such arguments in serious social theory shows that the pervasiveness, the self-evidentiality of the nationalist construction of the world is gradually fraying and disappearing. It has been argued forcefully in recent years, by social scientists like Chatterjee, Nandy and Madan,[12] that the state and the ruling elite uncritically adopted an orientalist, externalist construction of their society and its destiny reflected in the wonderful and tragic symbolism of 'the discovery of India'. Its initiatives were bound to be one-sided. To the world of India's lower orders, it simply refused or merely forgot to explain itself. Indeed to some it would have seemed that the Indian elite was more concerned about justifying its initiatives to external audiences than to its own. Historically its absentmindedness about cultural unity has driven apart the political diaglossia of the national movement, held together in a sense by the easy bilingualism of its political leaders and cultural intelligentsia. Today, that cultural terrain is increasingly broken into a unilingual English-speaking elite, and equally monolingual conglomerate of regional groups which are losing a dialogical relation not only with the upper strata but between languages as well, leading to greater friction and hostility among regions.

The implications of this critique must be seen clearly. It has brought into question the cognitive, the political and the moral legitimacy of the whole institutional regime constructed after independence. About the whole lot – the impersonal nature of public power, the rule of law, the democratic order, the idea of a complex and composite nation, a secular polity – it asks whether it is legitimate for a relatively small elite to impose their ideals on others who do not necessarily share them. It also asks if this political form, because of its unintelligibility, can be worked by this people. It must be seen that it moves from moral to cognitive questions to radicalise its critique. It must also be clear that these questions are addressed not only to the Indian political or modernist ruling elite, but also to social theory in equal measure – because they can be logically so directed, and also because it is these theories, which the elite believed, that gave them the intellectual justification to do what they had undertaken.

But some of the more general, abstract, epistemic implications of this kind of argument should be noted. In a sense, this sort of theoretical discomfort tries to break from the vulgar pretensions of being a policy science (which posited too direct a relation between social science and government policy) and seeks to return to a more classical conception of political theory, as a kind of historical self-reflection of society. It assumes that one of the tests of good social theory is whether it can relevantly comment on what is happening in society, and contribute to general management of social destiny. It rules out a distancing, reflective attitude to social and political questions. Its own performance must be as subject to this criterion of success as that of previous theory that it rejects.

The approach which I am proposing offers more promise than do reassessments either of Gandhian ideas or of traditional Indian or Hindu thought. Gandhi did not seek an answer to the problems of the modern condition. He shrewdly refused to deal in modernity's terms. His answer was not about how modern conditions can be brought under cognitive and moral control, but that modernity as a condition should be abjured. In a sense he embraced a deliberate obsolescence. His critique of modernity is of course powerful and lucid, but too radical, for he offers not an alternative solution to modernity's problems, but to modernity itself. I do not therefore seriously expect help from the side of Gandhian theory, though as a student of history of ideas, I can see that there can be a great deal of good theory which flies the Gandhian flag; that a lot of good, interesting theory could be done by illegitimately using Gandhi's name.

It appears that one of the curious things about the Indian, or at least the Hindu, tradition is that although it has a high tradition of philosophical reflection, and the political organisation of society was highly pronounced, it lacks for some reason any strong tradition of applying this apparatus to the analysis and justification of political (it is perhaps possible to say social) phenomena. As language gives a kind of condensed history of a culture, this is reflected in the constant trouble about translating basic conceptual terms like society and state into Indian languages. Thus, to find an indigenous vocabulary for making sense of the political world, going back to the indigenous tradition might not be very fruitful.

Even if there is a vocabulary, even if we pretend that it is interregionally sufficiently common, it will be a language that was adequate to state–society relations of the pre-modern form. The modern state cannot go back to the high ground in the middle of the circle of communities. The circles themselves cannot be made fuzzy again. There is certainly a great deal of humanity in the pre-modern languages of social living. Its sentiments are valuable, but its conceptual apparatus cannot work out solutions to modern calamities.

THEORETICAL QUESTIONS

It should be clear that the failures that we have examined here offer a potentially rich field for political theory to analyse. When even massive coercion fails to modernise or democratise nations, it is likely that these efforts are up against an intangible barrier, like the problem of conceptually reinventing a political world. That is why it seems necessary to return to the problem of theory for this whole field. This has been analysed so carelessly that it is still in a sense unnamed. For the 'Third World' is really the absence of a name. We must ask if this aggregation is defensible and look into its conceptual archaeology. It remains a negative and residual description, indicating the West's 'other'. And a negative otherness is particularly hard to theorise, because we are required to theorise what these societies are not.

Much of the blame for the blundering inadequacies of modern American development theory has been wrongly laid at the door of the Western tradition of high historical theory. This misreads the relationship between American social theory of the 1950s and its nineteenth-century European ancestry. It is to accept the past that American theory has given itself, shopping around in the earlier traditions of European social reflection. There were also critical self-limiting moves within European social theory which have not been studied with an equal seriousness in the eagerness to construct a paradigm. John Dunn, in 1979, wrote a book which sought to revive, in a more radical fashion, some of these self-limiting moves of Western theory.[13] He engages Western theory in an unaccustomed task – of finding its limits, something which in the last century at least it had become unused to doing. In India, Partha Chatterjee has recently offered the interesting and powerful hypothesis that nation-alists have accepted the Orientalist construction of the Indian society and the limitedness of social reconstruction and the present difficulties of the state begin from there. This is not a cultural complement or a version of the dependency thesis, for this line of argument is far more self-critical and modest. Dependency theory believes that most Third World states do what is wrong, but it has no doubt about what it means to do right. The new line of criticism is more radical: it appears to suggest that colonialism ruptures the self-relation of a society through time in such a fundamental way that it becomes difficult to imagine what would be right. It shows the task to be one of inventing right and wrong – the true function, according to one definition, of political philosophy.[14]

Dunn's book speaks in the cultured, civilised tone of withdrawing

97

into Europe as a region in history. But the withdrawal of Europe is not going to be such a simple affair. Others would object to its withdrawal; because that would amount to withdrawing not a familiar theory, but the assurance of a familiar world which made this theory relevant. Others have named their *lebenswelt* through these ideas and have started inhabiting them. This of course alters them unrecognisably, as happens with European languages which others have made their own. Dunn thus takes a rather narrow view of the responsibilities of Western theory. In much of the world, it faces the future of others.

NOTES

1. For an excellent discussion of the historical stratification of the meaning of the term 'state', see Q. Skinner, 'The State', in T. Ball, J. Farr and R.L. Hanson (eds) *Political Innovation and Conceptual Change* (Cambridge, 1989).
2. The term 'civil society' is used here in Gramsci's sense. But it appears that it is used in so many distinct ways, and that there are justifications for most of these, that there should be some rigorous discussion about its many, but somewhat confusing, riches.
3. In this section I have simply summarised my argument in a different but related paper, 'On the Construction of Colonial Power', presented at a seminar on Foundations of Colonial Hegemony, organised by the German Historical Institute, London, in Berlin (June 1989).
4. I use the word 'deconstruct' quite deliberately: for the critique of nationalism comes here as an internal critique, as the critique and rejection of those who, as Derrida would say, have been its inhabitants. Only then can it be called deconstruction.
5. B. Anderson, *Imagined Communities* (London, 1983).
6. The most celebrated work by Dadabhai Naoroji, which illustrates my point, is *Poverty and Un-British Rule in India* (London, 1901).
7. R. Kothari, *The State against Democracy* (Delhi, 1988); A. Nandy, *The Intimate Enemy* (Delhi, 1986) and *Tyranny, Science and Utopia* (Delhi, 1988); and T.N. Madan, 'Secularism in its Place', *Journal of Asian Studies* (November 1987). There are some serious differences which will become clear as we proceed. I have considerable sympathy with what they say has been happening in India, but not with their views about why it is happening, and what should be done about it, and finally, about how *we* relate to the relevant discursive structures.
8. I have advanced an argument of this kind in 'A Critique of the Passive Revolution', *Economic and Political Weekly*, Annual Number (March 1989).
9. R. Kothari, *Politics in India* (Boston, Mass., 1970).

10. For a detailed historical argument, rich in empirical detail, F. Frankel, *India's Political Economy* (Princeton, NJ, 1977).
11. Madan, 'Secularism . . .'.
12. P. Chatterjee, *Nationalist Thought and the Colonial World: A Derivative Discourse?* (Delhi, 1986); Madan, 'Secularism . . .'; Nandy, *Tyranny, Science . . .*.
13. J. Dunn, *Western Political Theory in the Face of its Future* (Cambridge, 1979).
14. T. Smith, 'Requiem or New Agenda for Third World Studies?' *World Politics* (July 1985) offers an understanding and wide-ranging critique of this whole field; but his criticisms of dependency are weaker and less pointed than they could have been. It seems that now it is time to do something like what Foucault would call an 'archaeology' of Third World studies, or to provide something like an in-depth narrative of its epistemic and methodological structures.

CHAPTER FIVE
Political Democratisation in Latin America and the Crisis of Paradigms*

Manuel Antonio Garreton

CONCERNING THE CRISIS OF PARADIGMS

We are currently witnessing a profound change in the way of analysing societies and social change. In the case of societies undergoing development – above all Latin American societies, and with due respect for the complexities and exceptions of each case – what one is dealing with is the surmounting of a type of analysis which viewed society as a system articulated in structures (economic, political, social, cultural). These structures in turn were determined by universal laws, where social action was in some way the emanation of the 'structural effects' of that society. Societies were conceived of monolithically, starting from some determining factor (this might have been 'structural' as in a Marxist approach, or 'cultural' as in a Parsonian[1]) which defined its character and potentialities. Thus, societies were socialist or capitalist, modern or traditional, democratic, authoritarian or totalitarian, depending on whichever determining factor might be chosen. Social change was defined in polar fashion as the passing from one type of society to another. One was dealing with processes which had been predetermined according to laws that were inferred prior to historical experiences and outside of the determining structural factor of that society.

A double determination, then, for developing societies. On the one hand, there was that produced by a factor or structure on the whole of society, whose other levels or components appeared as effects or reflections of that prior determination. On the other hand, there was that determination posited by the 'target society', which predefined

* Translated from the Spanish by Thomas Scheetz.

the type of social change. If in actuality it departed from the pre-set model, it was analysed as a deviation or deformation. Such a vision of society is transformed into a view of change, and history is seen as a succession of 'stages', whether they be of development, revolution, or modernisation.

Under this way of conceiving things, with all its variants, and recognising differences and complexities, all the social actors are defined from a position outside of both themselves and the context created by them. They are bearers of some role or historic mission, to which they have to adapt themselves. That is to say, they are 'agents' rather than actors, to whom someone (be it the scientist converted into ideologue or the party) must explain his mission. Strictly speaking, there is no action or historical creation on the part of these actors, but only the reading of general historical laws and an adequate or inadequate conformity to these laws.

In its more progressive currents, the monolithic quality of this theoretical viewpoint was translated into the identification of the concepts of 'exploitation', 'oppression' and 'alienation', all of which become fused into that of 'domination' or a 'system of domination'.[2] As a consequence, the principal collective action was the struggle against 'domination'. This defined the revolutionary character of every social struggle aiming at social change, even when the forms those struggles might take were not classics of a revolutionary process.

As I see it, both the so-called modernisation theories and dependency theories shared the same above-mentioned theoretical matrix.[3] Great emphasis has been placed on the antagonistic character of both schools, and it cannot be denied that they conceived of themselves as mutually exclusive, and that predominance of one in a given academic setting normally meant the elimination or subordination of the other. Nonetheless, both shared certain traits which were derived from the fact that they arose from global theories concerning society.

In both cases one was dealing with the passage from one type of society to another, and social change was viewed as a global process determined by a factor which in either case we might call 'structural'. In the one case the transition was from a traditional society to a modern one, in another from a capitalist (or semi-capitalist) society to one of a socialist type. In order to confront the diverse stages of either of these transitions, it was necessary to identify the social actors who were the main bearers of that grand project (the bourgeoisie, revolutionary actors) together with the obstacles or enemies who stood against this passage from one type of society to another.

This chapter is not the place to review all of these theories and assess their differences and similarities. Let us merely call to mind that the renovation of leftist thought in the world, the impact of neo-liberalism, the convulsions in the communist world since the 1980s, the formidable economic transformations which altered the world order in the 1960s,[4] the installing of authoritarian regimes of novel brutality, the struggles against these regimes and the ensuing democratic transitions,[5] and all the theoretical and practical reflections concerning these phenomena – all of these factors tended to undermine both these unilateral focuses and their antinomies, in a search for a more modest and secure characterisation of the problematic. It is not that the phenomena to which these approaches point did not exist, or that they were not basic elements in the explanation of Latin American processes. It is rather that, as totalising and (most especially) as deterministic forces, they lost their strength and analytical validity. Their elements have to be reintegrated into new approaches.

In studies of the state, or the revitalisation of civil society, or social actors, their discourse, social movements, cultural and political processes,[6] there has been growing over the past decade a crisis of paradigms. This has especially affected the modernisation and dependency theories which had been dominant over such a long period. Scholars have increasingly tended to abandon monolithic and deterministic visions of society. This necessarily implies the absence of a single overarching paradigm. It requires us to postulate several interpretative hypotheses and diverse theoretical currents to be interwoven in our assessment of each object of study. Rather than postulating new theories or globalising explanations of development and social change, we need to develop tentative concepts and theories of a 'medium range', aimed at the description, analysis and interpretation of relatively precise and delimited processes. We must do this not in order to give up on the total view, but rather to draw closer to it.[7]

This does not mean that there is no theoretical vision, but that we need above all a set of intellectual orientations aimed at proposing a series of concepts capable of enriching and being enriched by the study of concrete processes. One is dealing with an 'intellectual compass' rather than a single unified 'theoretical map' in which everything is already fitted into place and defined forever.[8]

It is worth indicating some of the analytical principles which are relevant to the study of particular socio-political processes.[9] In the first place, we must attempt to get beyond a structural determinism of a universal type, in which individual or national histories are mere illustrations of general laws. At the same time, once we get beyond the view of an essentialist and abstract correlation – defined once and for all among economics, politics, culture and society (the idea that a given economic system corresponds necessarily to a determined political or cultural form, or vice versa) – we must not deny that there do exist determinations between levels or components. We must develop a flexible scheme of determinations among *the economic model, the political model, the social organisation model* and *the cultural model*. There does not exist any *universal determination or relation* among these dimensions. Such determinations or relations vary for each national case and for each historical moment.

In the second place, it is necessary to emphasise the autonomy of social processes with respect to their 'structural base'. The task of the social sciences is not to do a 'natural history' of social structures and their dynamics, but rather to understand their sense. And that cannot be done without introducing the concept of the social actor. The whole problem of sociology and political science is rooted in describing how a structural situation or category is transformed into actor, and how those actors establish themselves within an historical and institutional context which they themselves help to produce and reproduce. Thence it is that society does not define itself starting from a structure or from a system of values, but rather from the particular configuration of relations in each society among (a) the state, (b) the regime and political parties, and (c) civil society or the social base. These historically bounded relations allow one to speak of a *matrix constituted by the social subject-actors* proper to each society, starting from which the analysis of its reality is possible.

In the third place, the meaning of the struggles – and more generally of the social action – of such actors is not given univocally by the struggle against 'domination as such'. This concept tends to obscure various dimensions such as exploitation, alienation and oppression, all of which do not necessarily coincide in the same actors or processes. These dimensions give birth to several conflicts and struggles and social movements, and for that reason to diverse goals of said struggles, and also to diverse utopian principles. A society's system of domination (it would be better to speak of systems of domination) is a combination of several axes or systems of actions and not the reflection of just one of them, even while there may be one or more of these sytems which predominate. In each axis or system of domination in a given society, confrontation exists over the principles and instruments which define its orientation and destiny. There is no single isolated subject of historical action, but rather

103

several, even when (in moments of condensation of a society's historical problematic into just one of those principles or axes of domination) there might exist a single privileged actor-subject. Nonetheless, this will always be in terms restricted to that given struggle or specific conflict. Under this approach, Utopia disappears as the architecture of a type of society in which history comes to an end (be it modern, democratic or socialist society)[10], and it gives way to partial Utopias which point to the temporary realisation of only some of the principles which define that society. There is no ideal society just around the bend; there is always struggle and process.

In the fourth place, the model or political system of a given society, to which we will make reference throughout this chapter, is made up of the *state*, the institutional relationships between state and society (that is to say, the *regime*), the *actors-subjects* who take part in the political arena in the name of social projects which point to that society's *historical problematic*, and the *political culture* or particular style of relationships among these elements.

The political regime is the articulation or institutional intermediation of the relations between state and society which resolves two of society's problems: how it is governed and how the people relate to the state (the problem of citizenship).

Democracy is a type of political regime which resolves these two problems: on the one hand, by means of principles such as the rule of law, human rights and public freedoms, the division of power, popular sovereignty; and on the other hand, by means of mechanisms such as the universal vote, the multiparty system, taking turns in office, etc. In this sense democracy is not a type of society, but rather only a regime which obeys no historical law or inescapable necessity, but only the will of the social actors. As such it is therefore an act of historical creation. The relationship between the political regime and society's other components is a matter for empirical analysis and there exists no relationship of essential necessity among them.

The study of political regimes and regime change – especially where we are dealing with transitions (and not revolutions) entailing the recovery by a regime of historically prior experience – can be accomplished with a certain autonomy for the analysis of the dimensions of social transformation. This perspective makes the weight of analysis fall on the actors, their constitution and interaction. Sociopolitical processes are seen as historical creations of those actors and not as the unavoidable results of factors and structural phenomena of which the actors are simply bearers or reproducers. Therefore, there exists no 'one' alternative paradigm to those holding sway in previous decades, but rather only analytical frameworks and conceptual openings.

POLITICAL DEMOCRATISATION IN LATIN AMERICA

In the case of Latin America, the transformations affecting the world economic system, the rise and consolidation of new poles of growth and influence, the crucial importance of information, communications, innovation and creativity in the development of contemporary society, the collapse of the so-called real socialisms – all of these oblige us to see in a very different way the reality of this continent. A diagnosis based on the characteristics of the 'present phase of capitalism', as one was accustomed to hear until recently, is totally insufficient. Nor is the culturalist and ahistorical analysis of 'Latin American identity'[11] sufficient. There is no possibility of returning to comprehensive and global historical projects, whether they be based on the overcoming of capitalism, or on the achievement of our identity, defined essentially. It is within the framwork of democratic regimes that the various historical actors and subjects set projects for themselves which attempt to overcome the most urgent contradictions defined historically and concretely for each society.

We will now attempt for these countries some analytical propositions which stem from an historical application of the concepts set forth schematically above. Such propositions will also be tentative.

The constitutive matrix of the social actors – that is to say, the matrix of the relations among state, system or political actors (parties) and civil society (social base) – was characterised during the major portion of this century by a kind of fusion among these three elements, whether by an interweaving between some of them, or by the subordination of some to others, or by the surpression of some.

Populism entails the fusion of various dimensions into a collective actor such as a party, the military, the state or a personal leader. It has emerged in diverse forms, such a corporatism, classism, basism, guerrilla style, etc. ('from below'), or militarism, technocracy, etc. ('from above').

The military regimes and the authoritarianisms of the 1960s and 1970s which devastated several countries, above all in the Southern Cone, set for themselves the task not only of replacing a regime, but also eliminating the old matrix of the relationship among the state, political parties and society. They sought to replace it (through control and repression) with a new matrix based on the market and technocracy, complemented by the striking of deals along corporatist lines.[12]

The termination of authoritarian regimes has given way to processes of transition towards political democracies. Just as the military regimes implied an attempt to break with the historical matrix of political activity, so these transitions appear to entail a change – still germinating and mixed up with other processes and bad habits of the past – in the historical matrix. Things are now moving in the opposite direction, towards the triple reinforcement of the state, the party system and social actors (or civil society). Instead of diverse forms of fusion, we are moving towards autonomy for and complementary tension among these elements. The degree of modernity of these countries can thus be defined by the way each one accomplishes its own reinforcement of these elements.[13] The regime changes and the consolidation of new democratic regimes also imply a change in politics itself and in the meaning which the several social actors give to it, with 'politics' defined as the strong link between these three elements which are themselves strengthened.

Similarly, this transformation is tied to the completion of three as yet unfinished historical tasks. First – and varying according to whether one is dealing with cases of transitions from authoritarian regimes or of democratisations of semi-authoritarian or proto-democratic ones – democratic regimes have been put in place without having completed the processes of political democratisation. These as yet incomplete processes include, on the one hand, the imposition of civilian control over the armed forces, the resolution of the issue of human rights and, on the other hand, the building of regimes which are genuinely effective at extending or generating channels of mass participation, particularly among ignored sectors such as the mass of the poorer classes, ethnic groups, women and youth.

To complete political democratisation in these countries and to ensure the consolidation of these democracies is the first task before them. This consolidation, and the completion of the transition from an authoritarian regime, are impossible without a reconstruction of the state and its guiding role in development – against all the forces which today seek its break up or disappearance through privatisation. But the reconstruction and fortification of the state demand at the same time the strengthening of civil society, the autonomy and ability of social actors to express themselves and participate through a strong system of parties which provide representation.

But neither the reconstruction of the state, nor the strengthening of civil society nor the construction or reconstruction of a strong party system can be democratically secured in countries which indefinitely hold down half or more of their population to subsistence (or even lower than subsistence) levels. Political democratisation (and there is located the autonomy of the diverse levels of collective action) can be maintained for a time if there is a strong desire for democracy,[14] even in situations of physical poverty. But undoubtedly the desire for democracy will disappear for many, if there is no social democratisation.

Second, the countries of Latin America are becoming modern without having finished their own processes of modernisation.[15] Their simultaneous membership in the developed world and the Third World is experienced dramatically, especially through the communications media and youth culture movements and by the marginalised poor.

There are simultaneously present in these countries struggles against exploitation, oppression and – especially acute today – the struggle against alienation infused by the still not totally defined principle of happiness. The need to be and fulfil oneself, to belong, to overcome loneliness and boredom, to express oneself and to be creative, along with the still unresolved problems brought forward from earlier times, such as misery, hunger, the minimal satisfaction of material needs for large sectors of people, all these are now syncretically mixed with Western individualism and belonging to the 'collective we' and the community. Such problems must be confronted all at once, and not step by step as could be done in developed societies. For this task there exists neither a model of society which can be offered as a solution, nor a model of collective action useful for confronting the task. This drives the masses (above all the youth) to question the traditional forms of organisation and representation.

This brings us to the third aspect or task that must be confronted. The tasks set out above cannot be accomplished by recourse to the development models which we have experienced up to the present, or by imitating other societies, or by the illusion that mere market expansion alone, and in all fields of endeavour, will automatically resolve the problems. While Europe is being restructured, Latin America has still not defined the mode of its autonomous insertion into this transformed world. We need to redefine a model of development and to do it together, conjointly within the region.[16]

In all of this, we must take care not to mix our analysis up with programmatic proposals and not to distort ideologically our examination of real social processes in these countries. However, it would seem that this analysis, starting from challenges and tasks, allows us to discern the context in which the political processes occur with greater clarity than did the paradigms which predominated in prior decades. The means by which a society confronts and resolves its problems are no longer predetermined.

In any case, from the viewpoint of the actors charged with these tasks, the very scope and complexity of these challenges forces one to look beyond structurally constituted classes and a single central idea or dimension of domination. The analysis cannot be reduced either to pure consensus or to pure antagonism, or to only a few privileged actors who are favoured by virtue of some pre-established theory.

All of the above makes only too clear the centrality of the problem of political regime, that is to say, the problem of the institutions which decide the way that a given society arrives at decisions, governs itself and resolves the problem of citizenship. It was precisely during the decades spent under military regimes associated with violent repression and profound social transformations that thinkers restated this issue, which in the theoretical and practical traditions of our continent had always been subordinated to the issues of development and revolution or to global social change.

Nevertheless, although democracy appears now as the ideal political regime (which implies the abandonment of revolution as the ideal political method and its replacement by the construction of political majorities), and although the legitimacy of democracy is not now subordinated to this or that historical project of some sector, it cannot be forgotten that in these countries the ideal democracy has always implied *social democratisation* (the elimination of inequalities, the inclusion of excluded popular sectors, social integration and participation).

In the study of political democratisation in the wide sense (that is, as a process of creating, widening or deepening the democratic political regime) one can distinguish several types. On the one hand, there are the *democratic foundations*, which refer to the creation of the first democratic regime in the history of a country. These foundations tend to acquire a more revolutionary character, that is to say, a coincidence between the change of regime and the creation of a new social order.[17] On the other hand, there are the *transitions*, changeovers from a modern authoritarian regime to a democratic regime, usually in the form of recovery of a democracy lost.[18] Then there are *democratic openings or deepenings*, which are distinguished from transitions by the fact that their point of departure is more diffuse, since they start from a semi-authoritarian or proto-democratic regime.[19] In each of these types of political democratisation there are, in addition, two other consecutive processes once a basic nucleus of democratic institutions has been attained. These are the *inauguration* or *installation* of the new regime and government (a not quite so clearly defined moment in the deepenings or openings from semi-authoritarian regimes) and the *consolidation* of the new regime. In what follows we will refer mainly to democratic transitions and consolidations.

Political democratisation does not assure the effectiveness of a democratic regime. It can be irrelevant in a society to the extent that decisions are made outside the regime by sectors not elected democratically, and citizenship is not respected, even though there be no other regime formally established.[20] On the other hand, the political democracies which we know under the form of *representation* or *delegation* solve well the problem of who governs and how. This raises the issue of the expansion (so difficult in complex societies) of direct democratic spheres of action.

Transitions from military or authoritarian regimes to democratic regimes are accomplished without institutional rupture and within the frameworks of the authoritarian regime, precisely in order to change such frameworks. These transitions involve complex processes – the decomposition and isolation of the authoritarian nucleus in power, together with processes of social mobilisation oriented towards an institutional formula for regime change for negotiations between regime and opposition over the time frame and the establishment of democratic institutions (especially elections), and for negotiations with actors and institutions beyond regime and opposition. Generally transitions are incomplete, leaving *authoritarian enclaves* in the new democratic regime – of an institutional type, an ethico-symbolic type (the problem of human rights) and non-democratic actors.

To overcome these enclaves and to complete the process of transition, is the immediate task confronting the democratic governments. Links undoubtedly exist among the diverse authoritarian enclaves. This makes it necessary that every strategy for their elimination confront them in both their specificity and globally as a group. If action against one of these enclaves is especially important for the success of the advance towards democratisation, such action ought to be made compatible with what is necessary regarding the others, keeping in mind that it is impossible to eliminate all of them at once.

Moreover, as we said, in democratic transitions other social problems are left unresolved, such as the redefinition of the development model and the question of social democratisation. In the resolution of these tasks which contribute to democratic consolidation, one factor which is especially important is the reconstitution of relations among state, party system and civil society. This entails, as we have noted, a strengthening of the autonomy of each of these elements, and of the complementary tension among them. The beginning of the processes of consolidation through the above-mentioned tasks constitutes the second great problem of the new democratic governments.

But there is also a relationship between the tasks of completing the transition and those of deepening social democratisation – namely, that of assuring democratic consolidation.[21] If the tasks outlined above get postponed or bogged down, this can – insofar as it makes more difficult the realisation of the latter tasks – have an impact among the poorer sectors of the populace, and among activists and militants supporting the regime. This can generate popular apathy, frustration, anomy, disillusionment or loss of interest, eroding the faith in and the desire for democracy. This in turn can cause people to seek corporatist or messianic refuges. Among the activists, this can produce ideological criticism of the government and regime, the abandonment of the government or nostalgia for heroic politics.

These things can occur because of inflated expectations about what a political regime can achieve, or as the result of something deeper. Amid these processes of transition and redemocratisation, a profound mutation of the political order is occurring. The meaning of politics as it has been lived for decades and under several different regimes is changing. People are seeking adequate modes of participation, solutions to individual and collective problems, the reformulation of the state's role, the questioning of traditional forms of representation, the absence of global ideological frameworks, the need to belong (combined with individualism), the presence of concrete and partial Utopias foreign to messianic and globalising Utopias, etc. The days of heroic politics are finished, and traditional or professional politics have not yet given rise to a new political culture. Technocratism, fundamentalistic sectarianism, corporatism, the flight towards individualism, all appear as spurious substitutes. To the extent that the elimination of the authoritarian enclaves is prolonged or gets bogged down, collective action is weakened and the processes of social democratisation and modernisation are held back, thus affecting democratic consolidation.

NOTES CONCERNING THE CHILEAN CASE

A complete analysis of the Chilean case is not appropriate here, but it is worth while raising a few fundamental ideas which can illuminate some of the general issues developed above.[22] We shall refer only to the broad historical problematic, without entering into detailed analysis of actors and specific processes.

The crisis of the Chilean democratic regime, which remained stable for several decades prior to 1973, cannot be attributed either to a single structural factor or to a conspiracy (whether national or foreign), although both were present. In this crisis and in the collapse of the democratic regime due to a *coup d'état*, which opened the way to a long spell of military rule, long-run factors were combined with some of greater immediacy. That which grows worse in the 1960s is the incapacity of the progressive political actors of centre and left to build a social and political alliance capable of performing, within the democratic framework, the pending tasks of modernisation and democratisation. In the absence of a project of democratic social change commanding majority support, ideological projects emerged both in the centre and on the left. The latter attempted radical social change without the socio-political and institutional majority needed for it, and that radicalised the conservative actors in an authoritarian fashion. In a climate of growing polarisation and deinstitutionalisation, the conservatives appealed to the traumatised middle class and to the military (insofar as it had automony from political and civilian control) in order to mobilise them to terminate the process of change which they felt menaced their survival.

How can we explain the durability of the military regime and the delay of a transition until 1988, after the victory of the opposition to the Pinochet dictatorship in the plebiscite called by him? Let us first consider the nature and evolution of the regime put in place following the *coup d'état* of 1973. On the one hand, the regime combined in itself traits of a personal dictatorship with those of a military regime. On the other, it undertook a project of transformation, employing enormous repressive weight. Moreover, one was dealing with a regime that achieved considerable institutionalisation prior to its crisis so that it was able to pass from a military regime to an authoritarian one (via the 1980 Constitution). This is to say that it failed to achieve 'a transition from above'. Lastly, the regime underwent a very slow and uneven erosion of its civilian block of support.

Also important was the opposition's inability to unleash 'a transition from below'. This was due to the fact that at the time of their

[margin note: ideological polarisation.]

111

appearance on the public scene (1983, with the protest movement), the forces of discontent did not transform themselves into a unified political force capable of proposing an institutional solution or way out that would dispense with the regime. Rather, by forming themselves into ideological blocks, they gave primary importance to their own problems of organic and ideological identities, which implied mutual exclusions.

Consider also the character of the transformations occurring within society. These had the effect of favouring atomisation, fragmentation, the shrinking of space for the emergence of new social actors, the 'backbone' of Chilean society, that is to say, the integration between party leadership and social leadership.

From the time of the Plebiscite of October 1988, which was intended to ensure the passage from a military regime to an authoritarian one (and to maintain Pinochet in power), hitherto unheard-of dynamics of transition were set in motion. For the first time, a politico-institutional confrontation occurred between regime and opposition (with all the limitations and arbitrariness that the case acquired) over the question of regime succession, forever the Achilles' heel of all dictatorships. At the same time and for the first time, all opposition forces appeared united around the same strategy of confrontation with the regime (seeking its defeat in the Plebiscite). Upon winning the Plebiscite, the opposition for the first time saw the possibility of undermining Pinochet's double legitimacy in the armed forces, which was both hierarchico-institutional and politico-constitutional. All of this made a new *coup d'état* by Pinochet practically impossible, given the very different national and international conditions from those in 1973.

The regime's defeat in the Plebiscite of 5 October 1988, in which the majority of the population voted against the continuance of Pinochet and his regime for another eight years, brought with it both the armed forces' gradual retirement from political power (while still maintaining its power of corporate pressure and political influence) and the splitting off of the civilian sector which supported the regime. This civilian sector crossed over in search of a role as the political right in the future democratic regime. To do that, it accepted an accord with the 'Concertacion' of opposition parties which proposed some adaptations to the constitutional framework through a reform plebiscite. The military government had no alternative but to accept.

For its part, the opposition had two tasks to confront. On the one hand, it had to search for a new institutional framework which would

dismantle the system set up by Pinochet. On the other, it had to ②
guarantee a majority-based democratic government which would
complete the transition after the presidential and parliamentary elections required under the Constitution and which would begin the task
of consolidation via global democratisation. All of this presupposed
constitutional agreements with the right (an indirect way of negotiat-
ing with the military) to which we have already alluded. But above
all, it presupposed the transformation of the coalition victorious in
the Plebiscite into a government coalition with a single presidential
candidate, a single agreed programme and a parliamentary electoral
pact. To achieve that, it was necessary to transform into long-term
allies two social and political forces whose past rupture had brought
about democratic collapse: the middle classes and the masses of the
poor. In political terms, this meant uniting the centre (the Christian
Democrats) and the leftist parties (especially the socialists, but also
the Communist Party which was implicitly bound by the agreement).
This way they might emerge victorious at the parliamentary and
presidential elections of December 1989, avoiding the 'Korean syn-
drome' of division among the opposition. Political democracy could
then be inaugurated in March 1990.

On 11 March 1990, the transition process from a military to a
democratic regime was concluded, a process begun on 5 October
1988 with Pinochet's defeat in the Plebiscite. Nevertheless, the
inauguration of the new regime and of the first democratic government were accomplished after an incomplete transition. This left two
great challenges facing this first democratic government: the transition's completion and the initiation of democratic consolidation.

Completing the transition implied overcoming the legacy of
authoritarian enclaves, that is to say, the elimination of the institutional remains which the former regime left behind and which
perpetuated authoritarian characteristics within the democratic regime
(parts of the Constitution, organic laws, labour legislation, etc.). The
new government also had to neutralise non-democratic actors (nuclei
of Pinochetism and the authoritarian right) and to solve the inherited
problem of human rights. If it were not to do these things, political
democracy would not be definitively re-established. It would be weak
and distorted, not fulfilling its functions as an authentic political
regime, and it would be at the mercy of possible authoritarian steps
backwards.

In order to begin the job of democratic consolidation – at the same
time as completing the transition with the destruction of authoritarian
enclaves – required, in the Chilean case, a deepening of social

113

democratisation (overcoming inequalities, bringing in marginated sectors of the populace, channelling of youth demands) along with the modernisation of the country, eliminating perverse and divisive traits left by the modernisations of the military regime.

In confronting this double challenge, Chile had two advantages over similar experiences elsewhere. On the one hand, it was not in the midst of a severe economic crisis which would force it to spend all of the energy of the new government dealing with inflation, the balance of payments, etc. This allowed leaders to give priority to the political tasks and institutional reforms to which we have referred. On the other hand, for the first time in these processes, and in the history of recent decades in the country, the democratic government was a majority government, socially, politically and electorally (although not institutionally due to some of the enclaves mentioned: designated senators, for example). It was a coalition whose axes were the centre (fundamentally, the Christian Democrats) and the left (fundamentally, socialists and the Party for Democracy). This majority-based governing coalition avoided the trauma of political democratisations in which one side administers the transition and the other side the social demands, mutually attacking one another and generating minority governments and destabilisation.

Both advantages were brought to bear as the regime set about destroying authoritarian redoubts and converting the social, political and electoral majority into an institutional majority capable of governing effectively on the basis of the immense democratic legitimacy with which the regime and government began. Because in situations like that of Chile, where there exists a social, political and electoral majority, the essential cornerstone of a strategy of destruction of authoritarian enclaves is found in the transformation of this majority into the capacity to govern.

Moreover, there was available for this task what has sometimes been called a 'honeymoon period', in which the government has everything in its favour in establishing its legitimacy. To this one ought to add that the division of the right between a democratic sector and a sector more tied to the former regime offered the opportunity for opening a space for the former by means of global democratising accords, which in turn isolated the latter. That was done by prolonging the accords supporting constitutional reforms made with this more democratic sector (the Renovacion Nacional Party) during the transition of 1989, which culminated in the above-mentioned Plebiscite in July of that year.

Thus, in the Chilean case, in spite of it being an 'incomplete

114

transition', one is dealing with one of the most successful democratic transitions on record.

Regarding the issue of the consolidation of a future democratic regime, over and above the destruction of the authoritarian enclaves, what seems to me crucial are three principles. First, we need to redefine our model of development and insertion in the international system, and to distance ourselves both from the traditional one exhausted in 1973 and from that set in place by the military regime. Second, we must accept the need for greater tension or separation between the party system and social movements. This new relationship between the state/regime and social movements, would restore the capacity to lead on the part of the state and get beyond the excessively tight 'interwovenness' between parties and social organisations which prevailed in Chile up until 1973. That takes us to a series of issues of an institutional and political-cultural nature. Finally, we must establish a long-term socio-political majority, taking in the centre and left which would overcome the ruptures of the past – especially that between the middle classes and the poorer masses.

NOTES

1. Suffice it to mention just two texts dealing with these approaches: L. Althusser, *Pour Marx* (Paris, 1965) and T. Parsons, *Societies* (Princeton, 1966). In Latin America Gino Germani's adoption of the Parsonian approach was extremely influential in *Politica y sociedad en una epoca de transicion* (Buenos Aires, 1963); similarly the spread of the Marxist approach in M. Harnecker, *Los conceptos elementales del materialismo historico* (Mexico, 1969).
2. A good example is the classic by H. Marcuse, *One Dimensional Man* (Boston 1963).
3. This is not the place to provide a bibliographical list of these approaches, each of which has many branches and which themselves do not recognise all the different development approaches. Besides the classic text of Germani already cited regarding the modernisation approach, one ought to cite the most important text for the dependency school, which is without doubt the least criticisable in the dimensions to which we will refer, F. H. Cardoso and E. Faletto, *Dependencia y desarrollo en America Latina* (Mexico 1969). Summaries and critical adaptations to these approaches can be consulted in R. Franco, J. Jutkowitz and A. Solari, *Teoria, accion social y desarrollo en America Latina* (Mexico, 1976); J. Graciarena and R. Franco, *Formaciones sociales y estructuras de poder en America Latina* (Madrid, 1981); Klaren and Bossert, *Promise of Development: Theories of change in Latin America* (Boulder, 1986); P. Morande,

115

Cultura y modernizacion en America Latina (Santiago, 1984); A. and S. Valenzuela, 'Modernizacion y dependencia: perspectivas alternadas en el estudio del subdesarrollo latinoamericano' in J. Villamil (ed.) *Capitalismo transnacional y desarrollo nacional* (Mexico, 1981); F. Zapata, *Ideologia y politica en America Latina* (Mexico, 1990); M. A. Garreton, *Proyecto cientifico y proyecto socio-politico. Esquema para una revision critica de la sociologia en Chile* (Santiago, 1978).

4. On these ideas see L. Paramio, *Tras el diluvio. La izquierda ante el fin del siglo* (Madrid, 1988).

5. On the topic of military regimes, among others, D. Collier (ed.) *The New Authoritarianism in Latin America* (Princeton, 1979). On democratic transitions see the already classic volume, edited by P. Schmitter, G. O'Donnell and L. Whitehead, *Transitions from Authoritarian Rule* (Baltimore, 1986). My own view of military regimes and contemporary authoritarianism in Latin America is found in *The Chilean Political Process* (1989) and in *The Failure of the Dictatorships in the Southern Cone* (1986), and on transitions see my 'Problems of Democracy in Latin America: On the Processes of Transition and Consolidation,' *International Journal* (Summer 1988).

6. See a review and interpretation of all these processes and bibliography on them in A. Touraine, *America Latina politica y sociedad* (Madrid, 1989). Also J. Nun, *La rebelion del coro* (Buenos Aires, 1989).

7. On medium range theories see the classic work by R. K. Merton, *Teoria y estructuras sociales* (Mexico, 1964). We employ this term here without all the connotations which have provoked such a long epistemological discussion (see P. Morande, *Cultura y modernizacion . . .*, pp. 36–45).

8. Special issues of the *Revista Mexicana de Sociologia* over the last 15 years, the FLACSO reprints in the journals *Critica y Utopia* and *David y Goliath* and in the collective work edited by F. Calderon and M. Dos Santos, *Hacia un nuevo orden estatal en America Latina?* (Buenos Aires, 1988, 5 vols), and many other works have contributed to the response to these earlier paradigms, while trying to rescue valid elements from them.

9. I have developed some of the concepts which follow here and in the paragraph about Latin America in *Dictaduras y Democratizacion* (Santiago, 1984); *Reconstruir la Politica. Transicion y Consolidacion democraticas en Chile* (Santiago, 1987); and in *Reconstruccion y Democracia. La doble problematica del sistema politico* in G. Martner, *Chile hacia el año 2000: Desafios y Opciones*, vol. I (Caracas, 1988); *Del autoritarismo a la democracia politica. Una transicion a reinventar?* (Santiago, 1991). In many of these positions I must give recognition to the intellectual influence of A. Touraine. See his *Production de la société* (Paris, 1973), *Le retour de l'acteur* (Paris, 1984), and *America Latina . . .*

10. Such is the historical vision, so profoundly ideological and wrong, widely spread about by F. Fukuyama, *El fin de la historia?* (Mexico, 1990).

11. A recent example, P. Morande, *Identidad cultural de America Latina* (Santiago, 1990).

12. See Collier (ed.) *The New Authoritarianism . . .*

13. On the originality of modernity for the case of each society, see O. Paz, *La busqueda del presente* (Mexico, 1991).

14. I have developed this term and the one which follows ('authoritarian enclaves') in *La posibilidad democratica en Chile* (Santiago, 1989).
15. Regarding the debate on modernisation and modernity in Latin America, see FLACSO, *Imagenes desconocidas. La modernidad en la encrucijada postmoderna* (Buenos Aires, 1988).
16. See the proposal of CEPAL, *Transformacion productiva con equidad. La tarea prioritaria del desarrollo de America Latina y el Caribe en los años 90* (Santiago, 1990).
17. Authors who analyse this type of process are Barrington Moore, *Social Origins of Democracy and Dictatorship* (1966) and D. Rustow, 'Transitions to Democracy: Towards a Dynamic Model,' *Comparative Politics* (1970).
18. See note 5.
19. This could be the process which Mexico is currently undergoing.
20. The situation of some Central American countries illustrates this affirmation.
21. M. A. Garreton, 'Transicion: Asimilar la profunda experiencia,' *Convergencia* (February–March 1991) and *Politica, cultura* . . .
22. The ideas expressed rather schematically here are more fully developed in my cited works.

PART TWO

The Theatrical and Imaginary Dimensions of Politics

CHAPTER SIX

Political Institutions, Discourse and Imagination in China at Tiananmen

Rudolf Wagner

The events in and around Tiananmen Square in May and June of 1989 can best be understood in the context of a severe and generalised crisis within China's political institutions. That crisis was in part triggered by economic problems following upon the partial liberalisation and modernisation of China's economy after 1978, but it was essentially political in character. Indeed the laws governing the institutional dynamics of socialist states in Europe and Asia are of a very particular brand and require a decisive devaluation of the role of the very factor that has been elevated to a pre-eminent position by Marx himself – the economy.

At most times, and especially in times of crisis, China's political institutions do not operate according to the rules set out in law and in the government's and the Communist Party's formal statements. Instead they function according to informal rules which render political institutions incapable of adapting and responding to the kinds of changes that occurred after 1978, except through the deployment of coercive force. This incapacity of political institutions, together with the fictional character of public discussions of institutional operations, had a destructive impact upon political discourse and the possibility of dialogue between the regime and those in Chinese society who had found a voice in the 1980s. It was impossible for those in power and the Tiananmen protestors even to define each other and to communicate with each other in any meaningful way, and the ghastly results are well known. To grasp all of this, we need to examine both the condition of China's political institutions and, more broadly, the character of political discourse and political imagination in China.

UNBUILDING THE INSTITUTIONS

It is commonly accepted by all, including Chinese leaders of every faction, that modernisation in bureaucratised economies and societies such as theirs will be a painful process. In the social rearrangements inevitably accompanying this process, conflicts, even violent conflicts, seem unavoidable because the discretionary monopoly of the hitherto ruling group is threatened, and various hitherto privileged groups like workers or cadres are in danger of being marginalised. In the socialist world, these modernising reforms have generally gone through two phases. In the first phase, which China experienced between late 1978 and the mid-1980s, the newly unleashed forces of a liberalised economy secure substantial growth rates and contribute to a general atmosphere of optimism and even buoyancy. In the second phase, which China experienced since the mid-1980s, the long-term structural problems of these economies and politics make themselves felt, problems that cannot be solved by patching and mending.

During the first phase, things are relatively easy, but in the second phase, the viability of the entire state structure is put to the test. We then discover whether the state is able to manage the inevitable conflicts by protecting contesting social groups from each other's worst (and best) impulses, and whether it is able to channel society's energies in a manner that contributes to the long-term solution of the problems.

China's 1989 crisis did not begin with the army marching on to Tiananmen Square. In March, Prime Miniser Li Peng had announced an austerity programme to cope with the mounting economic crisis and a return to stronger state control over the economy. Indeed since the inflationary rises in 1987, a sense of crisis had been driven home, especially to the state employees with their fixed salaries and to people in poor agricultural areas far from the cities and trunk lines.

Well before the massacre in and around Tiananmen on 3 and 4 June, the various institutions of the government had ceased to operate normally. The cause was not within the government itself, but rather within the leadership of China's ruling Communist Party. There, various factions and groupings were engaged in a fierce battle for control, the outcome of which would decide the future direction, personnel and operations of all the institutions involved. A closer look reveals that even the institutions of the party Centre were not actually in control. The party has legal institutions to handle such issues as appointments and policy guidelines, but in times of serious conflict, they instantly collapse, giving way to completely different and highly unpredictable methods.

In this case, the public learned from the party secretary, Zhao Ziyang, that in fact control over policy was even beyond his level. In a televised talk with Mr Gorbachev, Zhao declared that the relations between the Soviet and Chinese parties had not been reformalised during their talks – that is between the two party general secretaries – but a few hours before, when Mr Gorbachev met Deng Xiaoping (who held no senior party post). At the party Congress in 1987, Zhao declared that the party would refer in all major decisions to Deng and a group of old cadres convened by him. Institutionally Deng was head of the party's Military Commission. The other members of this top group, like Peng Zhen, Bo Yibo, Wang Zhen, Li Xiannian and Chen Yun, are no longer formal members of either the party Centre or the government, but belong to the various advisory groups who technically have no voting powers. The reason why these old cadres were invited to join in the policy-making group was not their institutional importance but the fact that they had built up, over decades, patronage systems in the civilian and military realms which enabled them to bolster their voice with the promise of delivering the support or the opposition of their cohorts.

The visible institutional leaders like Li Peng and Zhao Ziyang thus had little or no discretionary power. The actual decision-making was done in a body that had no formal institutional standing, the existence of which was revealed only by a disgruntled Zhao and he was promptly accused of leaking the secrets of the last party Congress to Mr Gorbachev. The personal patronage networks which provided the basis for the actual leadership's powers were essentially independent of political beliefs. This type of loyalty is owed in China under the following conditions:

1 Appointment received under the leadership or by the intervention of the given leader, an example being the heads of the military regions which for the most part have been appointed through Deng Xiaoping's influence in the military commission, and have been selected from his original military unit.
2 Work under a given leader; an example being the many people who had worked under the former and now late party secretary Hu Yaobang when he was head of the Youth League.
3 Admission into the party on the recommendation of a given leader; Hu Yaobang provides a good example as he recruited a large part

of the present middle-level leadership into the party through the Young League.

4 Family ties, either through blood or marriage; the details about state president Yang Shangkun's extended family have been widely reported; Li Peng is Zhou Enlai's adopted son, the new party secretary Jiang Zeming is Li Xiannian's son-in-law.

5 Same province of origin; an example is the grouping Deng Xiaoping, Yang Shangkun and Li Peng, all of whom are from Sichuan province. Another example is the Shanxi clique around Xi Jianxun.

6 Graduates of the same class in the military academy, and so on.

Institutions, accordingly, have no weight of their own in China. Their role and prestige is a direct function of their head's position in the invisible power structure of the Centre. This stands in radical contrast to a system such as that which prevailed, for example, in the Third and Fourth French Republics. There, dozens of governments manned by different party combinations succeeded one another at a rapid pace, while the professional administrators in the state institutions went on plying their trade, efficiently and unperturbed. Those administrators differed greatly in their political philosophies, but they shared a professional ethic and some political principles, among which was a commitment to basic freedoms and to the ongoing centrality of power under their direction. By sheer inertia, they blocked radical transformations planned by various governments. At the same time, the separation of powers between the courts and the bureaucrats safeguarded the citizens against abuses by the bureaucrats. This diffusion of power among political, legal and bureaucratic authorities was remarkably flexible in responding to the challenge of modernisation in France, mainly because it permitted competing models of adaptation to coexist and to compete. It also created enough latitude for a more or less rational discourse to occur amid the competition of the various powers and models.

In the People's Republic of China, the structure of politics prevents such a diffusion of power. Technically speaking it is even illegal. The state constitution contains the Four Basic Principles. These were articulated by Deng Xiaoping himself in 1979, on the basis of a Maoist precedent from the 1950s. The Principles are as follows: the leading role of the Communist Party; Marxism-Leninism-Maoism as the fundamental doctrine; the socialist system as the guiding system for relations of production; and the 'democratic dictatorship of the people' as the instrument to deal with the 'enemies of the people', that is counter-revolutionaries, a category now reserved for the participants in the democracy movement. In practice, this means that the National People's Congress and the government are led by the Communist Party. The Supreme Court and the other courts also operate under the four basic principles so that they must follow the directives of the party leadership, and the same is true for the various sections of the executive.

In a crisis like the one experienced by the Chinese body politic since 1987, and in particular in May and early June of 1989, the implications of this arrangement become vividly apparent. The separation of powers, which the formal constitutional order appears to promise, does not in fact exist. One day after the Tiananmen massacre, the Supreme Court published a statement requesting the speedy arrest, trial and punishment of all those involved in the 'counter-revolutionary turmoil'. The potential of the court to act as a buffer, protecting both the leadership and the people against the hysterics of the other is forfeited. There is no possibility to go to court against the military commanders of the units involved in the massacre or against individual soldiers who wantonly shot pedestrians in the week following 4 June. The Supreme Court did not shirk its real duties in doing this, but exactly fulfilled its duties, namely to follow the leadership of the party in defining the disturbances as 'counter-revolutionary turmoil' and then applying the 'dictatorship of the people' to the treatment of those involved, which meant execution or long prison terms.

Parliament (or the National People's Congress) might have been a second institution to mediate in the conflict between the leadership and the people. There had in fact been attempts to make it into an instrument for the representation of popular demands. Among the most outspoken theoretical advocates had been Yan Jiaqi, a political scientist with the Academy of Social Sciences. On the occasion of its meeting in March 1989, he petitioned in a published article for it to have a stronger supervisory role *vis-à-vis* the government. The budget for the year, he argued for example, is submitted to parliament fully three months *after* the government has started to act on it. The 1987 budget, furthermore, was changed considerably by the government without any parliamentary consultation. This, he suggested, should be changed.

Wan Li, a member of the Politburo, heads the parliament. During the last weeks before the massacre, he was on a visit to the United States and Canada. From there, he sent various telegrams in substance approving of the demands of the students whom he termed patriotic. He broke off his trip and returned home prematurely, warning his relatives in the United States before leaving that he might find himself arrested upon arrival. He was hospitalised in Shanghai and not permitted to go on to Beijing until he had publicly supported the imposition of martial law, and on Wednesday 8 June he appeared with Deng Xiaoping and others to congratulate the military for their heroic victory on Tiananmen. He had intended to call a meeting of the standing committee of parliament to discuss the crisis. People set great hopes by such a meeting which legally could have deposed Li Peng. In Nanjing, 600 students began a walk on 1 June over the 1,000 kilometres to Beijing to arrive on the scheduled date to present their request to dismiss Li Peng. The preconditions for summoning such a special meeting had long been met, but it was abruptly called off, obviously at the behest of Deng Xiaoping and in spite of legal problems, since Deng is not a member of the body whose meeting he cancelled.

When the meeting eventually took place, an important proposal for a new press law which would have given greater leeway to the papers was taken off the agenda, and the legality and legitimacy of the Tiananmen massacre was never mentioned. Technically, parliament heard without discussion the report by Li Peng, and approved it. Yan Jiaqi, the political scientist who suggested that parliament be made a powerful representative institution, is now on the most wanted list for counter-revolutionary crimes. Happily, he has made his way to Paris.

The formal institutions of the executive branch also had next to no influence during this crisis. The Minister of Defence was opposed to the use of the military, but the army was called in by the Military Commission of the Communist Party headed by Deng Xiaoping, overruling the minister, who is not a member of this body. Nor were minimal legal norms observed. Police arrested and paraded on television a number of suspected 'counter-revolutionaries'. Charges against them were in many cases legally invalid. One man was charged with 'spreading rumours', which certainly is no legal offence in the Chinese criminal code, but he was jailed. Another man was arrested for having made a speech demanding the abolition of one-party rule. Freedom of speech is guaranteed by the Constitution, but so is the leading role of the Communist Party. He was defined as a 'counter-revolutionary', which implies a heavy penalty. Within the leadership's understanding of the institutional structure, all of this was precisely according to the law, including the call by the Supreme Court to disregard niceties of legal detail and proceed to a speedy judgement and execution for the criminals.

As to the press, it comes institutionally under the control of the

Propaganda Department of the Central Committee, as do the arts including literature, cinema and theatre. The stated purpose of the press is to educate the masses in the spirit of the latest party directives. Within the leeway allotted by these directives, individual papers can operate without going through central censorship. If, as is the case since the Third Plenum of December 1978, the directive describes bureaucratism as an obstacle to desirable economic development, bureaucratism may be denounced. However, since bureaucratism is defined as a left-over from the old society, statements asserting, for example, that the state structure set up according to the Soviet model engenders bureaucratism are unacceptable and therefore unpublishable. Since the end of the Cultural Revolution a number of institutions have sprung up that could have been legalised. Consider, for example, the independent journals and newspapers: they were a part of the democracy movement between 1977 and 1979. After they had served their purpose by supporting Deng Xiaoping's bid for power against Hua Guofeng, they were outlawed and closed. Some of their authors were invited to write for official publications, and others like Wei Jinsheng and Wang Xizhe were jailed or put into labour camps.

This is not to say that there have been no independent publications, but instead to say that the party Centre continuously kept them in the shadow of illegality and could at any moment intervene when it felt this necessary. The Shanghai-based *Shijie jingji daobao* (*World Economic Herald*) may illustrate this. The paper is edited by the Shanghai Academy of Social Sciences, and has featured some of the more independent reporting and discussion in China in recent years. After failing to support the crackdown in late 1986 and early 1987, six of its editors were fired. When it again failed to toe the party line after the death of Hu Yaobang, Jian Zemin, then Shanghai's party secretary and now the new general secretary of the party, sent a 'leading group' to straighten out the paper. When the journalists failed to comply, the paper did not appear. The editor-in-chief was sacked long before the army crushed the demonstrations in Beijing. He was technically accused of 'violating party discipline'. He is a party member, which was the condition for his becoming the editor-in-chief, and by failing to abide by the directives of the leadership he indeed violated party discipline. He is an old man already, and has been put under house arrest while one of the younger men actually running the paper is on the most wanted list of intellectuals sought by police for counter-revolutionary activity.

During the days immediately preceding the 1989 crackdown, the content of all published papers shifted daily in direct reaction to who controlled the party Centre. The head of the propaganda department was Hu Qili, who did not support martial law. Thus the papers reported in a very friendly manner the actions of the students. Li Peng then set up a special media committee consisting of his spokesman and adviser Yuan Mu as well as another man whom he personally trusted. Although institutionally this unit had no existence, it took over from Hu Qili, who also held no government position. It turned the press and television into a desert of official proclamations and denunciations, showing the degree to which the entire media depended on informal channels of control. The authority of the committee was derived from the fact that Deng Xiaoping backed Li Peng, Li Peng backed Yuan Mu, and thereupon a simple Central Committee member overrode a member of the Standing Committee of the Politburo. The state organs played no role whatsoever in this.

It should be clear by now that the new party leadership after 1978 failed to build institutions that were able to mediate, diffuse or solve conflicts without resorting to the use of tanks, even though these leaders anticipated prolonged and intense conflicts. In fact, the policy of Deng Xiaoping has been less a failure to build such institutions than an active unbuilding of such institutions, even though these institutions were constantly growing in the public imagination. During the post-1978 decade, there was steady pressure for the establishment of such institutions. The parliament or National People's Congress tried to be more than an applause machine for party decisions; the government organs tried to professionalise themselves and become less dependent on day-to-day party directives; the papers tried to diversify and develop in new and more independent directions.

POLITICAL DISCOURSE AND POLITICAL IMAGINATION AT TIANANMEN

A similar distance separates appearance from reality in the workings of another key political institution, the Communist Party. And as we shall see, this and the charades discussed above have done enormous damage to political discourse and to channels of communication between state and society.

The party's constitution outlaws the formation of cliques or factions. As everyone knows, however, these factions exist and form the main organisational structures of power. This ban on forming factions means that the operation of the various factions is driven into a verbal underground. No one can claim adhesion to a certain faction as his reason to operate in a certain way, activity which is perfectly possible in a multi-party system. No one can claim the interests of a certain part of the population as a rationale for his or her policies. The legitimacy of controversial discourse in public as well as within the party is thereby eliminated. In a party of some 48 million members it can be assumed that the various interests in society, be they geographically or socially based, will be represented – an argument in fact advanced by the leadership against the necessity of a multi-party system. However, the lack of legitimacy for advocating particular and even parochial interests openly, and the heavily enforced and verbalised homogeneity of the party do not permit such a representation of interests.

There is always and in any polity a strong tension in politics between the rationale given for a policy or decision and the complex motives and compromises actually going into the decision. Still, the appearance of rationality is maintained and any demonstration that the official reasons were but disguises for ulterior interests is often considered devastating. Under Chinese institutional conditions, the conflict between the official rationale and the actual decision-making process is as fundamental as it is illegal to mention it publicly. The Hong Kong and Taiwanese papers, from a greater familiarity with cultural patterns, base all of their political analysis on the factions and alliances formed under the above-mentioned criteria. Therefore they are illegal contraband in China. Even if their perceptions are not altogether correct, these assumptions certainly inform the reading of the Chinese public and its political class.

The political discourse of the country is soured by this perception. Any news, any argument proffered, theory proposed or historical fact challenged is read as a potentially devious expression of some political purpose, and thereby stripped of its claim to rationality, which in turn would have made it challengeable on rational grounds. The political discourse is thus driven into the verbal underground of silent, symbolic or coded communication. While Pekinology might be an esoteric field in the West, it certainly is mass fare in China. Does a leader wear Western clothes or the Sun Yatsen suit? What type is used to set a specific article? Who is photographed with whom in published photographs, and how do the people photographed look at each other? Is there a difference between the printed and the performed version of a theatre play? The forms of esoteric communication developed to discuss controversial political issues are as old as they are endless in their variety.

In point of fact, China's institutions have been most effective over the decade leading up to Tiananmen at divesting themselves of their discretionary powers. Their partial self-dismantling freed substantial social forces that threw themselves into modernisation. The drive for this partial divestment of discretionary powers emanated from the reform leadership itself, and therfore was not in need of mediating institutions. The conflict, however, between the independent aspirations of parts of the populace and the Centre was constantly present, although only in a latent form. The various political campaigns against spiritual pollution and bourgeois liberalisation during the last decade showed a slowly rising temperature in the contention. But when the party Centre was confronted by the Beijing population and a substantial part of the political class with independent criticism of mismanagement and demands for institutional reform that would have transformed a paternalistic command structure into a contractual structure, this self-dismantling by party and state institutions left no structures through which to communicate, to mediate and to engage both sides in a negotiated settlement.

As this crisis developed, it turned out that both sides assumed and perceived the essential and, as far as the party was concerned, deliberate inability of China's state and party institutions to handle the stresses of modernisation and adaptation. This came as more of a surprise to Westerners used to the roles played by their own institutions rather than Chinese conditions. The protesters never seriously tried the institutions, and the party Centre treated them with the same disdain by languidly discarding them. And the members of the institutions themselves, well aware of their marginal existence, ceased to function even in their limited ways. The massive body of state and party institutions with their officials, papers, forms and language, with stability and continuity suggested by their sheer size and weight, turned out to be rather ethereal and highly unstable structures. They were subjectively and objectively unable to adapt to the new challenges from below, and they were paralysed by the dissonance in the party Centre itself.

Both sides were thus stranded for the occasion in an institutional desert, facing each other on Tiananmen Square. They had no well-established categories with which to define each other and each other's actions, and to communicate with each other and the public at large. Confronted with this situation they were searching in the imaginary stock of their historical and social experience for the words, the precedents and the model actions to express their concerns, to prop up their spirits and to earn themselves some legitimacy.

The students had a substantial problem defining themselves. Many of them wore the white headbands popularised by the Japanese, Korean and Philippino protesters. In the Chinese context this meant that they were not an organisation challenging the Communist Party, but the unarmed and non-violent masses articulating their basic aspirations. At the same time, this device likened the government to the Marcos regime, a brutal dictatorship basing its power on a mighty military machine and characterised by an extreme degree of personal corruption. Their legitimacy came from world opinion which had denounced Marcos, and their perspective and hope from the Philippinos' peaceful transition to democracy. In Beijing University, a photo exhibit in April and May showed many pictures from the Philippine revolution, by way of precedent. Institutionally this was a very broad and a very foggy construct taken from the imaginary world of the foreign post-socialist revolutions.

Their organisational forms – that is the independent unions of the students, the workers and the intellectuals – were taken from another stock, the Polish Solidarnosc experience. This implied an entire scenario, namely the broad and nearly complete popularity of the movement, the potential for a brutal crackdown such as that perpetrated by General Jaruselski, and the final demise of Jaruselski's socialist junta a few years later. The Solidarnosc model assumed that the military and the party would be willing to go along with a crackdown. It contained an ironic dialogue with Deng Xiaoping himself. On the occasion of the last major student protest, in December 1986, Deng had spoken approvingly of Jaruselski for having saved the Poles from their own self-destructive urges through his intervention. Coming back to the Polish experience in 1989, with the dramatic changes in Poland happening exactly at the height of the conflict in China, the students and workers took Deng at his own word by projecting what would happen to him if he copied Jaruselski. Of course, China is neither Poland nor the Philippines, but in this manner the students saw themselves and portrayed themselves as part of an irresistible world trend.

The hunger-strike as the ultimate means of pleading for a rapid and serious dialogue was another imported symbol from a world culture of dissidence. Generally linked to Gandhi's strategies of non-violent popular resistance, the immediate quote was from South Africa. There, students had staged a hunger strike to force the government to give up its apartheid policy. As the elimination of apartheid in

South Africa involved major changes in all areas of society which could not be managed within a few days, the purpose of the hunger strike was more to initiate this process than to see it completed. The main demand of the Tiananmen protesters, the elimination of corruption, as well as the clamours for democracy, involved long-term reforms. The purpose of the hunger-strike was thus to communicate to the world that the problems in China needed a solution as urgently as apartheid, and to achieve the establishment of an institutional structure of dialogue between the contestants and the government to tackle the problem. At the same time, the hunger-strike challenged the government. The South African government, gleefully described in the Chinese communist press with the entire arsenal of socialist curses, as 'capitalist, imperialist, reactionary', and 'racist', had positively reacted to the demands of the hunger strikers after two or three days. The Chinese socialist government was forced to don this South African garb through the students' symbolic action, and after three days the students were able to point out that the Chinese government had not even lived up to this modest model.

In February 1989, a very substantial number of leading Chinese intellectuals pioneered the use of such modern and Western forms by signing a petition for the release of political prisoners like Wei Jinsheng, a participant in the 1978 democracy movement who had been given a jail term of fifteen years and was reported to break down under the stress of solitary confinement. The resolution had been formulated by one of the least political of China's young poets, Bei Dao. Amnesty International and other organisations had kept the memory of these political prisoners alive, but Chinese intellectuals saw the 1980s as their period of greatest freedom and were not willing to speak out on the issue until 1989.

The use of this form as well as the language employed defined the Chinese government in an entirely Western framework of the 1980s, where human rights concerns, at least in theory, are seen as the main standard by which to measure a government. The Chinese leadership was thus defined by Chinese intellectuals as one of the regular repressive regimes running fair parts of this world. Since the beginning of the reforms, the leadership had proclaimed that from now on a patriotic commitment by intellectuals should suffice. They were no longer asked to be propagandists of socialist and communist values. The petition departed from this last common ground by criticising the Chinese leadership on the basis of a Western human rights concept although this might mean an 'unpatriotic' lowering of the prestige of the Chinese leaders. This courageous action also enhanced the credibility of many signatories in the West where their refusal to discuss problems of human rights and censorship in China had irritated many.

The standard song of all participants in this movement was, strangely enough, the 'Internationale'. Those who sang it might not have been aware that the song referred to the Communist International, but read the entire text afresh. Read unhistorically, it is indeed a song where the damned of the entire earth encourage each other to fight for the days of glory to come, socialism and communism not being mentioned. The refrain refers to the Communist International through the Chinese transcription *yindenaxiunaer* to the English word 'international', thus setting the Chinese movement into an 'international' world context so essential for its perspective and success, and disclaiming through the future tense in the refrain 'the *yindenaxiunaer* will free all mankind' the Chinese Communist Party's claim of having already achieved this liberation. In the context of the song, the party joined the ogres of exploitation and repression singled out in the text for rapid demolition. In terms of tactics, the choice of this very official song which is taught in all schools in Communist China permitted the singers to stay within the confines of state ordered Communist discourse, and still have their say.

Gorbachev's visit on 15 May linked the Chinese movement up with another world current, namely the radical restructuring of socialist states managed by groupings within the communist leadership itself. Gorbachev at the time, with his Western airs, stress on democratisation and close cooperation with the West, seemed to many Chinese to be just the figure needed in China, and some fantasies grew that Zhao Ziyang might grow into this role.

These quotes from and references to the modern *imaginaire* eventually culminated in the statue of democracy planted on Tiananmen Square. Its intention was to stand in lieu of the contestants, embodying their claims and virtues, while they themselves would return to their campuses and offices and not offer themselves up as victims for a military crackdown. The statue was based, both in idea and iconography, on the Statue of Liberty presented to the United States by France. This American statue, however, operates with the ambivalence of the word liberty, which might indicate national independence (from the British colonial empire) as well as civil liberties. In its former function, the statue had been often referred to in China when 'national independence' from the Manchu rulers and eventually from the foreign powers was the order of the day. The statue even made it onto the cover of the first best-seller in the world of modern

Chinese fiction, Zeng Pu's *Flower in the Sea of Retribution, Niehai hua*. The term used in 1989 for the statue, *minzhu zhi shen* – Goddess of Democracy – clearly came out for a new top priority, namely democracy.

These modern and foreign models were important and crucial, because they embodied the self-perception of the young, urban, and Western-oriented participants in the political movement, enhanced their stature and legitimacy, were understood internationally, and helped to build up much foreign support. For domestic consumption, however, for symbolically communicating their aims, aspirations, and problem definitions to a wide Chinese audience, the contestants built their definitions and their legitimacy with elements from the traditional arsenal of the Chinese *imaginaire*.

The death of the former Party secretary Hu Yaobang played an important role in this. In March, there had been a resolution calling for the release of Wei Jinsheng and other political prisoners, signed by many prominent intellectuals, a first in the history of the People's Republic. There had been signs, however, that Hu Yaobang was coming back. He had not been dismissed from the Politburo and, in March, his successor Zhao Ziyang had himself photographed with him and had the picture printed in the *People's Daily*. But on 15 April 1989, Hu Yaobang died after a heart attack during a bitter controversy in the Politburo where he reportedly charged that the Party would be finished if it was unable to get corruption under control. In the personalised structure of Chinese politics where the individual leader counts infinitely more than the institution he might be heading, Hu Yaobang seemed to be the only top leader with a record qualifying him to guide the country through the crisis. He had been head of the Youth League for decades, and in this function had promoted a good number of fairly outspoken young men and women into the upper ranks of the Party. From 1978 on, he had managed the rehabilitation of the victims of the Cultural Revolution and of the 1957 Anti-Rightist Campaign, he had suggested most of the more daring new slogans like 'seeking truth from facts' and had supported a much stronger divestment of Party control over government affairs. In addition, he was one of the very few leaders about whom no stories of nepotism circulated. His death closed what people saw as the last personal avenue of talk open to handle the economic and social crisis of the country. Mourning for him was much more widespread, more spontaneous and less tactical than that for Zhou Enlai which had been mostly organised by the children of cadres downed during the Cultural Revolution.

The death of Hu Yaobang and the state ceremonies for his burial set a date for the legitimate congregation of large numbers of people to show their grief. The massive and very emotional demonstrations contained a political demand. Hu Yaobang had been dismissed in 1987 for not suppressing the student movement against a reassertion of the conservatives. The Plenum in September 1988 had seen another reassertion of the forces supporting a stronger role for the central bureaucracy in the economy and had proclaimed the necessity to fight bourgeois liberalisation. Participating in the unofficial mourning ceremonies, people in fact demanded that the criticism against Hu Yaobang should be reversed, with the implication that the new conservative trend should be reversed.

The occupation of Tiananmen began with the unofficial mourning ceremony for Hu Yaobang. Next to his large portrait that had been dedicated by the students from the arts college, and was hung on the heroes' memorial, another smaller picture was mounted. It showed Hu Yaobang with the inscription 'New China's Bao Longtu'. Bao Longtu was a judge under the Song dynasty who became a hero of uncounted Chinese operas, which form the archive of China's historical *imaginaire*. There, he appears as the 'upright and clean official', *qingguan*, with daring uprightness even in the face of the ruler himself, incorruptible, with a great sense of justice, and a willingness to listen to the complaints of the common people. Of the two Peking operas performed in Beijing in mid-April, one had Bao Longtu as the hero. He comes on stage in times of crisis and corruption.

By depicting Hu Yaobang as the embodiment of the 'upright official', the students made a traditional comment about the state of China's institutions. The upright official operates without an institutional net high up in the eerie top of the hierarchy, daring to confront even the emperor. Two huge streamers appended to balloons floated in the Square, mourning Hu as '*Zhongguo zhi hun*' the soul of China. Assembling around his picture in mourning in Tiananmen Square put the assembled crowd into the imaginary role of this upright official who, risking his life, dares to speak up in times of need, and is morally utterly pure, a feature emphasised by the hunger strike which implied extreme self-deprivation and purity of motive, urgency, and a non-violent kind of pressure. In traditional China, a peasant would commit suicide in front of the house of the landlord who pressured him for rent payment when he was already starving. This put the landlord in the public role of the brute, forced him to pay for the burial, and exerted strong pressure on him to reduce or forfeit his claims on the family.

Acting out their historical role, on the same day as the unofficial mourning took place in Tiananmen Square, three student leaders, among them Wang Dan who was later to head the most wanted list, proceeded to the Hall of the People where the official mourning ceremony was held. They knelt down on the stairs in front of the door, knocked their heads on the floor, and asked to see the Prime Minister in person. They remained there for three hours. Li Peng refused to see them. In terms of symbolic action in a world where both sides see each other only as embodiments of imaginary constructs, the three student leaders had scored an important point. They had stressed the urgency of the crisis, maintained an unquestionably non-violent and non-threatening posture, thereby proving the purity of their motives and methods. Had Li Peng received them, he would have accepted their claim of being the pure officials confronting the ruthless leader. By not receiving them, he made the public accept it, and put himself into the situation of the corrupt emperor or premier presiding over the last and desperate hours of a waning dynasty, like a Jia Sidao from the Southern Song. Through this symbolic contest, Li Peng was transformed from an awkward and clumsy Soviet-trained middle-level engineer into a certified historical monster.

The students were using historical forms from the Han and the Song dynasties, when student demonstrations against corrupt government broke out, that had been vindicated by history although the students themselves were often brutally suppressed. For Deng Xiaoping a fine historical paradigm was found in the Empress Dowager Cixi of the last dynasty, the Qing. As a woman, she did not have an official role in the government and was not allowed to sit in court during the audiences. So she sat behind a screen out of public view, and directed things from there. In the same manner, Deng Xiaoping was caricatured as directing things from behind the scenes.

Tiananmen Square is not an old place. When Mao Zedong proclaimed the founding of the Republic in 1949 from Tianan Gate, there was little space in front of the gate. Tiananmen Square has been cleared, paved and circled off as a sacred space during the first decade after 1949 in imitation of Red Square in Moscow to become the symbolic centre of the nation, where the leaders on Tianan Gate and the people on the Square would face each other on national day and other occasions. In the tourist brochures and in songs taught in schools, in the streams of visitors guided there, in the buildings surrounding it and being gradually erected on the Square itself, and in the big rallies during the Cultural Revolution and after, the notion that this was the centre of the nation gradually became more specified.

The place is crossed from north to south by the imperial palace. In former days, the emperor sat on this axis facing south when he held court, and the officials would face north when presenting their memorials. The new Communist Centre was aligned with this imperial axis, and surrounded on both sides with new building that stressed the revolutionary character of the place, the Revolutionary Museum on one side, and the building of the National People's Congress on the other. The Centre, that is, the top leadership of Party and State moved not into the Imperial Palace, but into the Zhongnanhai compound slightly to the east. Within the geography of the *imaginaire*, however, Beijing was in the centre of the land, Tiananmen Square was in the centre of Beijing, and the people assembled on the Square faced the imaginary leadership on Tiananmen Gate. Quite independent of the actual situation, the occupation of Tiananmen Square meant that the occupants held the heart of the nation, and represented the best that China had to offer, and that in this constellation they faced the imaginary leadership in the Imperial Palace.

The buildings on the Square are all aligned along the imperial axis, but break its directionality. The heroes who had died for the revolutions since 1840 had a commemorative stele on this axis, but the inscription faced north, challenging the assembled leadership on whether they had lived up to the aspirations of those who had died for the revolution. Behind the stele stands another northward directed building, the Chairman Mao Memorial Hall which is dedicated to the ideological mainstay of the republic and houses the body of Mao Zedong.

The occupants of the Square were well aware of the symbolic and representative action they engaged in. Some 60,000 students from other schools throughout the country converged on Beijing to support the Tiananmen Square action, which for a long while was the only and central thing to happen. Many later actions in the regions were explicitly made in support of this. This was not only conditioned by tactical considerations of this being a big place near the seat of the political Centre with many people coming by, but primarily because Tiananmen Square is the symbolic centre of the nation.

In their actions, the occupants of the Square communicated through familiar associations. In 1976, the then Prime Minister Zhou Enlai had died. Mourning ceremonies for him were officially curtailed, whereupon hundreds of thousands of people congregated on the Square for three days until eventually the whole action was declared a 'counter-revolutionary incident' and was put down with the help of the factory militias; Deng Xiaoping who had just returned from being a leading 'counter-revolutionary' to an active leadership position under the protection of Zhou Enlai, was dismissed, and a new man was installed, Hua Guofeng. Two years later the crackdown was 'reevaluated', the mourning activities became the 'revolutionary April 5 movement', and Deng Xiaoping was back in power. The 1989 occupation of the Square used this precedent. Again, one of the few clean and widely accepted leaders had died. He had been criticised and slandered by a corrupt and ruthless clique in power. The new movement on Tiananmen might be put down again, but a few years down the line, the judgement might again be reversed and those not advocating suppression might be dismissed and face persecution themselves.

There is an old tradition in China, according to which officials and commoners, even foreigners could gain direct access to the emperor in case of a great wrong. They would proceed to the entrance of the palace or of a Yamen, where there was a big drum, the *dengwen zhi gu*, the 'drum that can be heard above'. They would beat the drum, and a censor on duty would come running out, take the writ, and bring it straight to the inner quarters of the emperor who would have to deal with the matter during the audience next morning. The institution was a safeguard for moments of institutional collapse. Only people who had tried all other avenues of remonstrance and redress and had failed to right the wrong were allowed to use this last instrument. The occupation of Tiananmen Square straight in front of the imaginary palace door, and the demands to the government voted upon the place and presented to the government, spoke the language of a largely imaginary imperial institution. All institutions have been tried, they have failed to right the wrong (usually corruption), now the emperor and the common citizen have to confront each other directly because no other solution can be found. The demand for direct and continuous dialogue between government leaders, that is Li Peng or other members of the Politburo, only epitomises the perceived absence and/or collapse of mediating institutions.

The definition of the main problem to be solved was again taken from the traditional arsenal. *Dadao guandao* was the slogan, down with nepotism. The modernist alternative, a demand for structural reforms towards democracy, could not compete with this slogan in its mass appeal. The slogan is based on the traditional assumption that bad character and personal corruption are the main causes for the ills of the country, and that 'clean officials' would be the panacea.

By using this slogan, the contestants staked a claim. They were in fact the 'clean officials' needed now to cure the country of its woes. The contemporary Chinese intelligentsia loves to see itself as the successor to the Chinese mandarins, those scholar-officials that ran the country for centuries before the collapse of the last dynasty. This certainly is a great misassessment. The modern intelligentsia in socialist states has no access to power except in a service function. Power is vested with the party with its own internal hierarchy. The contestants' attack against nepotism, their self-purification through hunger-strikes and non-violence and their projected selfless devotion to the common good of the people at large simulated a traditional scenario of conflict which was as satisfactory, effective, and popular as it was a misperception of themselves and the situation of the country. The traditionalist problem-definition at the same time saved the students from defining the problem of Chinese socialism in a harsh structural manner which would have landed the government onslaught on their heads with even greater brutality.

During the last ten days before the crackdown, the students from the arts institute built the statue of the 'goddess of democracy' there. In a characteristic merger of the two different layers from the arsenal of the *imaginaire*, the modern and Westernised statue was stationed right on the imperial axis. It faced north and stood before both the Heroes Memorial stele and the Chairman Mao Memorial Hall. It established a new priority, where democratic aspirations had precedence and would define how to live up to the expectations of the heroes who had died for the revolution and even how to live up to Mao Zedong's behest. In the appeal inscribed on the streamer next to this goddess as well as in some articles, it was made clear that the goddess represented the aspirations not just of the Chinese, but of the Asian peoples for democracy, reinforcing the Philippino connection. The statue again defined the imaginary other as the feudal, autocratic and militaristic authority in the palace of the party Centre.

The Centre had greater trouble in representing itself. It was in a passive position as the contestants managed to establish a definition in the public mind before the Centre even noticed in what corner it had landed.

In traditional manner, the Centre operated on the assumption that common people are by nature greedy, egotistical and oblivious of national interests, and therefore quite self-destructive if left to their own devices. The idea is best expressed through the standard metaphor used by the old imperial officials for the people. The people there are the river water. In China, the great rivers are diked up, and if they break through the dikes, much disaster and destruction follows. Metaphorically, they are not assumed to dig their own beds, but revert to their productive function only after a strong hand has forced them back behind the dikes of virtue. People need heavy-handed protection against their own destructive urges, which mostly come from their material greed. The danger also seeps into the lower ranks of officialdom, and it is the duty of the morally elevated top leadership to keep them at bay. The reform policy of China had whetted people's appetites and they had become receptive to Western ideas which support this moral depravity instead of combating it. This 'spiritual pollution' was therefore an extremely dangerous affair, and had to be fought tooth and nail.

It is the government's duty to establish a moral environment in the country which prevents people from mobilising their lower instincts, and to keep things under tight control. The worst disaster happens when leaders in the Centre tolerate, support or even encourage such spontaneous and irresponsible outbursts instead of suppressing them. This happened during the Cultural Revolution when Mao supported the Red Guards, it happened in late 1986 when Hu Yaobang refused to clamp down on the students, and it would happen again, when Zhao Ziyang opposed the use of the Army to restore order and thus in fact supported the contestants on the Square. In the perception of Deng Xiaoping and most of the senior communist leaders, China is an extremely unstable unit. Its stability cannot be reached through a contract between governing and governed, but only through paternal authority, which also would include strict punishment as an edu-cational device. The standard formula for the traditional and the modern bureaucrat's relationship with the people was that he was to be the 'father and the mother of the people'.

The public role of the Centre was accordingly taken from another stock of the *imaginaire d'histoire*. The Centre plays father and mother. The institutions governing relationships between parents and their children in China are not contractual as children and young people are considered incapable of independent and responsible action, but give full authority and responsibility to the parents. In traditional Chinese law, a father could legally kill his son for unfilial behaviour. The Centre thus proceeded to define the contestants assembled on the Square as 'children' and published numerous appeals to these 'chil-dren' to come to their senses.

Eventually the Chinese Women's Association came out with a dramatic appeal to the 'children' not to destroy their lives through the hunger-strike. The appeal assured the contestants that the party was in fact their 'mother who loved them dearly', but could not condone their irrational action. The government countered the 'Internationale' sung by the students with a song out of another archive, which ran 'I will sing you a song from a distant valley, the party is your mother and she loves you dearly . . .' which was endlessly broadcast over all stations in May and early June. To further substantiate its motherly role, the Centre sent medical teams to prevent the students from starving themselves to death, and buses onto the Square to protect them against a rainstorm. The Centre made sure that these measures were extensively covered on national television.

This caring aspect was combined with fatherly rigidity in matters of substance. During the few futile televised discussions with student representatives, the government spokesman Yuan Mu brought along a little sign which he put on the table where the government representatives sat. It read 'chairman's rostrum', *zhuxi tai*, and in this manner defined the students not as equal partners in a negotiation, but as the audience entitled to ask questions. Within this construct, the crackdown with tanks and machine guns came as fatherly punishment. The means used were not dictated by the visible threat posed. A dike breaks because first a little dribble of water leaks out. If this hole is not filled, destruction is immeasurable. The means used on Tiananmen were chosen with regard to the imaginary threat to the palpitating heart of the nation, not with regard to the few hundred students who were still on the Square on Saturday, 3 June, and who furthermore had voted the day before to go back to school on Monday. The crackdown was eventually justified in a translation into modern language, as one directed against a 'counter-revolutionary' onslaught, another part from the stock of the *imaginaire*, namely the onslaught against the Hungarian uprising in 1956 which the Chinese leadership re-enacted during the very time when the Hungarians themselves elevated the uprising from a counter-revolutionary attack to a 'popular uprising'. Both sides in this crisis drew and draw on a common stock of the *imaginaire* in terms both of institutions and experiences.

They also share this stock. Certain elements remain unthinkable for both sides, although on reflection they might have their merits. One of the greatest problems in this respect is the question of unity and homogeneity, both spiritual and geographic. Intellectual diversity and regional diversity or even independence have such a bad press in the *imaginaire* that they cannot be positively considered by any large segment of the political class. The same is true for the understanding of the role of the press. The contestants did not counter the propaganda press with sober, balanced, and factual information from their

side, but with counter-propaganda and thus remained victims of the
system they were criticising.

The Chinese Communist Party has all too neatly snuggled into the
roles and metaphors of the traditional Chinese state and has with
devastating efficiency eliminated all those entities that could help to
navigate this crisis. It is now but a bitter self-fulfilling prophecy when
the party asserts that, without its leadership, China would be done
for. A caricature in the Shanghai *Xinmin wanbao* in late May, 1989,
showed an axe proudly standing amidst felled trees, proclaiming itself
to be the only operative entity.

DOING AWAY WITH THE POLLUTION OF THE SACRED SPACE

After the crackdown, the Centre treated the sacred Tiananmen Square
like a living being that had been polluted, scarred, and maimed, and
needed to be cleaned, to be healed and to get rest. Still in the early
hours of the morning of 4 June 1989, the Goddess of Democracy was
crushed by a tank and the Square was cleaned thoroughly. For a few
days after, soldiers were made to sit in long rows around its edges,
with tanks behind them. Eventually they were replaced by fences and
armed guards. No one was allowed on the Square for months as if it
was healing. Eventually, in a bizarre ceremony, the leadership painted
the faces of a few hundred soldiers white, put gaudy costumes on
them, and had them perform a happy dance on the Square on the
occasion of National Day. For the same occasion, the leadership
erected a new statue on the very place on the imperial axis where the
Goddess of Democracy had stood. It undid the Goddess' pollution of
the spot by being its rigid counterpart, a bulging sculpture of the
emblem of 'the people', namely a worker, a peasant, a soldier, and a
bespectacled man with education. In a silent dialogue with the
sculpture that had been there a few months before, the new sculpture
proclaimed that 'the people' – which comprised the above-named
groups – had 'put down' the spiritual pollution represented by the
democracy movement.

It might be argued that the uses of historical moulds to form and
present oneself and one's action is unavoidable, and has its own merits
in enhancing the understanding, coherence and persuasiveness of
political actors and their utterances. The French Revolution did not

fare badly with its Roman nomenclature. In the Chinese case, this is much less convincing. In fact, the uses of the historical *imaginaire* show a profound misperception of all of the actors on stage – of themselves, their roles and the historical moment.

The young students or older intellectuals might see themselves as the successors of the virtuous officials praised in olden times, but their actual situation in a communist state – and a Chinese state to boot – is not elucidated by this self-perception. They are in fact not the future political class in a communist China, but at best the panegyrists of this leader or that. Historical identifications were useful in symbolically solving the problem of representativeness, but at the same time they produced a sense of self-importance and righteousness for which the actual behaviour of the intelligentsia after 1949 provided little evidence. The implied assumption of their being the future leaders based on their moral uprightness, as compared to the government's corruption, prevented them from properly defining their opponent and from developing a strategy based on something other than the interests of the educated city youths.

Their predominantly traditional self-perception meant that they had no eye for the causes of the success of their Polish counterparts, who effaced their own role and interests by subordinating themselves to the workers' movement. Neither inflation, nor the distressing material, social and political conditions of the working population in the cities and villages of China and among the non-Han-Chinese peoples living within the territory ever entered the representations of the students contestants. In fact, in their moralistic presentation of the conflict, the gigantic structural problems of the country at large, and of the transition to a more market-oriented economy in particular, were hardly ever addressed. By defining the main issue as the moral depravity of *guandao*, they were perhaps able to make a popular point, but they also landed themselves in a blind alley.

Most importantly, their symbolic scenario prevented them from seeing the actual complications of the situation. In the Centre, a bitter struggle had been on since the autumn of 1988 to oust Zhao Ziyang. The opponents of Zhao Ziyang cynically made use of the movement, attributing it to Zhao's mismanagement. It might even be argued that they manipulated the movement. After the big demonstrations commemorating Hu Yaobang's death, the students returned to their dormitories. The next day, 26 April, an editorial came out which managed to fan the storm again. After three weeks it died down again, and the students voted to go back to their dormitories. The next day, martial law was declared, and out they came. On Friday, 2

June, the students voted again to return to their dormitories. On 3 June, hardly a few hundred people were on the Square, mostly students from other cities. The tanks came at a moment when the movement had died down or was about to take other forms. The students failed to develop a scenario able to explain to them their situation, and to guide them and a broader populace in their understanding and action.

The party leadership fared no better. Eternally on the defensive, and clumsily reacting to a public opinion that had already cast them in the villain's role, they ended up defining their opponents as naïve children pushed from behind by some 'black hands' with counterrevolutionary purposes, and themselves in the double role of the protective mother of the people and the stern father who defends his family and prevents the children from doing harm to themselves. Within the Centre, they perceived each other as so many warlords going for each others' throats and forming tenuous alliances which would break down at the first opportune moment. The top leaders moved about among secret hide-outs to prevent arrest by their opponents. They spent their time shuffling army units brought into Beijing to prevent any one unit from managing a coup, and ended up in occupying Peking with a hodge-podge of frightened soldiers, without any communication among them, and an extraordinary level of military incompetence. The result was the foreiture of whatever respect they could still command among the population. Their 'victory' reduced them to a group of senile and ruthless men who have failed to notice that their time is over, and the population to a sullen silence, waiting for them to die and something 'to happen' thereafter.

With their lack of sophistication and inability to define at least the core features of the situation, both sides bear witness to a process of intellectual desertification in China. Chinese communism is a part of this process, and a great and successful promoter of it. But is has not instigated it. It just continued and systematised the pursuit of a core ideal of the traditional Chinese polity, the unification of thinking. In this way the Chinese communists have successfully prohibited the formation of a segment of the political class with enough credibility, maturity, cohesion and knowledge to lead the country out of its imbroglio.

CHAPTER SEVEN

The Show of State in a Neo-Colonial Twilight: Francophone Africa

Donal B. Cruise O'Brien

The inhabitants of African states, whether they should properly be designated citizens or subjects, do not readily regard their rulers as providing a legitimate authority, and state power does not rest on a secure foundation of popular belief in the right of rulers to rule. Nearly three decades of independent African government have led to situations where it is the decomposition of state structures, the tendency to de-institutionalisation, which are remarked. Richard Sandbrook puts it bluntly, but he speaks for many when he talks of fictitious states.[1] This may be a *mot juste* in certain African circumstances (Uganda, Chad at a certain period, etc.), but one should recognise a widely variable African capacity to sustain this fiction.

The African states have in general survived, some in better condition than others, after some thirty years of independence. It may be suggested that this survival of the state should redirect our attention to the pre-colonial history of the political entities subsumed within the state. While it is clear on the one hand that the state in its modern form (with bureaucracy, fixed boundaries, standing army, police) is largely a European import, or a graft, it may be on the other hand that the graft will take more readily where there is an approximate fit with some precedent socio-political reality. This 'fit' may not always (or ever?) be readily discernible, may not be explicitly recognised by the political actors concerned, but it is in principle an important issue for the success or otherwise of the European graft of state.

Three decades of independence seem to have witnessed the emergence of something like an African style of statehood, not indeed of reassuring institutional solidity, but remarkable enough in terms both of the political inventiveness deployed by those who have charge of the state, the political elite, and of skills deployed by those who seek to avoid the state. Between the ambitions of the elite and the survival strategems of the masses, the state often appears to survive essentially as a show, a political drama with an audience more or less willing to suspend its disbelief. The audience in question lies both within the boundaries of the state and in the international arena: the material basis of the African state lies in the manipulation of relations between these two sets of spectators. Jean-François Bayart's assessment is thus that 'the groups which hold power in Africa live, in the main, from the rents which they procure from their intermediary position towards the international system'.[2] In this intermediary role, it is the display of state which must satisfy the 'international system' with its increasingly impatient creditors and its frustrated multinational businessmen as well as its various bureaucracies and its information-gathering officials.

The show of state also plays to a home audience, with a display of institutional activity in the form of ministerial bureaucracies, of courts, of agencies of 'development'. Such institutions are unlikely to be accepted at face value by citizens with experience of the clientelistic political realities, but some benefit of the doubt may be extended to the state where the known perils of anarchy or internal war are remembered. Much better to have a state, even in this theatrical form, even as a cover for the most ruthless individual predation, than to have no state at all.

The show of state holds its audience, and the state survives, partly as a response to the presentational gifts of those on stage – the African personal ruler as star of the show, and then the cast of government (civil service, police, and other functionaries). The government may not in truth be discharging many of its nominal functions, as detailed examination tends to reveal, but it remains very important that it should with some plausibility at least seem to be doing so. Government, like paper money, is after all in part a confidence trick.

For the states of Francophone Africa it is, however, also clear that there is an important metropolitan contribution to the success of this political show. France may be seen to act behind the scenes, providing the lighting engineers and often the stage managers. A network of Franco-African cooperation agreements thus supports the state in a wide range of domains – military, judicial, educational, for example – and a special budget in the Ministry of Cooperation provides for the payment of civil service salaries in a range of Francophone African states.

It is worth noting in this context that the French may be seen as acting in a political show of their own, the show of France's national grandeur and world political power. That particular show has a consistent audience appeal in France, and it is significant that many politicians in France, from the Fifth Republic presidents on down, find it politically advantageous to be perceived as linked to Africa in some special way – Africa as an electoral resource in French politics.[3] But the African connection is also an increasingly expensive one, and may soon be beyond French means, even if it has thus far allowed France the illusion of world power at a discount price. Neo-colonialism may be coming into fashion now, in response to an insistent African demand, perhaps at the very moment when it is becoming financially unviable for the neo-colonialist French.

THE TWILIGHT OF NEO-COLONIALISM

Francophone Africa may be considered as a political unit, even if it is one which it is difficult neatly to characterise. The unit is only partially defined by the historical experience of French empire, as the ex-colonies of Belgium, Portugal, Spain and the United Kingdom seek affiliation to the institutions of *Francophonie*; it is only partially defined by a common language and culture, for African states where only a minority ever speaks French; it is only partially defined by the post-colonial institutions of cooperation, when the Franco-African Community was stillborn. But the appeal of the idea of Francophone Africa, at an elite level, remains so powerful that one may even see the French as being threatened by their own success.

The neo-colonial relation has made it possible for the ex-French states to maintain a minimum of institutional cohesion in the economy, in the apparatus of coercion, in the routine administration of the state. This should not, however, be understood as implying any altogether exceptional status to the ex-French states. The legal foundations of the state, in terms of the provision of a recognised code for arbitration between the citizens, are weak here as elsewhere in Africa, the tendency being for disputants to seek recourse to customary or neo-traditional arbitration – the informal sector of the law. The tax base of government (counterpart to legal provision) is no more substantial in Francophone than in other African cases, with impressive rates of tax avoidance.

The French connection has none the less given a significant element of surety to the ex–colonial states of Francophone Africa: civil servants are more likely to be paid than elsewhere in black Africa; the continued use of the metropolitan currency in a thinly disguised form has allowed a markedly superior economic performance to that of the states which have opted for a full financial independence; military cooperation agreements with France, finally, have contributed to the preservation of soldierly hierarchies, with a relatively reliable force available to the surviving civilian regimes (in Côte d'Ivoire, Cameroon, Gabon, Senegal, notably).

This may of course be less than warmly welcomed by some of the people who live in the states concerned, even less by those who make themselves the spokesmen of the people. Thus Achille Mbembe, in a passionate plea for political liberty in Africa, remarks that the record of 'twenty-five years of independence' is one where political power has been viewed as booty. More brutally, 'the state here is an alimentary space', politics being focused on the subject of who is going to eat. 'The state, the civil service, the police, the armed forces are perceived above all as alimentary deposits and as instruments of extortion.' Harassment on the part of the state has brought a collapse of legitimacy:

> the greater the number of 'directives' and 'instructions', the more the native has improvised strategies to escape the net, while exploiting official institutions for private purposes. The result has been a collapse of the moral authority of the State, of its capacity to win respect and obedience.[4]

The dire material predicament of those who live in such states is, for Mbembe, to be remedied among other things by the restoration of political liberty, since 'what has happened over the past twenty-five years is that the institutions of the state have operated to give society an inactive role, preventing it from realising its own potential'.[5] A cautionary note is, however, in order here: in plural social situations such as those that prevail in all African states (officially Francophone or other), in the absence of a significant degree of social consensus, liberty all too readily degenerates into anarchy. The survival of the state, in however dilapidated or theatrical a condition, is not to be devalued or taken for granted.

The French foundations of the African state refer one back to the period of colonial rule, and a centralising administrative model often contrasted with the British practice of indirect rule through African chiefs and notables. But in the post-independence period this contrast rapidly begins to blur, as the more successful of the ex-British states (Kenya, Zimbabwe) adopt a centralising position and as some repentant ex-French centralisers reconsider the possibilities of indirect rule.[6] More significant in the long run as a colonial legacy was the French allowance of significant possibilities for career advancement to colonial African politicians. The notion of belonging to a Francophone political entity is thus in part the legacy of those African politicians who have sat in the French parliament. (Indeed Félix Houphouët-Boigny has been a minister in a French government.)

The contrast with Westminster in this regard has not escaped African attention. The fact that such political openings obtained only for a narrow elite is self-evident. The elite in question was to inherit state command after 1960, and the connections made between French and African politicians in the terminal colonial period do much to explain the relative viability of Franco-African political linkages after independence. African politicians in Paris learned valuable lessons in the practicalities of parliamentary politics, where those in London were excluded from Westminster, but urged to adopt it as a political ideal. A very important example in this regard was the relationship between François Mitterrand and Félix Houphouët-Boigny, drawn together by converging political interest in 1950–1; Houphouët, at that time needing to abandon his damaging alliance with the French Communist Party, could not have found a better councillor in handling communists, and Mitterrand needed the votes of African deputies if his own party (the UDSR) was to be represented in the French government. Such personal ties as this have helped to secure the French foundations of the African state.[7]

The cultural dimension of political power has also been important here, the world-view focused on Paris. Again one is in African terms dealing with a small elite, some representatives of which have risen high in the French educational system, but this elite sets the terms of mass political ambition. Movements of political opposition in the Francophone states have tended to express themselves in the various idioms of Parisian Marxism. I well remember a leading nationalist politician in Senegal explaining a political point to inquisitive foreigners – '*Vous savez, ici en France . . .*'. There is of course sense in these unguarded words: the language of the state is French (thus the expression 'Francophone states' is appropriate although the bulk of the population does not speak in French) as is the language of instruction (vernacular languages having only a small place in the educational system). Where a multiplicity of African languages in any single African state indicates political problems for the future, the compromise of the metropolitan language holds the state together for the present.

Given some of these considerations, it is perhaps understandable that French politicians have not regarded African independence as constituting any sort of political rupture with the (ex) metropolitan power. The award of independence south of the Sahara was above all a means to prevent such difficulties as France had experienced in Indo-China, and was experiencing in Algeria. The Franco-British difference in this regard is reflected among other things in the historiographical treatment of this period: where British scholars have concentrated on the transfer of power, Francophone writers on decolonisation have emphasised the *longue durée*, 'a broad dialectic which transforms economic and cultural as well as political relationships established during colonial empire'.[8] Neither for historians nor for politicians does the moment of independence mark a clear dividing line in Francophone Africa.

The institutional network of Franco-African cooperation, put in place under General de Gaulle, has provided a clear continuity from the colonial period. De Gaulle's project for a Franco-African Community was stillborn, but as Hargreaves nicely remarks,

> a renovated and contractual community continued, like the smile of the Cheshire Cat . . . Its skeleton could be traced through a growing network of bilateral treaties and interstate associations. Its vital functions were sustained through the budget of the Ministry of Cooperation, installed in the offices of the Rue Oudinot, which had been the heart of the French colonial empire.[9]

The Centre of this network has, however, been at the Palais de l'Elysée, the personal prerogative of the President of France under the direction of Jacques Foccart for twenty-six years. Franc zone, military agreements and technical assistance were coordinated through his office as Secretary-General of the Community, which also handled

> personal family problems encountered by members of the [Franco-African] 'club', providing them with private secretaries and taking care of their children. This was the sense of belonging to a family. And even those leaders who proclaimed their independence in public did not, alas, do so in private when they eagerly requested personal favours on every possible occasion.[10]

Tamar Golan, who rightly stressed the personal and family quality of involvement in the Franco-African Community, tellingly illustrates her point with the tale of an encounter with the Liberian Foreign Minister, who spoke to her in the following terms:

> You spoke about the Francophone family as if it was a big joke. To me – to us – it is not. You see, the former French colonies have a feeling of belonging to a family. Bad or good, maybe – but a family. We Liberians are orphans.[11]

The French government underscored this point by its diplomatic efforts to save the minister in question, Cecil Dennis, from summary justice after the Doe coup of 1980 (although the efforts were unsuccessful).

The President under the Fifth French Republic has regarded Franco-African cooperation as a personal domain, perhaps, as is often said, as an escape from the frustrations of domestic politics and an opportunity to play the role of world statesman. All the Fifth Republic's presidents 'have cultivated their particular contacts in black Africa and have invariably sought to present themselves as "friends of Africa"'. Not only the Presidents of France, but also many other French politicians, assume that this is an advantage 'if they can present themselves, as did de Gaulle, as *l'homme d'Afrique*'.[12] African heads of state are thus welcomed at the Elysée Palace, given long audiences with the French President, encouraged to talk freely and at length – contrasting with the thirty minutes accorded in Washington. French familiarity is thus a political resource, although it can also become a trap for the French themselves, for example, with the adroit personal diplomacy of such as President Omar Bongo of Gabon.[13] African demand for membership of the Francophone family has also gone far beyond the frontiers of the French colonial empire, as is reflected in the composition of the Francophone 'summits', annual events since 1973: 'The myth of French universality has found its promised land in Africa.'[14] But the myth may be expensive to maintain, the clients too insistent, and the terms of international dependence not always to the French advantage.

If the institutions of Franco-African cooperation none the less have until now operated with success of a sort, an attentive examination of the internal workings of any particular African state brings out some of the tropical realities involved. Emmanuel Terray, an anthropologist with long experience of Côte d'Ivoire, proposes the model of two distinct systems of government in operation there, typified as that of the air-conditioner and that of the verandah. The system of the air-conditioner has all the apparent ingredients of 'State . . . President, Ministers, Parliament, Administration, Party, Constitution, Laws, Rules and airport with VIP lounge, company of paratroopers . . . motorcycle outriders with siren'.[15] It is to be noted that the motor-cycle outriders may in this model have a more important role than the Constitution. The function of all this apparatus is less of government than it is of presentation, to signify that the country holds its place in 'the ballet of nations', a message for internal as well as external use.

Real government business is done according to this model elsewhere, on the verandah, by a system of patronage 'governed by a logic which is no longer that of efficiency, but of the share-out'. Two key moments allow measurement of political strength on the verandah: the ministerial re-shuffle on the one hand, the opening of the school year on the other. The strength of a patron is known by his success in placing the children of his clients in the right educational establishments. Clients wield their own democratic resources, in choosing to abandon a patron who fails to deliver: 'The leader abandoned by his troops soon sees his career falter, his name become tarnished.'[16] Patron-client systems along the lines of Terray's verandah are widely agreed to provide much of the reality of African politics, but it is striking that this model is advanced for Côte d'Ivoire, then seen as one of the strongest states in black Africa. The institutional appearances of the air-conditioner model presumably accounted in their way for Côte d'Ivoire's success.

'*Le climatiseur et la véranda*' is a wittily presented model of state administration, with a serious content. Two models are involved, and although these are of contrasting characteristics, one is not to confuse that idealised contrast with a real political struggle: the same people are in charge under either system. The share-out of the verandah caters to a range of constituencies (ethnic, generational, professional, commercial, confessional) while the system of the air-conditioner is that of top-down bureaucracy. President Houphouët-Boigny is known to feel that since bureaucracy is a foreign system, it is best run by foreigners. And the many French residents of Côte d'Ivoire, in or out of government service, are much more comfortable with the air-conditioner although their role by Terray's model is an ironical one, that of conveying an impression.

France also makes a substantial contribution to the political stability of the ex-colonial states of sub-Saharan Africa, nowhere more clearly than in the provision of a stable currency – the French franc in its CFA disguise.[17] Dependency could not be more evident than in the continued use of a metropolitan currency, and the leaders of Francophone states in the past have chafed at the restrictions on their freedom of manoeuvre which are imposed by continuing membership of the franc zone. But if these leaders must forfeit the manipulation of the exchange rate as an instrument of government policy, or the short-term advantages of paying creditors and employees by printing money, they have seen elsewhere in Africa the perils of a full financial independence as currencies become subject to hyperinflation, worthless for foreign exchange. The franc zone countries have enjoyed a distinctly superior economic performance to their neighbours,[18] with much smuggling of produce for example out of the Anglophone Ghana and Nigeria into the Francophone Côte d'Ivoire and Togo.

The franc zone has made it possible for African member states to escape the devaluations and periodic interruption of supplies which have been general outside the zone. The financial stability of the zone also helps to attract foreign investment, and to retain a cadre of economic advisers. France thus helps to provide economic foundations for the state, with a financial medium which allows full participation in international trade. Currency more than any other matter maintains the French sphere of influence in Africa, although the trend of events since 1960 shows a changing reality to be involved.[19] Thus in the first decade of African independence the French Treasury maintained a tight discipline in the zone, being criticised in Africa for excessive financial prudence as well as an arbitrary imposition of French valuations in Africa. The decade from 1972 to 1982 then was to see an erosion of French discipline as a result of readily available foreign credit (with a hard currency, the franc zone countries were able to go more quickly into debt . . .) and grants to the poorest countries. The 1980s have brought a return to the original logic of the zone, the logic of tight money promoted by international financial institutions as well as by the French Treasury. But it is striking in overall terms that African criticism of the franc zone has very markedly declined over the years. African pressure now is from Anglophone or Lusophone states wanting to get into the franc zone, rather than from Francophone states wanting to get out.

The French Treasury is alarmed by the growing indebtedness of the franc zone, debts caused in part by African overspending: the foreign debt of any franc zone member is effectively a debt of the whole zone, including France.[20] The leaders of Francophone African states, on the other hand, are keenly aware of the perils of full financial independence, of being cut off from international trade by an unviable currency – when only barter agreements (for example with bauxite, as in Sékou Touré's Guinea) allow any imports to be maintained. The cautionary tale of Guinean financial independence has indeed served very effectively as a warning to any other Francophone states considering a break with the franc zone. The other peril for the Francophone states, that of future Nigerian domination in an expanded franc zone, finds the Francophone African leaders working in alliance with the French Treasury to the purpose of Nigerian exclusion, an excellent example of the intertwining of French and African politics in *La Francophonie*.

THE FRENCH MILITARY AND ADMINISTRATIVE PRESENCE

France's maintenance of a military presence in Africa has attracted much attention over the years since 1960, with the numerous occasions on which French soldiers have been deployed in protection of a valued ally or of a threatened territory.[21] From the viewpoint of the African head of state, the value of defence agreements with France has probably been greatest in providing a line of defence against the political ambitions of his own junior officers. The French military bases in key states (Senegal, Côte d'Ivoire, Gabon and Djibouti) and the 15,000 French paratroopers of the Rapid Deployment Forces in the Pyrenees also protect the territorial integrity of the Francophone states. French authorities are justified in pointing out that almost all of France's military interventions in Africa have been at the express demand of African heads of state, although, on the other hand, such demands have not always been met (as when Fulbert Youlou was allowed to fall in the Congo, Hamani Diori in Niger, or Félix Tombalbaye in Chad, despite their desperate calls for French military protection).

It has been suggested that there are grounds for a reassessment in French military circles of the long-run viability of the African commitment. 'For years, the French military authorities have relied on the following concept: speed of action is more important than firepower.'[22] P. Chaigneau then points to the effects of the arms race in Africa, with international arms dealers making modern weapons widely available and thus threatening the technological advantage of the French forces. Airborne troops using the bases as relay stations can reach any African state within twelve hours, and the paratroopers have been effective in quelling African military revolts or urban demonstrations on many occasions. But with the development of modern weaponry, such as heat-seeking missiles requiring no special training for the operators, and with the diversification of international arms suppliers, France would be unwise in relying on the lessons of the past. Thus one can see that as the franc zone is being reassessed in Paris as an economic liability, so the French military presence in Africa must also face perils ahead. The record since African independence is that French soldiers have made a substantial contribution to the stability of civilian regimes in the countries that France values most, those that General de Gaulle termed *les pays sérieux* – Côte d'Ivoire, Senegal, Cameroon.

The contribution of French personnel to the government and administration of the Francophone African states also deserves consideration here. Thus for Côte d'Ivoire it has been surmised that that country's superior performance in agricultural production was explicable more in terms of effective rural administration than in terms of market incentives.[23] The French presence in the country's administration has been particularly strong, and probably accounts for some of the performance of the administrative sector in Terray's air-conditioner. There may be more to that machine than mere show. French staff are often maintained in key administration positions, as in the Departments of Finance of all franc zone states (where they have struggled to contain government overspending) although the pressures for Africanisation are strong. In response to this pressure, France has been withdrawing technical assistants from civil service positions in Africa, favouring teachers instead: 'In 1960 slightly over 20 per cent of technical assistants were teachers, while by 1969 almost 60 per cent of the *co-opérants* were involved in teaching.'[24] But there are still a few states in Francophone Africa (notably the Central African Republic) where the civil service is heavily staffed by French 'advisers'.

A former French colonial administrator, now with Senegalese nationality, has stood at President Diouf's right hand: Jean Collin has been an obvious target for the Senegalese opposition (a white man as Secretary-General to an African Presidency) but his commitment to the President and to the country was to be taken seriously. The French embassy in Dakar found him a hard bargainer in his adoptive country's interest – 'among the most nationalist of Senegalese'. French citizens also occupy key positions in the government of Côte d'Ivoire, including that of Private Secretary to President Houphouët-Boigny.[25] African heads of state have often made use of European personnel in this manner, on the grounds of a more dependable loyalty. In a plural society such appointments may even be accepted as betokening a relative neutrality (between competing communal groups or political factions). The fact that such appointments are possible also testifies to the fragmented community existing within the frontiers of any given African state.

The elaborate network of French provision for African states – in the financial world through the French Treasury to the franc zone, in state administration by the multifarious cooperation agreements through the Ministry of Cooperation to individual African states, in the military field through defence treaties and agreements, supplemented by the institutions of the French linguistic community (*la francophonie*) – adds up to much the most elaborate post-colonial institutional network to be made available from any developed country to Africa. And there is an obvious continuity there with the colonial past, the official formula of cooperation being 'the reconversion of an indefensible colonial policy to a formula which made it possible to persevere with the *mission civilisatrice* in a new international context'.[26] In more immediate and practical terms the cooperation agreements have provided a mechanism for France periodically to pay the civil service bills of her ex-colonies, including those which have chosen a Marxist-Leninist or officially leftist ideological standpoint (Republics of the Congo and Benin).

The French government's willingness to make such provision for African client states is only partially to be understood in terms of French economic interests. The French taxpayer footing the bill for France's overseas business is a well-established tradition,[27] for example through tied aid from the Ministry of Cooperation: thus the pertinent economic interests may be those of French private business rather than of the French state. France's commercial interest in Africa has markedly declined since the time of African independence: thus French exports to the *Etats Africains et Malgache* were halved over the period from 1960 to 1979, and imports from the same states reduced to one-third of their previous level.[28] In business terms the French interest has been concentrated in a few African states: thus the three states of Côte d'Ivoire, Cameroon and Gabon accounted for two-thirds of French imports from the EAM in 1978.[29] In overall terms, commerce with Africa is a wasting asset, a protected field for declining French business which draws attention away from the dynamic overseas markets of Latin America or South-east Asia, a field in question. But then commercial considerations may be subordinate to those of international status in the formulation of French policy here: as General de Gaulle once superbly remarked, 'France's rank depends on the honour of the flag, not on increases in her Gross National Product'.[30]

France's strategic concerns do supplement the concerns of commercial interest in protecting an economic involvement in Africa. Thus for example it was through the Marxist-Leninist Republic of Benin that the railway ran to the uranium fields of Niger, a good reason for the French Ministry of Cooperation to extend generous grants to the two African states concerned. The states of Francophone Africa provide France with strategically valued supplies not only in the case of uranium, crucial for the extensive French nuclear power programme as well as for the defence commitment, but also in the case of a number of other mineral deposits.[31] But the language of strategic interest is notoriously one of double-talk and special pleading, most of the minerals concerned being readily available on the open market, and one remains unconvinced by the notion of a decisive French interest in Africa, whether commercial or strategic.

THE FRENCH LANGUAGE AND CULTURE

Franco-African institutions would appear to be validated by another logic, that of a latter-day imperial vocation. In the words of John Chipman:

> The whole idea of French power, from the nineteenth century to the present, is wrapped up with the exportability of French ideas and institutions and the active cultivation of overseas appreciation for the values of the French state . . .
> . . . as a symbol of power, an effective and persistent influence in black Africa is almost as important as possession of nuclear weapons and the status France enjoys as a permanent member of the United Nations Security Council.[32]

The neo-colonial vocation emerges for example from an examination of the institutions of the French-language community, from the Franco-African 'summit' meetings of heads of state, annual since 1973, to the *Agence de la Francophonie*, in operation since 1969. France's concern with the notion of *Francophonie*, a linguistic and cultural zone which could be the basis of political community, appears originally to have been conceived with French-speaking Canada in mind, but the idea has been more warmly welcomed in Africa than across the Atlantic. In Africa the notion of *Francophonie* is that of a cultural community of men of power, with a shared commitment to the French language. French being the language of power in the states of Francophone Africa, this is of course a commitment of the elite. That elite has responded warmly to the concept of a French-language community which could extend from the cultural to the political.

The expanding membership of the Franco-African summits indicates not only the wide range of official ideological commitments which are represented (Marxist-Leninist to conservative) but also more strikingly the extent to which the ex-colonies of other European powers have sought involvement in the French sphere of influence (the ex-Belgian Zaïre, Rwanda and Burundi since 1975; the ex-Portuguese Guinea-Bissau, Cape Verde and São Tomé since 1976; the Anglophone Liberia and ex-British Sierra Leone since 1979). This new membership is of course on the demand of the African governments concerned, and welcomed by the French government with a certain effrontery as corresponding to its 'wish for a pan-African opening'.[33] At the Nice summit of 1981 only sixteen of the thirty-three states represented were ex-French colonies, and Daniel Bach in writing of the event asks 'whether France has become the leading power of the African continent, a role to which she could not have pretended twenty years before?'[34] The expansion of the Franco-African summits beyond the historic boundaries of the French colonial empire does risk a dilution of the original *Francophonie*, although one can recognise a note of complacency in the reflections of President Mitterrand on this subject: 'We must be careful that the Francophones keep their originality and their identity, but why refuse the help of all the countries of Africa that want to debate with us?'[35] The summit is of course for 'debate' between top people, an occasion where the serious business is done in the corridors rather than the plenary sessions: President Giscard d'Estaing once suggested to the delegates that they 'Keep discussion of the most "political" subjects for mealtimes'.[36]

The French language is an instrument of power, a means of communication within the elite, those who have a stake in the state (in Achille Mbembe's terms, those who can eat thanks to the state). But French can also be a language of African political opposition: restrictions on press freedom, or indeed on liberty in any sense in many African countries, have made Paris a natural centre for African opposition movements – those of the counter-elite. French restrictions on political liberty are a lesser evil for African oppositionists who find a relatively welcoming environment in the universities of the ex-metropole. A certain ambivalence in attitudes towards France grows naturally from such a situation, which obtains also in its way for all African writers and intellectuals operating in the French language – like the recently deceased Wolof nationalist historian Cheikh Anta Diop, whose Senegalese political career rested in large measure on his studies in the Sorbonne, or in the Béninois philosopher Paulin Hountondji arguing in tightly controlled Gallic idiom that there is no such thing as an African philosophy.[37]

French is the language of the elite, cultural or political, but it must be remembered both that the bulk of the population in any 'Francophone' state does not write or speak French, and that the French language is only one among many languages used by any individual member of the elite. The social reality of the post-colonial African state is one of diglossia, where the prestigious social functions are dealt with through the European language (English or Portuguese as well as French). Other languages than the ex-colonial can begin to lay claim to a hegemonic status, as for example with the development of Arabic-language education in Mali, in the struggle for power between the Islamic fundamentalists of the Wahhabiyya and the more accom-modating Muslim traditionalists and pagans.[38] But in most of the Francophone states there is a general acceptance of the authoritative status of the French language, as revealed for example in the social institution of the 'concert party' in Togo, where the plurilingual situation of *diglossie* is seen as that of 'a society which takes account of its own domination'.[39]

The plurilingual realities of the social world encompassed by any single African state, Francophone or other, have tended to foreclose on the political possibilities of the development of any single African 'vernacular' language as an instrument of state authority.[40] There are in the first place technical problems in the provision of the necessary teaching materials, from grammar and dictionary to the textbooks requisite for secondary or even higher education: and in the Franco-phone states, where Protestant missionary activity has been weak to non-existent, the development of schooling in the African vernacular has similarly in the past been largely absent – excluded both by the Catholic Church and by the nominally secular state. But even more important than such pedagogical considerations are those of the political difficulties in the recognition of African languages in the educational process. These are familiar difficulties of the politics of primordialism – if one language is to be recognised, why not another? – and it may have been helpful for state survival that the French colonial tradition was so negligent of the development of African language instruction. The *pays réel* of the Francophone state is that segment of the population which is competent in French, the elite which can aspire to official positions and thus (in Mbembe's terms) a share in the booty. Those who are left outside under such political arrangements account for the bulk of the population.

One needs increasingly to differentiate between the states of Francophone Africa, as the years have elapsed since the time of independence (1960). States which inherited the same constitutional arrangements, modelled on those of the Fifth French Republic, and the same close ties with France, have taken on their distinct characters. Francophone Africa is thus less a political unit in 1989 than it was in 1960. Most obviously there is the distinction between the countries with a relatively stable civilian leadership (Côte d'Ivoire, Senegal, Cameroon) and the numerous military regimes, and the relatively viable economies which would also include Gabon, Togo and Mada-gascar. Beyond these six states the situation of economic crisis and institutional decay is general, although still with a marginal advantage over the states of Anglophone or Lusophone Africa. There is inequality also in disaster.

A blurring of the lines of colonially inherited division has none the less also resulted from Africa's crisis of indebtedness, with the hegemonic role of the World Bank and the International Monetary Fund and the standardisation of African government policies under the tutelage of Washington. One might perhaps have expected some of the normal dose of French national jealousies in the face of this new manifestation of the *Défi Americain*, as France is reduced to a secondary role in Africa, but it would seem that some French official thinking is more than happy to concede a leading role to the United States, as explained by Hugon:

> The pre-eminent role of the institutions of Washington is the more explicable as France is the most exposed country to African indebtedness, at the level of its banking system and its public institutions, and as the French Treasury . . . is concerned that the conditionalities should be those of the IMF and the World Bank.[41]

The French *Trésor* may be delighted to have somebody else take the risk of lending to the Francophone states, and of course there is not much evidence of a deliberate American challenge to the French role in Africa. The State Department has had its own reasons to be delighted with the French military assistance extended to the government of Chad in the expulsion of the Libyan forces, the humiliation of Colonel Qaddafi. The International Monetary Fund was indeed at one time hostile to the restrictive procedures of the franc zone, but thinking in the IMF has come to recognise the advantages of a convertible currency over the worthless paper available from many African states.[42]

The notion of an American challenge to the French position in Africa has been encouraged by some African heads of state, as part of the politics of international clientelism. This notion would appear to represent the trump card of a group of Francophone leaders (Houphouët-Boigny, Bongo, Eyadéma, Mobutu) who have manipulated the French press in its African coverage to put pressure on French leaders suspected of weakening in their commitment to the continent or to themselves. The technique here has been to work through pliable French journalists: under a socialist government articles appear in the French press insinuating the political incompetence of those in charge of the government's African policy, lamenting the decline of the French position in Africa, warning of the American threat. Jean-

François Bayart remarks that the African leaders concerned 'have managed to control Franco–African relations, dictating a particular policy to Paris, by their constant pressure',[43] in particular in preventing any excessive demands being made in the area of human rights ('moral colonialism'). The manipulations of the dependent are not to be underestimated:

> The bargaining power of these patrimonialisms is formidable, disposing as they do of the totality of the resources of their countries . . . the African governments use dependency as a carefully maintained resource – it is not enough to say that [they] have a relative autonomy towards France: often they compel her to act.[44]

Pluralism and democracy in France offer many possibilities to the intrigues of these dictators of dependency. But while the spectre of the United States is useful to these political actors, the Francophone leaders who threaten to leave the French sphere of influence for the hypothetical American one are surely bluffing.

FUN AND FEAR IN TOGO

The case of the state of Togo under the rule of General Eyadéma, the subject of a masterly study by Comi Toulabor, offers an appropriate conclusion here. The Togolese state is seen as dependent on France, a situation promoted by the General, who gains from it in many ways. But the state has also become viable in real terms as a structure resting on the twin principles of entertainment and fear. Entertainment is provided through the ruling political party in sessions of 'animation', slogans, music and dance; also through a dramatised version of the General's political career in the 'struggle against imperialism'. Fear on the other hand is inspired not only by the routine apparatus of coercion, but also by the great magical powers ascribed to Eyadéma on the strength of his 'miraculous' survival of an air crash in 1974. His escape from death on this occasion is the basis for a voodoo-inspired cult of Eyadéma as a spiritual medium, omnipotent and invulnerable. The air crash of Sarakawa is here presented as a 'victory over imperialism' (the two white pilots were killed) and the wrecked DC3 encased in concrete is made a place of pilgrimage.

General Eyadéma's success in building a cult around himself is to be set against the fact that the structures of the Togolese state appear to be 'virtually non-existent'. This 'state of nothingness' may do nothing for national integration or development, but it is enough that it maintains the privileges of a ruling elite.

> The State is thus no longer to be seen merely as something alien, grafted onto a society to which it is foreign. The African state has now been adapted, tropicalised and steeped in the ethos and the rationality of social actors who have reshaped it to their own purposes. The result is that this state can maintain itself in being, perhaps as a caricature of the Western state, but without the intervention of external forces. The graft has taken: it must be given time to reach maturity, become aware of itself and develop a real culture of the State.[45]

Structures and foundations may have to wait, but the show of state goes on.

NOTES

1. R. Sandbrook, *The Politics of Africa's Economic Stagnation* (Cambridge, 1985) p. 35: 'Fictitious states . . . exist in the minimal sense that other governments recognise a regime's claim to territorial sovereignty.' These are contrasted with 'a mere handful of healthy states' of which six are named, including three from the Francophone area (Côte d'Ivoire, Cameroon, Senegal), which 'are highly structured and capable of devising and implementing diverse policies'. A recent historical introduction to the subject is to be found in P. Manning, *Francophone Sub-Saharan Africa 1880–1985* (Cambridge, 1988). An excellent international relations treatment of the subject is to be found in J. H .W. Chipman, 'France as an African Power; History of an Idea and its Post-colonial Practice', D.Phil. thesis, Oxford, 1988.
2. J.-F. Bayart, 'Les Trajectoires de l'Etat au Sud du Sahara', paper to Congress of Association Française des Sciences Politiques, Bordeaux (5–8 October 1988) p. 48. See also J.-F. Bayart, *L'Etat en Afrique: La Politique du Ventre* (Paris, 1989). For the show of state in another place at another time, see C. Geertz, *Negara: The Theatre State in Nineteenth Century Bali* (Princeton, NJ, 1980).
3. Chipman, 'France as an African Power . . .', p. 335.
4. A. Mbembe, *Les Jeunes et l'Ordre Politique en Afrique Noire* (Paris, 1985) pp. 234–5. See also A. Mbembe, *Afriques Indociles: Christianisme, Pouvoir et Etat en Societé Postcoloniale* (Paris, 1988).
5. A. Mbembe, *Les Jeunes et l'Ordre . . .*, p. 220.
6. R Otayek, 'Burkina Faso', in D. Cruise O'Brien, R. Rathbone and J. Dunn (eds) *Contemporary West African States* (Cambridge, 1990) pp. 21–4, where it is argued that popular indifference to the fall of the Sankara government is partially to be understood against a background of that government's hostility to the popular Mossi chiefs.
7. One may name some notable examples of politically relevant Franco-African friendships: Léopold Senghor and Georges Pompidou, school-

friends from the Lycée Louis-le-grand; ex-Emperor Bokassa and Valéry Giscard d'Estaing, friends of the hunt; General Eyadéma and Charles Hernu, and many others. See P. Péan, *Affaires Africaines* (Paris, 1983) for the particularly interesting case of Bongo's Gabon, with the connections of the French secret services adroitly manipulated by Omar Bongo.

8. J. Hargreaves, 'Decolonisation: French and British Styles', at the conference on 'Les Afriques Francophones depuis leurs Indépendances', at St Antony's College, Oxford (29–30 April 1988) p. 1.
9. *Ibid.*, p. 16. The argument here is that 'Franco-British' differences will continue to be of some import in Africa, 'but only at the superficial levels of elite culture and administrative style', and that in the long run 'forces affecting the African continent as a whole will surely prove more decisive'.
10. T. Golan, 'A Certain Mystery: How can France Do Everything that it Does in Africa – and Get Away with it?', *African Affairs* (January 1981) p. 6.
11. C. Dennis quoted in *ibid.*, p. 4.
12. Chipman, 'France as an African Power . . .', p. 335.
13. See P. Péan, *Affaires Africaines*; also J.-F. Bayart, *La Politique Africaine de François Mitterrand* (Paris, 1985), where it is remarked that M. Bongo ogling Washington 'is a pastmaster in this sort of political blackmail', one of a group of Francophone leaders who say that they are being tempted by the United States, 'a temptation that is a little too obviously displayed if one thinks twice about it' (pp. 113–14).
14. J. C. Gautron, 'La Politique Africaine de la France', Travaux et Documents, Centre d'Etude D'Afrique Noire, Université de Bordeaux I, unpublished paper, p. 1.
15. E. Terray, 'Le Climatiseur et la Véranda', in *Afrique Plurielle, Afrique Actuelle: Hommage a Georges Balandier* (Paris, 1986) p. 38.
16. *Ibid.*, p. 44. See also D. Cruise O'Brien, *Saints and Politicians: Essays in the Organisation of a Senegalese Peasant Society* (Cambridge, 1975) ch. 5, 'Clans, Clienteles and Communities', pp. 146–85.
17. See J. Coussy, 'La Zone Franc au Cours des Trois Dernières Décennies (1960–1988)', to the conference on 'Les Afriques Francophones', St Antony's College, Oxford (29–30 April 1988) unpublished paper. The franc zone originates from 1948, based on the strict application of the principle of intra-convertibility between the franc of the Communauté Financière Africaine (CFA franc) and the metropolitan franc at a fixed rate of exchange. Chipman in this context talks of a 'vertical osmosis' between the French franc and the CFA. See the authoritative treatment of this subject in O. Valleé, *Le Prix de l'Argent CFA: Heurs et Malheurs de la Zone Franc* (Paris, 1989).
18. P. Hugon, 'Les Modèles et les Performances Economiques des Pays d'Afrique Francophone' (in 'Les Afriques Francophones . . .', St Antony's College) citing research by the World Bank and by French economists, shows that the growth rate for franc zone countries over the period from 1960 to 1982 was 'clearly superior to that of the other countries of sub-Saharan Africa', pp. 8–9.
19. J. Coussy, *La Zone Franc . . .*, pp. 18–32.

20. See 'Money: Inside the Franc Zone', *Africa Confidential* (13 May 1988) pp. 4–6; also A. Neurrisse, *La Zone Franc* (Paris, 1987). Thanks are due to Adrian Hewitt and Michael Hodd for their valuable comments.
21. See the table on p. 101 of R. Luckham, 'Le Militarisme Français en Afrique', *Politique Africaine* (February 1982). Luckham points out the 'striking contrast between the total French military presence, 7,800 men of which 6,700 are fighting-soldiers, and the 300 to 400 British troops stationed in Africa, almost all in training rather than operational capacities', p. 110.
22. P. Chaigneau, *La Politique Militaire de la France en Afrique* (Paris, 1984) p. 100.
23. Research in progress, Richard Crook, to whom my thanks. See R. Crook, 'State, Society and Political Institutions in Côte D'Ivoire and Ghana', Chapter 10 in this volume.
24. Chipman, 'France as an African Power . . .', p. 297.
25. Golan, 'A Certain Mystery . . .', p. 7.
26. P. Quantin, 'La Vision Gaullienne de l'Afrique Noire: Permanences et Adaptations', *Politique Africaine* (February 1982), pp. 17–18. 'From 1962 onwards De Gaulle's speeches kept the themes of French generosity and genius in the foreground, while the theme of material interest was discreetly maintained for French voters.'
27. R. Aron, 'Les Conséquences Economiques de l'Evolution Politique en Afrique Noire', *Revue Française de Science Politique* (Sept. 1959).
28. P Hugon, 'L'Afrique Noire Francophone: l'Enjeu Economique pour la France', *Politique Africaine* (February 1982) p. 79.
29. *Ibid.*, p. 81. See also P. Hugon, 'Les modéles et les performances économiques des pays d'Afrique Francophone', paper delivered to the conference on 'Les Afriques Francophones . . .', St Antony's College, Oxford (29–30 April 1988).
30. Chipman, 'France as an African Power . . .', p. 349.
31. Francophone Africa has been estimated to have supplied 60 per cent of France's uranium and 30 per cent of her manganese; also chrome and other minerals of strategic significance. P. Hugon, 'L'Afrique Noire Francophone . . .', p. 81.
32. Chipman, 'France as an African Power . . .', pp. 30, 175–6.
33. J. L. Dagut, 'L'Afrique, la France et le Monde dans les Discours Giscardiens', *Politique Africaine* (February 1982) p. 19. In these speeches France is put forward as the 'champion of the Third World', and sponsor of the ideal, 'Africa for the Africans'.
34. D. Bach, 'Dynamique et Contradictions dans la Politique Africaine de la France: Les Rapports avec le Nigéria (1960–1981)', *Politique Africaine* (February 1982) p. 74. France is thus seen as 'the only European power which has not seen a weakening of its economic and political relations with Africa, on the contrary a consolidation of these ties' (p. 73). See also D. Bach, 'Régionalismes Francophones ou Régionalismes Franco-Africain', paper delivered to the conference on 'Les Afriques Francophones', St Antony's College, Oxford (29–30 April 1988).
35. Mitterrand quoted in J.-F. Medard, 'La Conférence de Paris (3–4 Novembre 1981), le Changement dans la Continuité', *Politique Africaine* (February 1982) p. 31. Medard here remarks on the continuity of France's

African policy: the Socialist government at first seemed to favour a break with the existing structure, but soon repented.

36. *Ibid.*, p. 32.

37. P. Hountondji, *African Philosophy: Myth and Reality* (London, 1983) originally, *Sur la Philosophie Africaine: Critique de l'Enthnophilosophie* (Yaoundé, 1980). This work is centrally concerned to reject the outlook expressed in P. Tempels, *Bantu Philosophy* (Paris, 1959). Where Tempels regards the outlook of the Bantu people as amounting to a philosophy, Hountondji insists that a work of philosophy must be expressed in a text, which can then be the subject of analysis and criticism. Tempel's work is thus relegated to the status of 'ethno-philosophy', a collection of folk wisdom written up by an outsider to the folk in question.

38. On Muslim education and political power in Mali, see L. Brenner, 'La Politisation des Institutions Islamiques au Mali', in C. Coulon and D. Cruise O'Brien (eds) *L'Etat et les Communautés Musulmanes en Afrique Noire* (Paris, forthcoming).

39. A. Richard, 'Les Parisiens de Concert: Discours Métissé ou Discours Dominé?', *Politique Africaine* (February 1982) p. 36. The concert party dealt with here is a 'show based on the foreigner's prestige – which is sometimes opposed, but never in fundamental terms' (p. 45).

40. Somalia is the exception here, a potential African nation-state with a community of language and culture at the foundations of state authority. This community, however, raises important questions for the political future with its endemic factional strife and its territorial claims on four neighbouring states including Somali minorities. See D. Laitin, *Somalia: Nation in Search of a State* (Boulder, Colo., 1987).

41. Hugon, 'Les Modèles et les Performances . . .', p. 18.

42. *Ibid.* See also Coussy, 'La Zone Franc . . .'.

43. J.-F. Bayart, *La Politique Africaine* . . .. Chapter 1, 'Le Phantasme d'une autre Politique Africaine', sees the Socialists as torn between a 'moralising neo-interventionism . . .', 'the angelic concept of co-operation' and the hard realities (p. 44). Chapter 3 is then, 'L'Abdication Idéologique de la Gauche': 'Anglo-Saxon analysts are surprised that the Left has taken over the inherited African policy. Could things have been different? Almost all the African states wanted a continuation, and not just the Francophone states'.

44. *Ibid.*, pp. 44–5. A crucial example here is that of Gabon, with its tiny population and enormous mineral wealth, resources used to pay for election campaigns in France (party expenses) and to suborn French officials to the political or other purposes of Omar Bongo. See Péan, *Affaires Africaines* . . . The notion of power based on entertainment and fear may emerge from an African tradition going back as far as the seventeenth century. Asante power thus rested on the fear of being sold into slavery, and on the entertainment provided at parties where consumer goods were displayed and obtained. I am grateful to Richard Jeffries for this suggestion.

45. C.M. Toulabor, *Le Togo sous Eyadéma* (Paris, 1986) p. 313.

CHAPTER EIGHT

Power and Obscenity in the Post-Colonial Period: The Case of Cameroon★

Achille Mbembe

In this chapter I shall analyse the banality of power in the post-colonial period. By 'banality of power' I do not only mean the prevalence of bureaucratic formalities, and the implicit or explicit rules, in brief the routines. I refer to what has come to be predictable, through its repetition in everyday actions and gestures. I also mean the grotesque and obscene elements, which Mikhaïl Bakhtin seems able to find only in 'non-offical' cultures,[1] but which in reality are part of all systems of domination, and of all ways of deconstructing such systems. 'Post-colonial' simply refers to societies in a distinct historical trajectory: those that have recently emerged from the colonial experience, which is a period of violent relationships *par excellence*.

In reference to societies of this type, I ask in which ways state power

1 politically creates its own world of meanings, which it aims to make so central that it aspires to affect all other worlds of meaning that exist in the society
2 makes every effort to institutionalise its world of meanings as the 'social-historical world',[2] in other words to turn it into reality by instilling it not only into the consciences of its subjects or targets,[3] but also into the world-view of the period.

Finally, I am interested in the results of such endeavours: in the world orders they end up creating; in the types of institutions, knowledge systems, norms and behaviour they produce; in the role of the grotesque and the obscene which are indissociable from these endeav-

★ Translated from the French by Mary Harper.

ours. Cameroon, which will be the focus of this discussion, shows that the grotesque and the obscene are an integral part of these post-colonial systems of domination. The particular characteristics of the obscene and the grotesque must, however, be researched in the banalities of everyday life. In other words, for the purposes of this study, they should be researched in the places and times when the state shows off its splendour, and in the ways that it exhibits its majesty and prestige, and presents them to its subjects.

THE CREATIVITY OF ABUSE[4]

This method of analysis – as well as the types of questions being asked – requires additional explanation. The notion of 'obscenity' will be explored first of all. In a study made some years ago of what he calls 'political mockery' in Togo, C. Toulabor analysed some of the ways in which the populace gave double meanings to normal and conventional words, and how in this way they created an equivocal vocabulary alongside official discourse.[5] But Togo is an example of a post-colonial system of domination which maintains an image of a society without conflict. The state considers itself both as indistinguishable from society and as the keeper of the law and the truth. State power is incorporated into one person: President Gnassingbe Eyadéma. He alone controls the law, and can grant or abolish liberties. The single party, the *Rassemblement du Peuple Togolais*, claims that it controls the whole of social life – subjecting it in order to pursue communal ends – and that it expresses the unity of the people, who are undivided. In this context of advanced authoritarianism, any opposition is challenged and deprived of legitimacy. Although one would expect to find this society deprived of its spirit, a dissociation persists between the image that the state presents of itself and of society, and the ways in which civil resistance contradicts this image and attempts to counter this hegemonic enterprise.

There are therefore some zones in society which escape from state control, either with or without interruption. This 'escape' is verified in social rhetoric, which is one of the best examples of banality. This rhetoric may be obscene, but it never lacks poetry. For example under the pretext of declaiming party slogans, in reality the people sing about the brusque erection of the 'enormous' and 'rigid' presidential phallus, of how it stays in this position, of its contact with 'vaginal liquids'. Another example is the identification of the party acronym with 'the sound of fecal matter falling into a septic tank' or with 'the sound of a fart emitted by wobbling buttocks' which 'can only smell disgusting'.[6] Such obsessions with orifices, smells and genital organs must be interpreted in relation to the fact that the state is constantly engaged in defining and elaborating an image of itself and of the world, an image which it is forcing onto its subjects. It wants to be a world order in itself.

But it is precisely this eccentric world order that is being deconstructed by public mockery. In this context, obscenity exists not so much in the constant references to genital organs as in the way in which public mockery catches hold of power and forces it to face its triviality at the same time as power tries to detach itself. In other words, in the post-colonial era, splendour and prestige have truculent and baroque elements within them that the state tries to hide,[7] but which the public tries to remind it of. This double 'effort' of forgetting and reminding is an expression of a deep conflict between antagonistic worlds of meaning. In considering these factors, it becomes clear that in the context of advanced authoritarianism faced by most sub-Saharan African countries, the notion of 'political mockery' does not fit well with the systems described by Toulabor. This becomes apparent if one subscribes to the idea that in the post-colonial era, state power defines itself as a world order and African rulers claim to be deities of a sort. It is thus better to speak of blasphemous practices, taking account of the part played by the grotesque and the profane which characterise them. Furthermore, the notions of excess and transgression are inadequate explanations for what is in fact a 'devouring'. For, if one carefully follows Bakhtin, and if we accept (even provisionally) that the carnivalesque praxis attacks a cosmology and creates a myth whose central part is the body, we must conclude that in the Togolese case, as in other post-colonial countries, what one actually faces are 'theophagic' operations[8] – involving the sacramental eating of gods. Totem is no longer protected by taboo,[9] and a gap is opened in the prohibitory system.

However, if the populace can dismember and 'devour' the deities which African powers aim to be, the opposite is also true, as shown by the following account of the public execution of two lawbreakers in Cameroon:

> At dawn on August 28 . . . they were driven to the 'Crossroads of Billes', alongside the main road from Douala to Yaoundé [where] they saw the crowd . . . As well as the local population – which was several hundreds in number – there were the authorities: the Governor of the coastal region, the Prefect of Wouri, the Public Prosecutor, the Deputy-

Prefect, the GMI squadron leader, the steward of Douala central prison, a priest, a doctor, one of their lawyers . . . several gendarmes as well as . policemen, soldiers impeccably dressed in combat gear, firemen . . .

Inside the police car which had driven them to the site of execution, food was brought to them. They refused to eat their last meal, preferring to drink instead. They were served whisky and red wine which they knocked back rapidly . . . At seven o'clock . . . they were driven to the execution posts, one separated from the other by a distance of about 10 metres. Whilst Oumbe allowed himself to be tied up, Njomzeu continued to struggle . . . He was forced to his knees. It was now his turn to break down and cry . . . The priest and the pastor who were present approached them and asked them to pray. This was in vain.

There were 24 soldiers in the firing squad, that is 12 for each man – they advanced, marching in time under the captain's orders, and took up position at a distance of 30 metres, 12 kneeling and 12 standing . . . At the captain's order to 'Take aim!', the soldiers cocked their guns and aimed. 'Fire!': a short and terrible blast drowned the cries of the condemned . . . bullets were propelled at the speed of 800 metres per second. Then it was the death blow. And then unbelievable but true, the crowd started to applaud wildly, like at the end of a good show.[10]

Here, since we face a relatively similar situation, we could adopt the narrative structure used by Michel Foucault in his account of the punishment of Damien.[11] However, it must not be forgotten that the case we are interested in occurred in a post-colonial state. It does not imply the same degree of physical pain as in the case of Damien. The status of the condemned is not the same, for one had made an attempt on a king's life, the other two were accused of a low-level criminal offence. Apparently in the Cameroonian case, the execution was held only to bring about death: the condemned had their limbs broken only once and so brutally that the *coup de grâce* served only to mark dramatically the end of their existence.

But, as in the case of Damien, the act of execution was *public* and visible. Even in deciding over the life and death of two individuals, the state tried to dramatise its splendour and to define itself. The state's appropriation of two lives and two deaths, which is in principle a private affair, is organised as a public performance for people to remember. But the public performance must have an intimate and non-constraining air. A crowd is summoned because without it the execution would lose its glamour; for it is the crowd which must ratify its purely sumptuous form. In order further to show the all-powerful nature of the state, the public execution becomes a social transaction. Domination may then show its menacing innuendos to the public. Does one of the condemned refuse to be tied up? He is forced to his knees. Does he refuse the food offered to him? He is given the choice of whisky or red wine. The ceremonial order (first the governor, then the prefect, then the representatives of the law, the police, the gendarmes, the clergy, the medical profession . . .) witnesses the fact that power is not an empty space. It has its hierarchies, institutions and methods.

But in the post-colonial period it is above all an *economy of death*. More precisely it creates room for pleasure even in the way it brings about death: this explains the frenzied applause which, like the bullets, drowned the death cries of the condemned. It is this that gives it its *baroque* character – an eccentric and grotesque art of representation, with its taste for the theatrical, its violent and shameless pursuit of dereliction. In this context, obscenity lies in this mode of expression which could be seen as macabre or vertiginous, but which, according to a more cynical point of view, is a feature of power, in its rush to instil itself into the public belief system. That which I refer to as obscenity in the post-colonial period is characterised by its obsession with the brightness of things and with the suppression of life which includes a hermeneutic of folly, pleasure and drunkenness.[12]

In the following pages, I shall try to track down certain examples which show the positive uses (at least from the viewpoint of the rulers) of obscenity in the post-colonial era. The examples will be limited to Cameroon, and I shall choose above all the facts and discourses which involve power itself, or those that speak for it. The question of their deconstruction by popular obscenity will be the subject of another study.

THE DOMAINS OF DRUNKENNESS

On 5 October 1988 the head of state, Paul Biya, returned from a trip to the United Nations where, like most world leaders, he had addressed the General Assembly. His speech was extremely short and contained nothing that was likely to be of interest to a distracted and cynical international opinion. It was an altogether ordinary speech for a leader of one of those singularly unknown small African countries, which could engender no conflict likely to upset the balance of world power.

In spite of this, the speech was televised in Cameroon. The journey itself was described as a 'triumphant voyage'. Maybe this was the reason why, on the President's return, the governmental delegate from the district borough of Yaoundé (who was Mayor of the capital) published a communiqué inviting 'the entire population' of the town 'to gather as one person to show the support of all Cameroonians for His Excellency, Mr Paul Biya, champion of the Third World and creator of cooperation without discrimination'.[13] And, in order to facilitate the 'spontaneous' participation of the crowd in this 'exceptional welcome', the markets were closed from 1.00 p.m. onwards. All traders from the Chamber of Agriculture and all merchants from the centre of town were 'invited to fill the 20 May Avenue from the post-office roundabout to the Warda crossroads'.[14] And that is what they did.

Of course this was not the first time the head of state had returned from travelling abroad. Nor was this the first time the governmental delegate invited the people to 'fill the 20 May Avenue from the post-office roundabout to the Warda crossroads'. This is the common practice, which has ended up 'banalising' itself. It is part of the permanent public demonstration of grandeur which perhaps sets Cameroon apart from other sub-Saharan post-colonial states.[15] In this way, and despite appearances, the return of Paul Biya had nothing about it that was particularly unusual. The performance which accompanied his return served only to mark an instance of the dramatisation of a particular system of domination which was installed before Biya's rise to power, which has now had time to become 'routinised', to create its reactions, the aim being, on each occasion, to use an event that is banal (in this case addressing the United Nations' General Assembly) and anodyne (if one takes the way in which such an event is perceived elsewhere in the world as a reference point) to increase its prestige.

This is especially evident during the visits of foreign heads of state to Cameroon. In October 1987, when a reception was organised for the arrival of Abdou Diouf, the President of Senegal, forty-two dance groups were brought to the airport several hours before the plane was due to land. Beforehand, the governmental delegate had published the usual communiqué requesting

> public and private sector employers to be kind enough to allow their employees to leave work for a short time so that their massive and enthusiastic presence could contribute to the success of the welcoming celebrations which such an illustrious host deserved to receive.[16]

This is why 'a human fence comprising pupils in school uniform, party militants, men, women and children of all ages' lined the route that the convoy would take from the airport to the host's residence.[17]

This thirst for prestige and the accompanying desire for recognition have been incorporated into the state liturgy since Ahmadou Ahidjo's presidency. This causes the 'grammar' of official discourse to resort constantly to rhetoric which may be picturesque, but is not very persuasive. Therefore Paul Biya's visit to Belgium in May 1989 was described in the following way:

> Belgium, which was so over-excited that it could no longer contain its eagerness and impatience to honour the Cameroonian presidential couple, received yesterday afternoon the head of state and his wife with a warmth and enthusiasm which people here say is unusual for such an occasion. Belgium, and Brussels above all, was so glorious and sunny yesterday that it seemed that the sun had deliberately chosen to shine in all its splendour to show that this day was a particularly special one.[18]

Should the above be seen simply as verbal extravagance which carries no special meaning? This would be to forget the fact that in the post-colonial period, the actual process of power involves the production of the absurd.[19] The creation of vulgarity must itself be understood in the context of the struggle to constuct a make-believe world, and it must not be given any moral connotation. It is a deliberately cynical process. It is political in the sense that, as Willentz argues, all political subjects are governed by *master fictions* which, little by little, become indisputable.[20] But the fiction produced by the post-colonial polity tends towards the realms of fantasy and hallucination.

Take for instance the following extract from a speech given by Henri Bandolo, Minister of Information and Culture, during the ceremony for the appointment of Gervais Mendo Ze as Director-General of Radio-Television Cameroon on 31 October 1988:

> Four years of experimentation, repetition and installation have gone by since the rise of Bamenda. Our public has been fidgeting with impatience. It has become less and less tolerant. It has been waiting for the spark of creativity and ingenuity for which you have just received the fuse, the gunpowder and the light.
>
> With all their instruments tuned, and the musicians well positioned, you, as conductor of such a grand and large orchestra, face the public.
>
> With the magic and authority of your baton, let us listen to a crystal-clear symphony, in harmony with the aspirations of the Cameroonian people who, liberated by progress, have increased their demands for excellence in harmony also with the choices and ideals of the 'Renouveau national camerounais'.[21]

Then, after having stressed the need to turn one's back on these 'disoriented and insipid broadcasts, in which most programmes consist of deformation, disinformation, obscenity, biased commentaries and outrageous gossiping', the minister added that such practices are 'designed to tarnish the good image' of the country. Because of this he thought it 'necessary to denounce these escapades, these bunglings and these erring ways as results of incompetence, naivety, narcissism, laxity and deception'.[22] The preoccupation with social rank and pomp upon which the minister so insisted did not only manifest itself through rhetorical devices (the repetitions and lists, contrasts between words and things, frequent antitheses, the tendency to exaggerate resulting in the systematic use of superlatives, frequent use of hyperbole, and the use of expressions that go beyond reality).

This preoccupation is present above all in the diverse 'liturgies' organised so often by the state and party. Prior to examining them in detail, it is necessary to point out that what here takes on the characteristics of a real 'tangential language' is in fact a way of thinking that belongs to a closed society.[23] It is the expression of a domestic mentality which has its 'jargon' and fulfils its own needs. It is a local, coherent and codified genre which strings facts and events together in a fantastical way in order to produce the incredible. *Master fictions* can be created only in this way. This is why the post-colonial rhetoric of power can be compared to that in communist regimes, in the sense that it is, above all, a regime given to producing untruths. It is also comparable in the sense that it uses the 'banal' during public 'events'. Thus, during visits abroad by the head of state, it is necessary to give, in great detail, a list of all the people to whom he granted an audience:[24] 'All these businessmen told the president of their willingness to back the development activities he was embarking on in Cameroon by offering investments and services in various areas.'[25]

But the theatricality of post-colonial power is most apparent during the ceremonies listed in the state's liturgical calendar. In its rush to decolonise, Cameroon consciously developed a ceremonial system which is similar, in many respects, to that of communist regimes.[26] The symbolic system institutionalised during Ahidjo's presidency (1958–82) was closely linked to communist ceremony in the way it took on para-religious and dogmatic aspects, which are perceptible in the general economy of public life. The ceremonies organised in the last ten years of his presidency almost always involved a degree of emotional expression and intense symbolism. They tended to become stereotypical in form. They had the repetitive nature of myths and cyclical time. In the end their regularity transformed them into custom. A 'massive, spontaneous and enthusiastic' participation was demanded of the crowds. The official calendar marked the different sequences of social life.[27] The regime ended up by creating its own rhythms of time, work and leisure. At the same time, it had to construct a suspect genealogy to compensate for a lack of legitimacy which prevailed in the early years since, when decolonisation began in 1958, the French colonial administration decided that it was in its long-term interests to cut itself off from the nationalists and to grant the spoils of independence to its clients. This enterprise to legitimise a regime born of contempt was accompanied by a violent reaction against certain historical figures from the nationalist period.[28] One of the most remarkable features of Cameroonian regimes has been the state's obsession with reconstructing the past in its own image.

It was also during Ahidjo's presidency that – in addition to public holidays – all successes, especially in inter-African sports competitions, were celebrated. It was also during this period that the head of state's portrait was hung in the main public places. Admittedly there have been no statues in his honour, but the largest stadium in the capital as well as some of the main roads and public places were named after him during his lifetime. 'Slogans of support' also appeared during this period. This accentuated the personality cult which resulted in his being bedecked with various titles by his courtesans: 'Father of the Nation', 'Great Camarade', 'Untiring Builder of the Nation', 'The Man of February 1958', 'The Greatest Peasant'. The acrobatic character of such declamatory rhetoric was revealed in 1984 when, following the discovery of a plot, Ahidjo was tried and condemned to death in his absence, then pardoned. Today, it is as if Ahidjo never existed. The regime that succeeded him has made every effort to banish him from memory in the same way that Ahidjo himself organised the 'forgetting' of the heads of nationalist resistance.[29] As we have seen, in the post-colonial era, the 'manducation' of *theophagic* time and facts is not only the act of 'plebians'.

Biya's regime has inherited these practices, has routinised them and has created new ones. For instance, with the objective of showing off the omnipresence of authority in daily life, a medallion featuring the head of state accompanied by a 'thought for the day' is published every day on the front page of the government newspaper. In addition to a celebration of his rise to power every 6 November, the regime has added another holiday to the calendar, this one to exalt the party. The first one lasted for three days in Bertoua, a region in the east of the country; this was in April 1989. The people danced to balafons and drums. Sports competitions were organised and, as usual, speeches were given. The festivities ended with a five-kilometre 'long march' of support which ended where it had begun. Not only local people, but also religious, political, administrative and 'traditional' authorities participated in the celebrations. During these parades, political subjects engage in an act of self-denigration while they attempt to enhance the splendour of power. In an improvisation, Samba Letina, president of the party's Lom and Djerem section, invited his fellow citizens to support 'the Renewal government thanks to whom we enjoy so many marvels and charitable acts today . . . and an unprecedented, rapid economic, social and cultural development'.[30] But the art of 'normatively' regulating a society is already well known.

THE INTIMACY OF TYRANNY[31]

But what really deserves attention is the way in which what Michel Foucault calls 'the politics of coercion' increases subjection and overdetermines the limits of normality. In the post-colonial period, power does not only act upon the bodies of dancers writhing about under the sun as they wait for the arrival of their own or a foreign head of state. Because the post-colonial mode of domination is, above all, a punitive system, studies should focus their attentions on the thousands of ways in which local people resist. These escapes – which seem like the work of Sisyphus – must be assessed on the understanding that local people are always caught up in the constraints of rituals of ratification.

The logistics of this ensnarement have not been analysed in enough detail in recent African studies. However, the knowledge that we have of the role of voluntary servitude, disorder,[32] and the baroque in post-colonial authoritarian systems is closely bound up with this ensnarement. In fact, at a given stage in the post-colonial historical trajectory, the authoritarian mode can no longer be interpreted solely in terms of 'control', 'surveillance' and 'the politics of coercion'. In the same way as obscenity is the other side of munificence, and vulgarity a condition of state power, an intimate tyranny links together the dominant and the dominated. If subjection is increased, it is also because the subjects themselves have internalised the part of the system that they blame, to such a degree that they end up reproducing it as if it was their own. (They reproduce the authoritarian epistemology with its taste for obscenity and folly in the small details of everyday life such as social networks, secret cults and societies, cooking methods, leisure habits, systems of consumption, fashion tastes, rhetorical devices, and the political economy of the body.) It is in this sense that the body which dances, eats, drinks, gets dressed, forms a crowd along an avenue and applauds at a passing procession in a ritual of confirmation, proves the abundance of state power. And by dramatising its subordination, it protests its loyalty and confirms the existence of an undoubted institution.

Take for example ceremonies known as the 'transfer of office' which mark bureaucratic time in the post-colonial period and deeply affect the minds of individuals, elites and masses alike. One such ceremony took place in October 1987 in the small town of Mban-komo in the central-southern region. Essomba Ntonga Godfroy, newly elected municipal administrator, had to be 'installed' in his post, in the company of his two assistants, Andre Effa Owona and Jean Paul Otu. The protagonists of this liturgy were, at the same time, its most decorative aspects. The ceremony was presided over by the prefect of Mefou, Tabou Pierre, assisted by the sub-prefect of Mbankomo district, Bekonde Belinga Henoc-Pierre. Among the main personalities on the 'official' stand were the president of the party's departmental section, representatives of the elites from 'within and without' the district, 'traditional' authorities and cult priests. The dancers were accompanied by drums and balafons. A religious choir also participated in the festivities. According to one witness

> The paroxysms of elation were reached when the tricolour scarves were presented to the municipal administrator and his two assistants, and the badges of the municipal councillors to the elected of 25 October. Well before this outburst of joy, the prefect, Mr Tabou gave a well-received and brilliant brief speech explaining the meaning of the day's ceremony to the elected men and to the populace: the celebration of retrieved democracy.[33]

He also presented a list of positions held by the newly elected administrator. The prefect mentioned not only his age, but also a complete list of the positions he held as well as his sporting triumphs.[34] But it was during the 'installation' of Pokossy Ndoumbe as head of the borough of Douala that the most detailed presentation was given:

> Mr Pokossy Ndoumbe was born on 21 August 1932 at Bonamikengue in the region of Akwa. He attended the main school in Akwa, obtaining his certificate in 1947. Then he left for France. At the Jules Ferry school in Coulonniers he passed the first cycle without difficulty. In 1954 he passed the baccalaureate in experimental science at the Michelet lycée in Vanves. He was interested in studying pharmacy and he diligently attended the faculty of pharmacy in Paris, where he obtained his diploma in 1959. During his final years at university he worked as an intern at the Emile Roux hospital in Brevannes before returning to his homeland in 1960.[35]

Such attention to detail should not come as a surprise for it is a part of the system of 'prestige'. Mentioning even the smallest educational achievements touches one of the post-colonial codes of prestige, especially if they were made overseas. It acts as a sign of distinction. Such ostentation is not only limited to state liturgies. A transubstantiation must take place whereby the new position shines upon the person being 'installed' in it so that he is immersed in its radiance. In such parodical deference, the setting out of a person's educational history, and diplomas and titles obtained, constitutes a sign of rank, status and professional qualification.[36]

There are plenty more examples of decoration and medal-giving ceremonies. In the 20 May 1989 ceremonies alone, more than 3,000 people were decorated, with 481 receiving gold medals, 1,000 vermeil medals, and 1,682 silver medals. The medals, which employers obtained from the Ministry of Works and Social Providence, cost CFA 11,500 each for the gold ones, CFA 10,500 for the vermeil ones and CFA 8,500 for the silver. The 'contributions' given by businesses to the recipients of the medals for family festivities should be added to this sum.[37] Family festivities are 'libations, feasting and diverse orgies [which] are the norm in such circumstances'.[38] One could analyse the purely lavish form of such expenditure during these ceremonies, where it is rare to find a recipient of a medal who is not heavily in debt the day after the festivities. But that would be to forget that in this context decoration should be considered as a political performance based on prestige and ostentation. The generous distributions of food are of interest only in the sense that they put those at the receiving end in a position of 'obligation'; they establish hierarchies and show off superiority. Distributions are made to prove wealth and to subordinate people.[39]

> The day they told me I was to be decorated, my wife and I were so excited that we stayed up all night talking about it. Up till now, we had taken part in the festivities only when other people received decorations. This time we would celebrate our own medal . . . On the day I received my medal, my wife prepared a pretty bouquet of flowers which she presented to me on the festival stand to the sound of public applause.[40]

In the post-colonial period, magnificence and the desire to shine out are not only the prerogative of the state; the populace also wish to be honoured and to engage in festivities:

> Last Saturday, Cameroon's Muslim community celebrated the end of Ramadan. For 30 days, Muslims had been deprived of many things from dawn until dusk. They refrained from drinking, eating, smoking, indulging in sexual relations and saying anything against the belief and

177

the law. Last Saturday marked the end of these abstentions for the whole Muslim community of Cameroon.[41]

It can therefore be said that, in the post-colonial period, the obscenity of power is partly nourished by the public's desire for grandeur. Because this period is characterised above all by scarcity, the question of 'eating' and 'tipping' is a political style *par excellence*.[42] But the question of 'eating', like that of 'scarcity', is indissociable from particular systems of 'death', from specific ways of rejoicing and from given therapeutic methods.[43] This is why 'the night',[44] 'the invisible',[45] 'the stomach', 'the mouth',[46] or 'the penis' must be seen as historical phenomena in themselves, as institutions and political powers in the same way as the economy of pleasure (mainly sex) or of fashion is understood:

Cameroonians adore slick gabardine suits, Christian Dior outfits, Yamamoto shirts and crocodile skin shoes.[47]

Designer labels are a real sign of 'class'. There are certain names which make a big effect, and it is these names that should be worn on a jacket, a shirt, a skirt, a scarf or a pair of shoes if you want to be respected.[48]

Do not be surprised if one day, coming unannounced into an office, you discover piles of clothes on the desks. The corridors of ministries and other public or private offices have become the market place *par excellence*. The market for these goods is so flexible that everybody – from the director to the orderly – can find what he wants. Due to the current economic crisis, traders give large-scale reductions in price and offer long-term credit facilities . . .
     This is such good business that many people are not hesitating to become involved. Sophisticated ladies are rubbing shoulders with every breed of hoodlum and yobbo. The root of the whole 'system' is travelling. It is no secret that most of the clothes on the market come from the West. Those who have the 'chance' to travel there regularly, quickly latch on to the benefits they can reap from these frequent journeys. Just make a few 'agreements' with customs and the deal is on.[49]

Even death does not escape from this wish to shine out and be honoured. The dominant and the dominated do not only wish to feast in order to show off their splendour. Those who have accumulated goods and profits, prestige and influence are not only involved in the 'constraint of giving',[50] but also want to 'die well', to be buried with a certain amount of pomp. Funerals are one of the occasions when power gazes at itself in a narcissistic way. Therefore, when Joseph Awunti, the presidential minister in charge of relations with parliament, died on 4 November 1987, his body was met at Bamenda airport by the governor of North-West province, Wabon Ntuba Mboe, accompanied by the grand chancellor, the first vice-president of the party, and several administrative, political and 'traditional' authorities. Many other personalities and members of the government were also present, including the 'personal' representative of the head of state, Joseph Charles Dumba, minister in charge of missions to the presidency. The Economic and Social Council was headed by its president, Ayang Luc, the National Assembly by the president of the parliamentary group, and the central committee of the party by its treasurer.[51]

During the funeral of Thomas Ebongalame, secretary of the National Assembly, member of the superior council of the magistracy, administrative secretary of the central committee of the party, board member of many different businesses, and 'an initiated member of his tribe', the procession left Yaoundé by road. The funeral procession was awaited by huge crowds who had come from various parts of the South-West province:

> At Muyuka, Ebonji, Tombel and Nyasoso, primary and secondary school students formed human fences several hundreds of metres long. When the body arrived in Kumba, the main town of Memee, the town transformed into a procession. At the head was the ENI-ENIA fanfare playing a sad tune. People were weeping profusely . . . In this town with a population of 12,000, socio-economic activities had come to a halt since 30 April when the tragic news was heard. People were waiting for instructions from Yaoundé. No fewer than ten meetings were held to organise the funeral programme.[52]

As we have seen, obscenity constitutes one of the post-colonial forms of power, although it does not have moral connotations. But obscenity is also one of the ways in which subordinates deconstruct this power. Bakhtin's mistake was to associate obscenity only with the subordinates. The production of the burlesque does not only belong to them. The real inversion is that while the masses involve themselves in folly in their desire for splendour and put on the flashy rags of power in order to reproduce its epistemology, power, in its violent quest for grandeur and prestige, adopts vulgarity as its main way of existing. It is in the context of this narrow *intimacy* that the forces of tyranny in sub-Saharan Africa must be analysed.

NOTES

1. I am mainly referring to the way in which he explains how non-official cultures invert and desecrate official values by carnavalesque activities.

179

See M. Bakhtin, *Rabelais and his World* (Bloomington, Ind., 1983). For a recent criticism, see R. Lachman, 'Bakhtin and Carnival: Culture as Counter-Culture', *Cultural Critique* (Winter 1987) pp. 115–52.

2. I owe this idea to C. Castoriadis, *L'Institution Imaginaire de la Société* (Paris, 1975) p. 475.

3. I use the word 'target' in the way that Michel Foucault uses it in reply to the question 'what does the art of governing consist of?' He explains how the subjects of power are, on the one hand, the territory, and, on the other hand, the people who live in this territory, the population. See M. Foucault, *La Gouvernementalité* (Paris, 1989).

4. I have borrowed this heading from D. Parkin, 'The Creativity of Abuse', *Man* (March 1980) p. 45. The author uses it in the context of ritualised verbal exchanges, although I am using it to interpret political situations.

5. See C. Toulabor, 'Jeu de Mots, Jeux de Vilain: Lexique de la Derision Politique au Togo', *Politique Africaine* (Sept. 1981) pp. 55–71. Also see his book *Togo sous Eyadéma* (Paris, 1986) especially pp. 302–9.

6. For an example of the poaching of rhetoric in the pseudo-revolutionary regime of Burkina-Faso under Sankara, see C. Dubuch, 'Langage du Pouvoir, Pouvoir du Langage', *Politique Africaine* (Dec. 1985) pp. 44–53.

7. I am extrapolating an argument developed in another context by E. Tonkin, 'Masks and Powers', *Man* (June 1979) pp. 237–48.

8. I am using, at my own risk, a character taken from Greek mythology. Dionysos was dismembered by his mother and other women and eaten according to a fixed ritual. See J. Kott, *The Eating of the Gods: An Interpretation of Greek Tragedy* (New York, 1970). For a similar dramatisation see G. Bataille, *Death and Sensuality: A Study of Eroticism and the Taboo* (New York, 1962).

9. S. Freud, *Totem and Taboo* (London, 1983) p. 140.

10. This is taken from *La Gazette* (Douala) (September 1987).

11. See M. Foucault, *Surveiller et Punir: Naissance de la Prison* (Paris, 1975) pp. 9–11.

12. I am using to my own advantage an idea contained in Bataille's work, *Death and Sensuality . . ..*

13. *Cameroon Tribune* (5 October 1988).

14. *Ibid.*

15. For a historical and sociological perspective for the successive regimes in Cameroon, see R. Joseph, *Le Mouvement Nationaliste au Cameroun: Les Origines Sociales de l'U.P.C.* (Paris, 1986); J. F. Bayart, *L'Etat au Cameroun* (Paris, 1977); P. F. Ngayap, *Cameroun Qui Gouverne?* (Paris, 1984).

16. *Cameroon Tribune* (2 October 1987).

17. See M. Bakoa, 'Une Fete Africaine pour Diouf', *Cameroon Tribune* (2 October 1987). In the same article there is a description of the outfits worn by Madame Diouf (a red skirt, with a green, red and black shirt) and Madame Biya (a yellow silk dress).

18. See *Cameroon Tribune* (9 May 1989). For a more explicit account of 'the growing prestige' that Cameroon and 'its president' are supposed to be gaining from these frequent journeys abroad, and of the glowing effects

this has on the 'international scene', see Abui Mama, 'Un Pays qui Compte', *Cameroon Tribune* (18 May 1989).

19. This aspect is well reflected in the post-colonial African novel. See for example the works of Sony Labou Tansi or, to a lesser degree, those of Tchicaya U'Tamsi, *Ces Fruits si Doux de l'Arbre a Pain* (Paris, 1988). For a study of a case that is not nearly so extreme as is generally thought, see D. Bigo, *Pouvoir et Obeissance en Centrafrique* (Paris, 1989) pp. 58–64 and 143–71.

20. S. Willentz, *Rites of Power: Symbolism, Ritual and Politics Since the Middle Ages* (Philadelphia, Pa, 1985) p. 4.

21. See H. Bandolo, 'Radio-Tele: Les Nouveaux Defis', *Cameroon Tribune* (15 November 1988).

22. He says they must be condemned, 'not only because we regret its bad effects, but to curse and exorcise them as evildoers', *Cameroon Tribune* (15 November 1988).

23. In the sense that R. Horton, 'African Conversion', *Africa* (1971), 'On the Rationality of Conversion', *Africa* (1975) uses the idea of 'microcosm' to which he fixes the existence of a domestic way of thinking that is closed in upon itself.

24. For example, we were told that during his trip to Belgium he dined with M. Jacques Delors, President of the European Commission. Then he held discussions with M. le Vicomte Davignon (President of Belgian branch of Société Générale), M. J. P. Schaeker Willemaers (Director of the Tractebel group), M. Fontaine and M. Lebeau (Compagnie française d'enterprise), M. Stulemeyer (Six BBM), M. Albert Frere (Brussels-Lambert group), M. Sylvain (Director-general of the European Investment Bank), M. Jacques Saverys and M. J. de Wilde (Belgian Maritime Company), M. Jo Goes and M. Alain Rozan (Société Sopex).

25. See P. C. Ndembiyembe, 'Une Journée Intense', *Cameroon Tribune* (11 May 1989).

26. See the two works of C. A. P. Binns, 'The Changing Face of Power: Revolution and Accommodation in the Development of the Soviet Ceremonial System: Part I', *Man* (Dec. 1979) pp. 585–606, and 'Part II', *Man* (March, 1980) pp. 170–87.

27. See E. Leach, *Culture and Communication: The Logic by Which Symbols are Connected* (Cambridge, 1976) and S. Lukes, 'Political Ritual and Social Integration', *Sociology* (Dec. 1975) pp. 298–308.

28. See J. A. Mbembe, 'L'Etat-Historien', in R. Um Nyobe, *Ecrits sous Maquis* (Paris, 1989) pp. 10–42; or J. A. Mbembe, 'Pouvoir des Morts et Langages des Vivants: Les Errance de la Memoire Nationaliste au Cameroun', *Politique Africaine* (June 1986).

29. See J. A. Mbembe, 'Le Spectre et l'Etat: Des Dimensions Politiques de l'Imaginaire Historique dans le Cameroon Postcolonial', paper presented at the 'Memory and Identity' conference, Laval University, Quebec (October 1987).

30. See D. Ibrahima, 'Bertoua: Rejouissances et Meditation', *Cameroon Tribune* (19 April 1989). For an analysis of ceremonies see Y. A. Faure, 'Celebrations Officielles et Pouvoirs Africains: Symboliques et Construction de l'Etat', *Revue Canadienne d'Etudes Africaines* (3, 1978) pp. 383–404;

T. C. Callaghy, 'Culture and Politics in Zaïre', doc. pol. (October 1986); C. Lane, *The Rites of Rulers* (Cambridge, 1981).

31. I have inverted the title of R. Sennett's book, *Les Tyrannies de l'Intimité* (Paris, 1979).

32. In the way R. Boudon, *La Place du Desordre* (Paris, 1981) uses it to create a methodology.

33. See P. Essono, 'Installation de L'Administrateur Municipal de Mbankomo: La Fête de la Democratie Retrouvée', *Cameroon Tribune* (4 December 1987).

34. Among other things, one learned that he was the old champion and record holder of the 400 metres in Cameroon and a gold medallist in the French African school and university competition in May 1957.

35. See M. Bissi, 'Communauté Urbaine de Douala: Place à M. Pokossy Ndoumbe', *Cameroon Tribune* (19 April 1989).

36. For a discussion of rituals of government and private behaviour see E. Goffman, *La Mise en Scene de la Vie Quotidienne: Les Relations en Public* (Paris, 1973) pp. 19–72.

37. Figures from R. Owona, 'Un Prix Fort', *Cameroon Tribune* (18 May 1989).

38. P. Ntete Ntete, 'Un Privilege qu'il Faul Meriter', *Cameroon Tribune* (18 May 1989).

39. See M. Mauss, *Essai sur le Don*, p. 269.

40. *Cameroon Tribune* (18 May 1989). See, for a similar phenomenon, the ceremonies for the decoration of army officers, *Cameroon Tribune* (18 April 1989).

41. J. B. Simgba, 'Le Communauté Musulmane du Cameroun en Fête', *Cameroon Tribune* (7 and 8 May 1989).

42. In the way that J.-F. Bayart, *L'Etat en Afrique: La Politique du Ventre* (Paris, 1989) uses Foucault's idea of 'governmentality' and for sub-Saharan African speaks of a 'governmentality of the belly'.

43. See M. Taussig, *Shamanism, Colonialism and the Wild Man: A Study in Terror and Healing* (Chicago, Ill., 1988).

44. See E. de Rosny, *Les Yeux de ma Chevre* (Paris, 1977).

45. See P. Bonaffe, *Nzo Lipfu, le Lignage de la Mort: La Sorcellerie, Ideologie de la Lutte Sociale sur le Plateau Kukuya* (Paris, 1978).

46. See E. P. Brown, *Nourir les Gens, Nourir les Haines* (Paris, 1983).

47. See R. Owona, 'Branche sur les Cinq Continents', *Cameroon Tribune* (27 April 1989).

48. D. Ndachi Tagne, 'Le Venin Hypnotique de la Griffe', *Cameroon Tribune* (27 April 1989).

49. C. Mien Zok, 'Le Bret-à-Porter fait du Porte-à-Porte', *Cameroon Tribune* (27 April 1989).

50. P. Veyne, *Le Pain et le Cirque: Sociologie Historique d'un Pluralisme Politique* (Paris, 1976) p. 230.

51. N. Mbonwoh, 'Le Corps de Joseph Awunti Repose Desormais à Kedju Ketinguh', *Cameroon Tribune* (12 November 1987).

52. M. Bakoa, 'Heures de Tristesse dans le Sud-Ouest', *Cameroon Tribune* (14–15 May 1989).

PART THREE

Political Institutions and State–Society Relations

CHAPTER NINE
The Historical Trajectories of the Ivorian and Kenyan States

Jean-François Medard

Surprisingly, Côte d'Ivoire and Kenya have been very rarely compared, perhaps because they are too similar. If we follow the
distinction proposed by M. Dogan and D. Pelassy between comparisons of analogous and contrasting countries, Côte d'Ivoire and Kenya
fall into the first category, while Côte d'Ivoire and Ghana – which
Richard Crook compares in Chapter 10 – fall into the second.[1] Let us
begin by recalling the main characteristics which make these two
countries analogous, as well as a certain number of differences which
are too often overlooked.

It is generally agreed that Côte d'Ivoire and Kenya have deliberately
chosen a capitalist path of development combined with an economic
and political opening towards Western countries with relative success.
Both countries have been considered showpieces of capitalism in
Africa, whether negatively or positively, placing the debate concerning their relative successes and failures on an ideological as well as a
scientific plane. Observers agree on a number of points: both
countries sustained a positive rate of economic growth[2] until the end
of the 1970s and both have enjoyed political stability.[3] Observers
disagree, however, on whether one should talk merely about growth
or about development. Depending on their viewpoints, they emphasise the costs evaluated in absolute rather than relative terms and
underline the structural obstacles to full-fledged development; or they
forget about the cost, emphasising how much better the performances
of both countries are with comparisons to the other African states.
Let us add that the two countries, deprived of mineral resources and
of oil, have given a priority to agriculture, financing industrial
development on surpluses from agriculture and mostly on foreign
capital. The two political regimes are authoritarian, though moderate

185

for Africa. For all these reasons, these two countries are the most similar cases to be observed in their category in Africa.

However, if we want to compare the two states from a political point of view, we have to keep in mind some basic differences.

First, geographically: Kenya is slightly larger than Côte d'Ivoire. Côte d'Ivoire is marked by a contrast between the forest in the south, near the ocean, and the savannah in the north near the desert. In Kenya, the main contrast is between the agricultural highlands, in the centre, surrounded by semi-arid pastoral land, and the Indian Ocean on the east, Lake Victoria on the west. The economic geography of the two countries has been superimposed on these oppositions.

Second, demographically: it is important to remember that Kenya has twice as many inhabitants as Côte d'Ivoire (22 million and 10 million respectively) while both countries have extremely high demographic rates of growth (4 per cent and 3.7 per cent respectively).

Third, historically: while Côte d'Ivoire was opened to Western influences by way of the Atlantic Ocean, Kenya was opened to Arabic and Eastern influences through the Indian Ocean. In Côte d'Ivoire the population living on the present territory was divided between acephalous societies in the west, and chiefdoms in the east. But as Crook underlines, 'The peoples of Côte d'Ivoire were scattered groups of refugees and migrants from other core areas.'[4] In Kenya, apart from the coast, there were mostly acephalous societies based on clan and age set ties. Côte d'Ivoire was colonised by the French and Kenya by the British, but this is not the most important point since both colonies were under direct administration. More important is that Kenya was a settlers' colony and Côte d'Ivoire was not. This had two consequences: the cultural, social and economic impact of colonisation went further and deeper in Kenya than in Côte d'Ivoire. The issue of land control has been, from the beginning, the main economic and political issue. It fostered anti-colonialism and still is a serious problem. Only 17 per cent of the land is arable, with ownership still highly concentrated and great demographic pressure. In Côte d'Ivoire there was plenty of land with free access to it. The land was owned by those who cultivated it. Economic growth in Côte d'Ivoire was based on clearing and cultivating the forest areas. This has had important economic, social, ecological and political consequences. There was no global scarcity of land, even if the search for land and the internal migrations towards the West which followed, fuelled local conflicts over land rights between the Baoulé migrants and the native Bété.[5]

Finally, economically: if the growth rates in the two countries have been roughly the same over a long period (about 7 per cent in the 1960s and 1970s), per capita income is twice as high in Côte d'Ivoire as in Kenya (more than $600 as opposed to $300). Economic growth in Côte d'Ivoire has been higher than the demographic growth, but slightly lower in Kenya. This means that the standard of living is higher in Côte d'Ivoire, in spite of the bad economic performances of the 1980s. Another important difference is that economic growth in Côte d'Ivoire is largely based on non-qualified African manpower, imported from Burkina, Mali, etc. (about one-third of the active population is of foreign origin including qualified French experts);[6] the manpower in Kenya is largely Kenyan. The rate of urbanisation is higher in Côte d'Ivoire (46 per cent) than in Kenya (15 per cent). But towns and industries are more scattered in Kenya than in Côte d'Ivoire.

We contend that a comparison between these two states has to be dynamic and historical and not static. Even more it has to follow a socio-historical perspective, comparing the states not as if they were atemporal phenomena, but specific historical trajectories. Such an enterprise will necessarily be sketchy and superficial, but it may help raise comparative analytical questions. In comparing these states, we do not follow the classical distinction between states, regimes and government (or authority) because the degree of differentiation between these three levels of political organisation is not important enough to be relevant in this context.

In both countries, the state appears with the colonial state. But the colonial state was not a full-fledged state, it was truncated, bereft of its indigenous political dimension and thus reduced to its repressive and bureaucratic nature by its foreign and imposed origins. The first section of this chapter analyses the genesis of the independent state which begins in both countries shortly before independence.[7] Then, in a second section, we observe the initial crystallisation of each state around a charismatic leader, the patriarch,[8] the founding father. This coincides with a period of economic growth. In a third section, starting at the end of the 1970s in a context of economic crisis, the political paths of the two states diverge somewhat; while the succession crisis is faced successfully in Kenya, Côte d'Ivoire has simultaneously to confront the economic crisis and the succession problem. On the whole, politics in both countries remained relatively autonomous, despite the deepening economic crisis.

THE GENESIS OF THE STATE IN COTE D'IVOIRE AND KENYA

At independence (1960 for Côte d'Ivoire and 1963 for Kenya), the two countries inherited the administrative and coercive apparatus bequeathed by their respective colonial states. While taking hold of this apparatus (very slowly in the case of Côte d'Ivoire) and developing it tremendously in both cases, they appropriated the political dimension of the state which fed back into the administrative dimension. We need to see all of this as an evolutionary process, occurring both before and after the date of formal independence – without seeing that date as entirely meaningless.

One can say that, in each case, the colonial state's legacy is roughly the same because the two colonial states were based on the same Napoleonic principles.[9] There is no point here in stressing the differences between direct and indirect administration. It is more important to emphasise the differences in the two decolonisation processes which had an effect on the nature of the political power coalition crystallising around the two founding fathers. In both cases, a political leader arose as the charismatic guide of the people and built the new state around his person. This is why we call these states by the names of their leaders – the Houphouët state and the Kenyatta state.

In both cases, we can distiguish three phases: the decolonisation process, the compromise of independence and the consolidation of the leadership.

The Decolonisation Process

Côte d'Ivoire The present one-party state in Côte d'Ivoire originated from the 'Parti Démocratique de l'Indépendance' (PDCI), a branch of the 'Rassemblement Démocratique Africain' (RDA). The PDCT-RDA grew largely from the Syndicat Agricole Africain (SAA) founded by Houphouët-Boigny, a traditional chief, a doctor and a wealthy Baoulé planter. The SAA was set up to defend the interests of African planters against French planters who were favoured by the colonial administration. The SAA was led by big planters, but recruited among all the planters, except the smallest ones. Taking advantage of the favourable political conjuncture at the end of the war, it entered the political arena by promoting the creation of the PDCI together with come urbanised and educated people trained by the 'Groupes d'Etudes Communistes' (GEC).[10] Félix Houphouët-Boigny was elected to the Assembly in 1946 and his name was associated with the abolition of forced labour and the code of *'indigénat'*. This was the basis of his popularity. In this way, the big planters were taking the leadership of the anti-colonialist movement in contrast with what happened in neighbouring Ghana.[11] The PDCI as part of the RDA became part of the parliamentary group of the Communist Party which was the only metropolitan party to adopt an anti-colonialist position. With the beginning of the Cold War the communists had to leave the government. The PDCI-RDA was faced with violent repression from the colonial administration for the double reason that it was anti-colonialist and pro-communist. The situation became very conflictual and Côte d'Ivoire seemed in 1951 at the eve of revolt and war, when Houphouët-Boigny broke with the Communist Party and chose compromise instead of war.

Kenya The processes of decolonisation and state-formation in Kenya were much more complicated and less peaceful. Several anti-colonialist movements were involved instead of a single one. The anti-colonialist struggle started earlier in Kenya, but ripened at about the same time, just after the war. But it was a rather regionally diversified process articulating both ethnic and class factors. More violent than in Côte d'Ivoire, it led to independence at a later date.

In 1946 Jomo Kenyatta, a Kikuyu, who had been educated in Britain, took the leadership of the Kenya African Union (KAU): this was the beginning of a nationalist movement, divided between moderates and radicals, with Kikuyu hegemony.[12] Other anti-colonialist associations with an ethnic base existed, such as the Luo Union. Meanwhile, a strong and aggressive union movement was developing. In the background, a clandestine movement was organising in the central part of the country, known as the Mau Mau. It launched a guerrilla war in 1952. A state of emergency was declared and tens of thousands of Kikuyu were detained preventively in Nairobi. This movement, mostly a Kikuyu movement, was more anti-colonialist than Kenyan nationalist.[13] It was basically a peasant movement without the leadership of intellectuals, isolated internationally and geographically. It was aimed at the recovery of the land taken by the settlers and against the missions. Military operations lasted from 1952 to 1956, while emergency was abolished in 1959. The Kikuyu leaders, among them Jomo Kenyatta (wrongly accused of being a member of the Mau Mau), continued to be detained.

The insurrection forced the British into a process of decolonisation at both the economic level, by facilitating the transfer of land to Africans, and the political level through the Lyttelton Constitution, opening the political system to Kenyans. During this period, since political organisations were forbidden, the lead was taken by the unions. Tom Mboya, a Luo, became the general secretary of the Kenya Federation of Labour in 1953.[14] In 1955 Kenyans were authorised to constitute political associations at the district level. In 1957 the Lennox Boyd Constitution introduced parity within the Legislative Council. In 1959 the British authorised the creation of multiracial parties. London accepted the principle of a constitutional conference to which the Africans presented an united front. But later, they divided into two parties: Kenyan African National Union (KANU) based on a Kikuyu–Luo coalition, and the Kenyan African Democratic Union (KADU) made of a coalition of minority ethnic groups (Kalenjin, Masai, Luyia, Coastal . . .) who were afraid of the hegemony of the former. Finally, under growing nationalist pressure, the British freed Jomo Kenyatta, who became the leader of KANU.

The Politics of Compromise

Côte d'Ivoire From this time on, Houphouët-Boigny and the PDCI on one side and the colonial administration on the other were slowly drawn together. Among the Ivorians themselves, there was a political realignment. The leaders of the other parties which had been supported by the administration against the PDCI were coopted within the party. Much before independence, the PDCI became hegemonic and Houphouët became the leader, if not yet the ruler, of Côte d'Ivoire. In 1957 Côte d'Ivoire obtained, according to Deferre's *loi cadre*, a statute of self-government, while Houphouët had become in 1956 a 'Ministre d'Etat' in the French government. As a French minister, he was in a position to strengthen his own position even more within his country. In 1960 Côte d'Ivoire moved reluctantly towards independence. The terms of the compromise were the following: PDCI and Houphouët-Boigny were going to rule the country, but Côte d'Ivoire would remain economically and politically bound to France. Hence, the accusation of neo-colonialism, assumed without any complex by Ivorians. It does not follow that one should see Houphouët, as his opponents maintain, as a puppet of the French. This is too easy and simplistic an interpretation. But what remains is that in choosing the economic kingdom before the political kingdom, Houphouët sacrificed the ideological and nationalistic aspiration to economic growth and he not only accepted, but asked for, a very strong French presence in the country.

Kenya   The principle of independence was established at the Lancaster House Conference (April 1962). The elections of May 1963 saw the victory of KANU, receiving two-thirds of the vote. In June, self-government commenced and Jomo Kenyatta became the prime minister. Independence was proclaimed on 12 December 1963, much later than in Côte d'Ivoire, after the third Lancaster House Conference, on the basis of a double compromise – among Kenyans, and between Kenyans and British. The first compromise led to the so-called 'Majimbo' constitution based on regionalism, for which the British pressed in order to satisfy the aspirations of KADU which they favoured. The second compromise, linked to the first, organised the transfer of land from the settlers to the Kenyans and created the basis of an independence preserving British interests. Jomo Kenyatta emerged, like Houphouët-Boigny, as the national hero, but not as strongly hegemonic as the Ivorian leader: the single party was not established yet, the country was more divided politically and the consolidation of his leadership took more time and was less firm than Houphouët's.

The Consolidation of Leadership

Côte d'Ivoire   Having reluctantly asked for independence, Houphouët-Boigny replaced his friend Auguste Denise, who was the prime minister under the *loi cadre*, and was elected President of the Republic. His power then became formal and not just informal as before. As the head of the PDCI and as a minister in France, with the popularity accumulated through his share in the fight against colonialism in the old days, he had considerable authority. But the compromise on which Houphouët and the party acceded to independence, within a neo-colonial framework, was not accepted by many militants and intellectuals. In 1963 and 1964 Houphouët denounced plots against the regime and had dozens of militants arrested. They were tried; some were condemned to death but never executed; later, Houphouët freed and rehabilitated them, a few became ministers and he pretended the plots had been invented by his police. Whatever the truth of this, the repression of the 'plots' marked the consolidation of Houphouët's state: no other policy than the president's was possible.

The PDCI, which already was a single party, became monolithic and was reduced to a tool in the hands of the leader.

Kenya   In Kenya, a different process led to a seemingly equivalent situation. The consolidation of leadership has been twofold: administrative and political. The colonial state apparatus, which had been dismantled by the regionalist Majimbo constitution, was quickly rehabilitated and the central administration was re-established as early as December 1964. The Senate was merged into the House of Representatives in 1966, and all trace of regionalism had disappeared by 1968. Very soon a presidentialist regime was emerging from a parliamentary mould.[15] More important, KADU was soon absorbed by KANU, bringing in political reunification and a *de facto* one-party system. But, within KANU a deep ideological cleavage existed with a left wing leaning towards the Soviet bloc under the leadership of Oginga Odinga, and a conservative pro-capitalist and pro-Western wing under the leadership of Tom Mboya and Jomo Kenyatta. This led to a schism and the creation of the Kenyan People's Union (KPU) in April 1966 under the direction of Oginga Odinga. First marginalised after the 'little elections', the KPU was later outlawed.[16]

From this period on, Jomo Kenyatta's leadership was consolidated. It was based on a single party with a multi-ethnic coalition under Kikuyu hegemony coopting the leaders of the KADU and, after Tom Mboya's assassination, excluding the Luo. But KANU did not attempt to control political life in as tight a manner as PDCI in Côte d'Ivoire. One notices an open and lively factional political life under the distant but effective leadership of Jomo Kenyatta.

In conclusion, one observes the emergence of two states that basically share the same values and the same pro–Western and pro-capitalist orientation, under the leadership of two patriarchs, the founding fathers of the republics based on both a single party and a centralised administration. But the relations between Côte d'Ivoire and France were tighter than between Kenya and Britain. The style of leadership of Kenyatta was more flexible and indirect than the style of Félix Houphouët-Boigny, and correlatively a more open and pluralistic political life followed.

THE HOUPHOUËT AND KENYATTA STATES: THE 'FAT YEARS' (1960–78)[17]

Similarities

Whether we consider the economic bases or constraints, the economic policy, the political structures (single party, presidentialism, centralised administration) or the political mode of functioning (authoritarianism, paternalism, patriarchism, patronage, patrimonialism and prebendalism) and the dominant values (getting wealthy), the similarities between Houphouët's Côte d'Ivoire and Kenyatta's Kenya in the 'fat years' (1960–78) are striking.

Within the economic context of contemporary Africa, the most effective path towards wealth and thus towards social stratification is through the access to state resources, whether direct or indirect.[18] Economic power supposes political power, private enterpreneurship being dependent on the state, whether for accumulation or for protection. On the other hand wealth, combined with the control of coercion, is the principal means of political influence. This is the basis of what is called straddling. This is why we have to reason in terms of production, extraction, accumulation and distribution of resources, whether these resources are economic, political or both.

The production of economic resources is based on roughly the same foundations in both states: cash crop agriculture and extraversion – coffee and cocoa in Côte d'Ivoire, coffee and tea in Kenya, completely controlled by nationals in the first case, partly in the second, but in any case dependent on the international market and complemented by wood in Côte d'Ivoire and tourism in Kenya largely controlled by foreigners. From that starting-point, there developed a partial diversification of the agriculture (pineapple, palm oil, sugar and rubber in Côte d'Ivoire, fruits, flowers and vegetables in Kenya). Local industries were developed through a policy of welcoming foreign capital investment and the extensive use of parastatals. They were more oriented towards import substitution in Kenya than in Côte d'Ivoire. Foreign capital was nationally more diversified in Kenya than in Côte d'Ivoire still retaining strong ties with the French economy. This economic policy has been mistakenly described as a 'liberal' policy, mistakenly when one observes the importance of the parastatal sector and of state capitalism in both countries.

The extraction of resources is not exclusively for the profit of foreign capital, but also for the benefit of the state and those who live from the state. This ruling class has been exceptionally instrumental in extracting resources from both internal and external sources in order to strengthen both its economic and its political power. Its nature has been extensively discussed in both countries and wrongly described as 'bourgeois' (whether 'petty', comprador, national, bureaucratic or state), confusing the idea of a privileged class and a bourgeois class: not every privileged class can be described as a bourgeois class. This ruling class was based on a coalition, a power bloc built around a dominant ethnic group, the Baoulé in Côte d'Ivoire and the Kikuyu in Kenya; the members of these two ethnic groups do not monopolise the resources, but control a disproportionate share of them. This ruling class, through straddling, has proceeded to primitive accumulation of both economic power and political power. In both cases, the patriarch has been the supreme regulator of this double accumulation and, through this, of the coalition. The inherent contradiction between the logics of extraction and of economic accumulation (the predatory state) on one side, and the logic of political accumulation through economic redistribution (the prebendal state), has not been resolved, but has been managed through a rather moderate use of political coercion, an absence of ideological mobilisation and through a skilled use of political patronage in a favourable context of economic growth.

This question is, as many authors have noted, more complicated than the simple interaction between political and economic resources, between political stability and economic growth. The contradiction remained latent in the period of economic growth, but it was going to be clearly manifest with the arrival of the economic crisis. When that occurred, the contradictions between the administrative state with a technocratic and developmental outlook and the predatory and prebendal state based on patrimonialism were to become acute.

This mode of analysis is not peculiar to Côte d'Ivoire and Kenya, but corresponds to the more general model of the sub-Saharan state. Our task is to identify what distinguishes Côte d'Ivoire and Kenya from the other African states. I agree with Richard Crook that the explanation is related to a higher level of state capacity.[19] Both states have been more skilful in mobilising internal and external resources in a favourable context of international economic growth. In particular, they have been able to use, instrumentally, both foreign personnel and capital. The level of efficiency of administration and parastatals was higher in both countries than in the rest of Africa. In Côte d'Ivoire, a generalised and long-term use of foreign expertise, in spite of its cost, has been instrumental in that respect. This is much less true in Kenya, where the level of efficiency is more based on local expertise, since the process of Africanisation has gone much faster in Kenya than in Côte d'Ivoire. For whatever reasons, the elite in Kenya seem to have been better trained than in Côte d'Ivoire. These questions must be explored more thoroughly in order to give more specific answers.

Differences

The differences between the Houphouët state and the Kenyatta state are most evident when we consider the relationship between the state and social differentiation on the one hand and political regulation on the other.

The State and Social Differentiation In both countries the state has the key role in the process of social differentiation, but this process appears more advanced in Kenya than in Côte d'Ivoire.

Côte d'Ivoire: Access to the state is at the core of the process of social differentiation, for it is the centre for the accumulation process. This is why we must review quickly the question of the Ivorian elite, social classes, ethnic groups and the state.

Since the publication of the book *Etat et Bourgeoisie en Côte d'Ivoire* (1982), the existence of the 'bourgeoisie of the planters' is generally considered a myth. More recent publications, in particular the study of Tessy Bakary on the political elite, confirm this.[20] Once we recognise the role of the big planters in the constitution and the direction of the Syndicat Agricole Africain (SAA) and then of the PDCI from its beginning (although not everyone agrees on the respective roles of the SAA and the Groupe d'Etudes Communistes or GEC),[21] the expression 'bourgeoisie of the planters' can be abandoned. This does not mean that the production of coffee and cocoa and the connected interests are not predominant factors. However, the small planters form the vast majority of the planters and only a minority of the big planters have direct political influence, the most influential of these being the absentee planters who live in towns. Côte d'Ivoire is definitely the planters' republic: a republic of all the planters. We must also take into consideration that certain planters hold government posts, whether low level, intermediary or high. The significant point remains that wealth is gained through access to the state.

On the other hand we cannot define Ivorian businessmen as a private economic bourgeoisie.[22] Should we then speak of a state bourgeoisie? Bakary disagrees with our definition because he hesitates to use class analysis in a society which is as yet poorly differentiated and where classes are still in formation.[23] This objection does not convince me. It is true that we are confronted with a double, correlated process of the formation of the state and the formation of social classes, but must we await total differentiation before speaking of social classes? I believe that we can use these terms if we do not confuse the classes 'in themselves' and the classes 'for themselves', and avoid taking analytical categories for groups considered as actors. Nevertheless, the process of differentiation of the classes seems more advanced in the upper part of the society than the lower. However, I hesitate to use the words 'state bourgeoisie' because I accept Callaghy's arguments.[24] The word 'bourgeois' must not be taken as a generic term to designate any privileged group. It is true that there is a contradiction in the term 'state bourgeoisie'. The bourgeoisie cannot be of the state. It is not impossible, however, for a political class to become an authentic bourgeoisie in certain cases.[25]

The ethnic cleavage is another distinction to be considered. Donzon's studies on the Bété show how this ethnic group is the result of colonisation and of state influence. This type of analysis, although it cannot be generalised as Amselle would like to do,[26] indicates the importance of the ethnic factor in Côte d'Ivoire from a political point of view. However, I still believe that the principal cleavage is between foreigners and Ivorians, which make the ethnic differences fade in spite of the predominance of the Baoulé (as the comparison with Kenya shows). I do not foresee any ethnic explosion in Côte d'Ivoire. There is no reason to consider ethnicity and national integration as a zero sum. It is only the exceptional and extreme case where ethnicity produces separatism. Usually what we call 'tribalism' is precisely the sign of the existence of a centre, if not a state, for which the control and the stakes are the source of political mobilisation of ethnic groups. The interaction of the process of social differentiation and the construction of the state is therefore inseparable from political regulation. This is also true in Kenya.

Kenya: Whether there is a national bourgeoisie in Kenya or not has been much debated ever since the publication of Colin Leys's book, now a classic.[27] The Kenyan debate is now more or less at a standstill. The question has been covered very well by Kitching,[28] who, after presenting both theses on the absence or presence of a national bourgeoisie, observes that to reach a conclusion precise information on the fortunes of the higher circles is needed, but that this information is impossible to obtain. The debate on Kenya underplayed the importance of the state by concentrating excessively on distinctions between ruling class and governing class. In fact, their relationship to the state seems to me a very significant element in the making of the Kenyan bourgeoisie. For an illustration, think how the political mechanism of land distribution, which did not solve the problems of landownership, allowed the ruling class to establish an economic foundation. On this base, and with the help of patronage, access to wealth was controlled more or less directly by Kenyatta who with his 'family' felt no scruples about serving themselves first. Here again, what is important are the political ties. It is my impression that in the same way that economic differentiation went further in Kenya than in Côte d'Ivoire, social differentiation and particularly social stratification went further, too. I feel that social classes function more autonomously in Kenya than in Côte d'Ivoire. Kenya's much discussed national bourgeoisie, even if less national than some scholars admit, constitutes a proto-private bourgeoisie which, it seems to me, has no equivalent in Côte d'Ivoire. This is why I would hesitate less to speak of a bourgeoisie, in the full sense of the term, in Kenya than in Côte d'Ivoire. Goran Hyden is right to draw our attention to the still important roles of the 'economy of affection' within the Kenyan 'bourgeoisie'.[29] Conversely social stratification seems more advanced in Kenya at the bottom of the social scale because of the problem of landownership which could provide for an eventual political mobilisation, and because of the concentration in Nairobi of workers and unemployed who have not yet been the object of any political mobilisation.

Ethnic identity appears to be more important in the political arena in Kenya than in Côte d'Ivoire, including sub-ethnic groups. In both countries the ethnic group and the family of the president were found at the centre of political-economic power. The other ethnic groups do get a share, however. At every level we find the political game played in this way. Historically we know that KANU was based on a coalition of the Luo and Kikuyu, and the KADU on the coalition of the other minority ethnic groups. Tom Mboya, the Luo leader with a nation-wide platform, was assassinated. His Luo rival Oginga Odinga, leader of the KPU with national support also, was excluded when the one-party system was established. Oginga Odinga had to resign himself to being the leader of the Luo who became marginalised themselves. In this way the Kikuyu became relatively stronger. At the same time the ethnic parties which made up KADU were absorbed. On the basis of this relatively stabilised ethnic balance at the time of the accession of the vice-president Arap Moi, the sub-ethnic politics tended to play a predominant role, favoured as it was by semi-competitive elections. Thus the political game of ethnic factions is inseparable from the methods of political regulation.

The Method of Political Regulation Both political systems are presidentialist with a one-party system which is characterised by authoritarianism compounded with paternalism. In Kenya the mode of regulation is very flexible, more indirect and leaves more room for politics than in Côte d'Ivoire; however, it is more violent and conflictive.

Côte d'Ivoire: Houphouët is the great regulator of the state, the society and the political class. His relative capacity to forgo the use of force should be seen as an indication of strength rather than weakness. Côte d'Ivoire has an authoritarian government, but not a police regime. Houphouët strikes quickly and hard if necessary, as in Gagnoa or in Sanwi. He quells strikes of students, teachers and workers. But he excells in later recuperating and coopting the leaders.[30] When tension runs too high, he knows how to release pressure by holding his famous 'dialogues'. Ably using inducements, force and persuasion, he has prevented the crystallisation of any real opposition movements until very recently. Of course, the presence of French military units is dissuasive. Still more convincing is his great popularity in spite of claims made by his opponents, which is nothing but wishful thinking on their part.[31] An amazing combination of authoritarianism and liberalism coexist: there is no freedom of the press, but *Afrique-Asie* is sold on the sidewalks and you may speak freely in public places. Those who are jailed are freed soon afterwards; often beaten, but not tortured. The regime has killed very few people; the highest toll was at Gagnoa. We must also mention the suspicious death of the president of the Supreme Court at the time of '*l'affaire des complots*'. Obviously this is still excessive, but it is less so than elsewhere.

The single party, well controlled by the general secretary Yacé, was monolithic until the end of the 1970s. The central organs of the party controlled nominations for secretaries of the sections. Elections were organised on the principle of a single candidate appointed by the party, and the candidate once elected did not represent one '*circonscription*', but all of Côte d'Ivoire. The deputy, thus elected, was the representative of the president. Conversely the president chose the deputies in such a way as to have all the regions represented. He strongly encouraged them to plant and invest in their home areas. Sometimes the deputy's ties with his home continued, but more importantly he now became a member of the political class with all the material advantages that went with it. Bakary has shown the extraordinary political longevity of the ruling class.[32]

It is paradoxical to see a relatively moderate state establishing a one-party system, not tolerating independent workers' unions or any social protest movements, inhibiting all political activity and evacuating all ideological debates without great use of coercion. Cohen has shown how Houphouët undermined social protest movements by cooptation and patronage: 'the politics of distribution', as he calls it.[33] Houphouët was able to convince Ivorians to concentrate on their material welfare at the expense of pursuing ideological concerns. Patronage was facilitated by economic growth, which was great enough to allow the top level of society to increase their wealth through corruption. The state and Houphouët, in particular, were able to make financial outlays on grandiose projects for which the economic rationale, if not the political, was very questionable. A visit to Yamoussoukro is enough to make one reject the vaunted self-image of Houphouët, 'premier farmer' of Côte d'Ivoire, and the fatherly image. But actually everyone benefited either directly or indirectly from the Houphouët state.

Kenya: The great difference between Côte d'Ivoire and Kenya in this early period was that Kenya had a competitive electoral system within the single party, whereas Côte d'Ivoire adopted the system of a unique candidate. Of course, this was only for legislative elections and not for presidential elections. However, this permitted political activity in Kenya with contested elections and the institutionalisation of factional conflicts arbitrated by President Kenyatta. What was at stake in these elections was not general national policies, but local, specific policies, which does not mean that they were without importance.[34] The important national policies were made by the president and remained outside of the electoral game and political debates as the candidates had to adhere to the policies of the party. The party exercised a certain control over the choice of candidates which undermined the democratic game without eliminating it. Political life was reported by a relatively open press, which was and is much freer than in Côte d'Ivoire. The newspapers reported debates in parliament which were at times very lively when back benchers vigorously confronted ministers. In spite of the party filter, a minority of radical deputies managed to get elected and animated debates. The justice department also preserved a certain independence and had more legal weight than in Côte d'Ivoire.

The regulation of the political game has been described very well by Okumu and Barkan.[35] It consisted in the leader arbitrating between the clientelistic factions at the different levels of differentiation. Kenyatta coopted regional leaders by appointing them to ministerial posts. They in turn became the masters of lesser leaders. The test of a political leader was his capacity to deliver the goods. The final arbitrage was made by the president, who was often ready to award an alternative leader. The president's control was flexible, indirect and permitted an autonomous game on the periphery. The deputies came and went quickly, as they could not meet all the expectations of the electors. However, government ministers who disposed of direct access to important resources had more chances of being re-elected. In this kind of system, it is obvious that politicians must be very rich and have a lot of connections. As Daniel Bourmaud has shown, this factional and clientelistic regulation of the relations between the centre and the periphery gives rise to tension with the authoritarian administrative mode of relations between the centre and the periphery.[36]

The political game was not as calm and controlled as this description might make you believe. It was violent and political assassinations were not rare at the base between candidates and at the top. Political detention was frequently used and torture, officially forbidden, was often used. Although the succession to Kenyatta occurred according to constitutional procedure, the conflict over the succession was of rare violence, in proportion with the power at stake.[37]

While the problem of succession in Côte d'Ivoire did not become insistent until the end of the 1970s, the problem in Kenya had to be faced almost from the start as Kenyatta was already advanced in age. Kenyatta's power once consolidated was never seriously contested, but in the background the potential successors were in continual conflict. This was part of the explanation of the violence which constantly marked the political life of Kenya. The assassinations of Tom Mboya and of Kariuki were certainly connected to the struggle for succession. At the end of Kenyatta's reign the tendency towards authoritarianism and racketeering increased. The Kariuki affair is an excellent example because it shows that while parliament had the autonomy and the initiative to open an inquiry into his death, the government had the power to suppress and imprison the protesters. As you observe the political game in Kenya, you realise how very different it was from Côte d'Ivoire.

Moi came to power in the context of an international economic crisis. After a brief interruption, the authoritarianism and racketeering intensified. At the same time, in Côte d'Ivoire, the political system became more liberal and semi-competitive.

THE HOUPHOUËT AND THE MOI STATES: THE LEAN YEARS (1978–present)

Although economic hardship has badly affected Côte d'Ivoire, the political system shows a remarkable capacity to adapt to the situation. However, the problem of succession has become more pressing and this has had repercussions on the capacity for adaptation. In Kenya the problem of the succession to Kenyatta was resolved by the arrival of the Kalenjin vice-president Arap Moi in the presidency, according to constitutional procedure. Kenya fell into the pervading economic crisis less brutally than Côte d'Ivoire, but the authoritarianism of Moi has developed increasingly. In different ways both countries have faced a crisis which is not exclusively economic.

The Houphouët State and the Economic Crisis

The Extent of the Crisis The nature of this crisis is more complex than what may appear at first sight. It has not only an economic dimension, but also a political dimension that must be emphasised.

The Economic Crisis: As the effects of the economic crisis are well known, I will review them only briefly: the growth of GNP slowed towards the middle of the 1970s, followed by a sudden substantial increase of international coffee prices in 1976–7 which stimulated a short economic boom that ended abruptly when coffee and cocoa prices collapsed. As a result, Côte d'Ivoire found itself severely indebted just as its exports lost value. In 1984 came the first drought in the history of Côte d'Ivoire; it was the ecological consequence of the rapid deforestation of the preceding years. In 1985 world commodity prices began to go up and some Ivorian observers recklessly proclaimed the end of the depression. Cocoa prices soon sank again and Houphouët tried to influence world market prices by stocking his cocoa. The cocoa crisis, however, was not caused by speculation, as he believed, but because African cocoa now had to compete with more cheaply produced cocoa from South-east Asia. Côte d'Ivoire found itself without reserves of foreign exchange.

The Political Dimension of the Crisis   There are several aspects to be considered here. First, the succession problem has become more and more acute with time as the president has grown older and the economic crisis has got worse. Not only has the president had to face the crisis, but he has also had to settle the factional conflicts activated by the anticipation of a succession.

As B. Contamin and Y.A. Fauré have argued, the economic crisis was accentuated by a patrimonial crisis.[38] This has two aspects: a crisis of the patrimonial economy and a crisis of patrimonial leadership. As to the crisis of the patrimonial economy, Louis Gouffern has helpfully shown that what Fauré called dysfunctions (corruption, etc.) were inherent traits of the Ivorian model.[39] The contradiction between the patrimonial management of the economy and the logic of economic development was not sufficiently emphasised by Fauré. Added to this, at the time of the coffee boom, patrimonialism had run out of control and got beyond acceptable limits. From the economic point of view, a limitation of patrimonialism became necessary. Contamin and Fauré show that it has also become a political necessity. There was a crisis in the patrimonial leadership, as Bakary demonstrates.[40] Although we have seen how much Houphouët centralised his management of patronage, it seems that he lost control of it to the benefit of his 'barons' towards the second half of the 1970s. The reforms undertaken at this time corresponded not only to an economic necessity, but also to a political imperative.

Responses to the Crisis   Aside from the economic aspects, a double response – both political and administrative – was made, revealing a remarkable capacity to meet the situation, but contradicted by other measures.

At the Administrative Level: We must mention here the tentative attempt to reform the administration for technocratic reasons by Becchio, the young Minister of the Public Service, who showed a great deal of political courage and determination. However, he was not supported all the way by Houphouët and this reform managed only to reform his ministry. In the sociological context of Côte d'Ivoire even during the depression, it was difficult to imagine such a radical reform of the administration.[41]

On the other hand, the restructuring of the public sector was relatively well done.[42] When Mathieu Ekra was named minister of the parastatals in 1977, no one believed that the reform would materialise, in spite of the strong personality of the man in charge.

When the reform was made public in 1980, it made an immense impression. Mathieu Ekra announced the dissolution of a large number of parastatals, returning them to the private sector or transforming them, aligning salaries and allowances with the public administration, forbidding the direct borrowing from overseas (this was the cause of half of the national debt), and so on. Contamin and Fauré show that these measures were not taken because of pressure from the IMF as everyone thought, and that the changes did not bring about a return to the private sector as was generally believed, but rather a reorganisation of the parastatals by transforming their statutes. In particular, the reform separated the functions of financial appropriations and accountancy. If the results of the reform do not correspond exactly to the objectives anticipated, the degree to which it was realised is nevertheless remarkable. It was successful particularly because Houphouët gave it constant support, even though at times he was forced to make temporary retreats when protests grew too strong.

Other measures include the elimination of administrative bails which triggered the teachers' strike in 1983, but which was maintained none the less. Above all we must mention the establishment in 1977 of the '*Direction du contrôle des grands travaux*' (DCGT) headed by Cesaero, a French engineer, who was directly accountable to Houphouët. This became the key instrument for the ministerial reforms beginning in 1982, which centralised all the public works markets. They had been handled separately by each ministry up until then and, for ministers, they had been a major source of wealth. This change, unlike the preceding reforms which were made for technocratic reasons, actually constituted a patrimonial mode of controlling patrimonialism. The president chose a man who had his complete confidence to repair the damage caused by an exacerbated patrimonialism. This also shows another use of foreigners in Côte d'Ivoire.[43] These administrative measures can be best understood in relation to the political measures.

Political Measures: In 1977 Houphouët dismissed the four ministers who had been the most directly associated with the 'Ivorian Miracle'. In 1980 he took over party leadership, dismissing Yacé from the post of general secretary, and instituted elections within the single party. In this way he opened the system to semi-competitive elections very similar to those in Kenya. The elections of 1980 were effectively free and were responsible for an important renewal of political leadership.[44] Although the elections were very successful in drawing out large numbers of candidates, they did not mobilise voters who abstained en masse, in Abidjan more than in the country (we find the same phenomenon in Kenya). The elections in 1985 had a slightly greater number of electors, but not nearly as many candidates.[45] Bakary suggests that the party filtered the candidates more the second time which diminished their number. I would add that the candidates had learned that it no longer paid to be a deputy.[46] No one took Houphouët seriously when he announced that a deputy would no longer be allowed to hold office while performing other public or private functions. The deputies who had spent a fortune getting elected found themselves bankrupt.

How should we interpret this? Actually it illustrates less a desire for democracy than great political ingenuity which consisted in having the electors purge the political leaders. The happy result of this manoeuvre was to incorporate a certain degree of democracy into the political game. Bakary speaks of the 'centralising of political decentralisation' (*décentralisation politique centralisée*). The effect of this measure was nevertheless disappointing when you consider the poor electoral turn-out, particularly in towns. The explanation that Bakary gives is the same as the one Daniel Bourmaud gives for Kenya: the rural and urban areas are becoming more differentiated and a political marginalisation of the urban population is taking place.[47] This makes us less optimistic over the prospects of liberalisation in Côte d'Ivoire.

If we return to our opening question, when we consider all these measures together, we are struck by their congruity. As Bakary has shown, the political class is characterised by great stability (unlike other African countries where the president's patronage resembles a game of musical chairs). This stability had allowed the 'barons' to create autonomous economic bases while still preying on the national economy. This triggered a double crisis of patrimonial leadership and patrimonial economy. The measures applied provided a solution to both problems.

Taken together, these measures show a great capacity to meet the crisis, which may not suffice in getting Côte d'Ivoire out of the depression, but which have permitted the Ivorian political system to reduce the political consequences of the economic crisis.

This does not mean that there is no interaction between political resources and economic resources, but it suggests a less mechanical interpretation. The 'digestive capacities' (Bakary) of the Ivorian system and the political inventiveness of its leader are great. Nevertheless the recent measures concerning cocoa and the sumptuous expenditures on the cathedral of Yamoussoukro do not make us optimistic. Even if Houphouët manages to control the patrimonialism of his subordinates, will he restrain his own? The contradiction between the political logic and the economic or technical logic is difficult to resolve. From an economic viewpoint, Houphouët should lower the price at which cocoa is bought from the farmers. Politically this would be suicide, or at any rate the abnegation of his self-image.[48]

The Moi State[49]

At the end of his reign, given his great age, Jomo Kenyatta controlled the political system from a distance, but he was there and he did not allow his family to organise his succession exactly as they would have desired. With the backing of Njonjo and Kibaki who opposed the Kiambu clan and Gema,[50] the vice-president Arap Moi succeeded Kenyatta in accordance with the constitution. In spite of (or because of) the underground struggle for succession, this was an undeniable sign of political stability and the institutionalisation of the state. However, the Kalenjin Moi did not come to power under favourable auspices. He had to prove his authority and overcome the deepening economic crisis, without the benefit of the prestige of his predecessor. His political actions, however, cannot be analysed solely from the viewpoint of the economic crisis.

The Pervasive Economic Crisis   During the 1970s the economic growth rate dropped and then continued to decrease steadily. At the same time, high population growth, the lack of land, increased prices of imports, higher cost of petrol, lower revenues from exports, inflation, stagnation of industries and lack of employment make Kenya feel the economic crisis just as in Côte d'Ivoire. In addition, Kenya faced a drought in 1984, but recovered as well as could be expected. The effects of the crisis in Kenya were less spectacular than in Côte d'Ivoire, but in certain ways (such as unemployment, slums) they seemed more serious. Kenya experienced the same coffee boom as Côte d'Ivoire, but it did not set off an explosion of patrimonialism as in Côte d'Ivoire. As a result the national debt did not reach such catastrophic proportions. Political discontent increased with the pressure of economic and political frustrations. Foreign investors lost confidence in the economy and the Kenyan political system, spurring disinvestment and withdrawal by multinational companies.

Establishing the Moi State and Political Restructuring   When Moi came to power, he was very popular. The end of Kenyatta's reign had been difficult. Moi renewed hope for the future by fighting corruption, which had increased seriously, freeing political prisoners, making an opening towards Oginga Odinga and adopting a few populist measures. He promised to follow in the footsteps of his predecessor (*nyayo*). He looked to the churches for support, but this did not last. Moi consistently sought, as David Throup showed very well,[51] to dismantle the Kenyatta state, to eliminate the Kikuyu from their predominant political and economic positions and to replace them with his own men. He continued playing Kenyatta's game of faction politics, but he played it in such a way as to divide, weaken and finally eliminate the Kikuyu. The systematic replacement of Kikuyu by Kalenjin in important posts and the failure of Kikuyu banks which no longer had support from the Central Bank illustrate this. Njonjo's disgrace fits into the same policy, even though this does not prove his political innocence.[52] Replacing vice-president Kibaki by Karanja confirms this tendency, even if he is Kikuyu.[53] Denouncing corruption and tribalism is very often a way of replacing one system of corruption and tribalism by another. In pursuing this policy, Moi may be sawing off the branch he is sitting on. Can Kenya be governed without the support of the Kikuyu? Yes, if the Kikuyu remain divided and Moi has become a master at keeping them divided. But can the country be ruled very long solely by political manoeuvring and authoritarianism, particularly at a time when the resources of patronage are decreasing?

The Political Lock The Kenyatta system, as Daniel Bourmaud[54] showed so well, relied on the tolerance of the political game at the periphery so long as it did not question the supremacy of the central government, the president providing the regulation of the administration and the party. This system has been reversed by Moi by introducing the District Focus reform which was made for technocratic reasons on the administrative level and reinforced the authoritarianism on the political level to the point of defying the pluralistic elements of the system.

At the administrative level, the reform provides that the districts propose the development policies under the direct control of the president's office. This dispossesses the local political leaders and the local provincial administration by giving the control not to the ministers, but to the president himself. The relative predominance of the district officer over the local administrative and political leaders is now well established. The result is clear: the political pressure of the periphery by way of local leaders has lost its effect, which limits the demands and centralises the decision-making process. Will the rural periphery tolerate this new situation?

As to national politics, we must emphasise that with the increase of authoritarianism, the regime can no longer be described as moderate. KANU became a constitutional single party system in 1982. Arrests and political imprisonments have continued to increase, culminating in the repression of the Mwakenya movement. Torture and brutality, according to a large number of witnesses, have become frequent and widespread. The independence of the magistracy has disappeared, although, in contrast to the majority of African countries, there remained traces of it for a period of time. The press is forced to autocensor whatever is published.[55] Parliamentary debates are no longer centred on the essential issues. The system of voting by queueing was established to control the voter. The control of candidatures has also been increased by the party whose role has grown more than ever disciplinary. The attempted *coup d'état* in August 1982 showed how fragile the political system was. It took place at a time of economic depression, but in addition one wonders if Moi's policies are not rather destabilising. The tactics of Moi will not suffice for long in disguising his strategic weakness in the face of accumulating basic problems – especially the growing social, economic and political marginalisation found in Nairobi and the other big cities.

After this rapid comparison of Côte d'Ivoire and Kenya we need to ask two questions. What, beyond the similarities of the two countries, differentiates them the most? What distinguishes the two countries from other African states? In Chapter 10, comparing Côte d'Ivoire and Ghana, Richard Crook suggests that the crucial variable is the weakness of the civil society in Côte d'Ivoire as opposed to the strength of civil society in Ghana. In Côte d'Ivoire the strength of the state was encouraged by the weakness of the society and vice versa. In Ghana the state, which was strong at the outset, was unable to resist the strength of the society. In Kenya we observe a balance between a strong state and a strong civil society. This is what explains both the pluralistic and conflictive character of political life. The decolonisation process in Kenya did not allow the state to gain as much power over civil society as in Côte d'Ivoire. Beyond these differences both states are well established and here to stay, even if factional conflicts, economic crises and other constraints threaten the stability of the regimes and leadership.

What distinguishes Côte d'Ivoire (and Kenya) from other African states has also been considered by Crook. He suggests that it is not the economic strategy that explains the better performances of Côte d'Ivoire (and Kenya) so much as the superior capacities of the state and in particular, administrative capacities.[56] If we look at the economic strategies of African states, with the exception of those with socialist tendencies, we see that they are very similar, but the efficiency of the states varies greatly. Côte d'Ivoire and Kenya have shown superior political and administrative efficiency in comparison with other states, and it would seem plausible to explain the greater economic success by this. Crook then asks whether the term neo-patrimonial can be applied to states as different as Côte d'Ivoire (let us add Kenya) and Zaïre since, elsewhere, we hold neo-patrimonialism as responsible for the political and economic collapse of African states.[57]

First let us emphasise that the performances of Côte d'Ivoire and Kenya are only relative to the general economic and political failure of African states. Neither has gone beyond the primitive accumulation of power and capital. We definitely believe that the word neo-patrimonial applies to both Kenya and Côte d'Ivoire. Corruption, or as J.-F. Bayart would say, 'belly politics', works exactly as elsewhere in Africa. Let us examine the term neo-patrimonial more closely.[58] Patrimonial refers to an ideal type where the public domain is not distinguished from the private. Neo-patrimonialism refers to a modified type which supposes an articulation between two contradictory logics: patrimonial logic and bureaucratic logic. The distinction between the public and private domains exists, but it is not respected. The system that is generally found in African countries is neo-patrimonial; patrimonialism corresponds only to extreme cases such as Zaïre and Bokassa's Republic of Central Africa. Varying according to the African state, the distance in relation to the ideal patrimonial type is larger or smaller.

From this point of view, Côte d'Ivoire as well as Kenya are clearly neo-patrimonial, and not patrimonial, with the 'neo' part more important than in other African states.[59] You find there a distance, compared to patrimonialism, which allows for a certain latitude of action and permits certain areas to be more or less protected. Sandbrook's analysis gives the impression that patrimonialism must be considered as an irrational practice but, quite to the contrary, it corresponds exactly to the logic that any realistic political entrepreneur would have in the same situation. It is what I would call 'the logic of the big man' by which the political entrepreneur multiplies his economic resources by the use of his political resources, and multiplies his political resources by use of his economic resources. However, as

Marshall Sahlins[60] has shown in quite a different context, but transposable here, the big man is caught in the contradiction between accumulation and distribution, between economic power and political power. This contradiction may be faced in more or less rational ways. Thus purely predatory behaviour would in the long run be political suicide; even the patrimonial political entrepreneur must know how to renew his resources which are the base of his power, and how to articulate judiciously his economic and political resources. On this point, Kenyatta, Houphouët and, to a lesser degree, Moi managed their resources in a fairly rational manner.

The Ivorian and Kenyan experiences illustrate, through their strong points and weak, how the newly forming African states must maintain a precarious balance. There is no administrative or economic efficiency without political efficiency; for if the effort to rationalise the administration and the economy ends in social and political implosion, it has failed. This political efficiency must be realised largely through good neo-patrimonial strategy. Conversely, if everything is subordinated to political logic, as in patrimonialism, with no consideration of the administrative and economic restraints, that strategy will also backfire.

NOTES

1. M. Dogan and D. Pelassy, *Sociologie Politique Comparative* (Paris, 1982) pp. 135–53.
2. The economic strategy followed by both states has been basically the same as the one followed by the other non-socialist African states. But it produced better results.
3. Political stability was greater in Côte d'Ivoire than in Kenya. There was the same ruler, the same political leadership and the same regime in Côte d'Ivoire. In Kenya, the succession was consititutional, but was followed by a relative turnover of the political leadership. The regime became more authoritarian and the president faced a serious coup attempt.
4. R. Crook, 'State, Society and Political Institutions in Côte d'Ivoire and Ghana', Chapter 10 in this volume.
5. J.-P. Chauveau and J.-P. Dozon, 'Au Coeur des Ethnies Ivoiriennes . . . l'Etat', in E. Terray (ed.) *L'Etat Contemporain en Afrique* (Paris, 1987).
6. For more details, see Crook, 'State, Society . . .'. The Lebanese community, though not quite as important in Côte d'Ivoire, plays a similar role to the Asian community in Kenya.
7. Because of lack of space we cannot give sufficient attention to the precolonial period and to the colonial state. A deeper comparative analysis

of the trajectories of the two states should go further in the exploration of the '*longue durée*' (J.-F. Bayart) of both societies.

8. Daniel Bourmaud speaks of 'patriarcat' for the Kenyatta state in *Histoire Politique du Kenya* (Paris, 1988) pp. 153–60 and Tessy Bakary of 'patriarchie' in his not yet published work *La Démocratie par le Haut en Côte d'Ivoire*.

9. See the relevant observations of Daniel Bourmaud on the colonial administration in Kenya: 'Les Préfets de sa Majesté', in *Histoire Politique* . . ., pp. 7–44.

10. M. Amondji, *Félix Houphouët et la Côte d'Ivoire, l'Envers d'une Légende* (Paris, 1984); *Côte d'Ivoire, le PDCI et la Vie Politique de 1944 à 1985* (Paris, 1986). In reality, the big planters were '*évolués*' themselves. See the basic work on Côte d'Ivoire, A. Zolberg, *One Party Government in the Ivory Coast* (Princeton, NJ, 1964). More recently Bakary insists that the big planters were educated (*La Democratie* . . .).

11. R. S. Morgenthau, *Political Parties in French Speaking Africa* (Oxford, 1964) p. 170.

12. D. Martin and M.C. Martin, *Le Kenya* (Paris, 1983) p. 96; C. Horrut, *Les Décolonisations Est-Africaines* (Paris, 1971).

13. R. Buijtenhuis, *Le Mouvement Mau Mau: une Révolte Paysanne et Anti Coloniale en Afrique Noire* (Paris and The Hague, 1971); *Essays on Mau Mau: Contributions to Mau Mau Historiography* (Leiden, 1982).

14. D. Goldsworthy, *Tom Mboya: The Man Kenya Wanted to Forget* (Nairobi and London, 1982).

15. Bourmaud, *Histoire Politique* . . ., p. 75.

16. C. Gertzel, *The Politics of Independent Kenya* (London, 1970).

17. On the Houphouët state, Zolberg, *One Party* . . .; S. Amin, *Le Développement du Capitalisme en Côte d'Ivoire* (Paris, 1967); M. Cohen, *Urban Policy and Political Conflict in Africa* (Chicago, Ill., 1974); Y. A. Fauré and J.-F. Medard (eds) *Etat et Bourgeoisie en Côte d'Ivoire* (Paris, 1982); B. Campbell, 'The Ivory Coast', in J. Dunn (ed.) *West African States* (Cambridge, 1978); *L'Etat Post Colonial en Côte d'Ivoire* (Paris, 1982); I. W. Zartman and C. Delgado (eds) *The Political Economy of Ivory Coast* (New York, 1984); and the following by T. Bakary, *Les Elites Politiques en Côte d'Ivoire* (Université Paris X Nanterre thesis, 1983), 'De l'Etat Providence à l'Etat Impécunieux' (to be published), *Les Elections Legislatives Ivoiriennes de Novembre 1980 et le Système Politique: Essai d'Analyse des Comportements Electoraux* (Bordeaux, 1985), 'Développement Socio-Economique et Comportement Electoral en Côte d'Ivoire', *Cultures et Développement* (1985), 'Côte d'Ivoire: Logique du Recrutement Politique', *Le Mois en Afrique* (1985), 'Elite Transformation in Ivory Coast', in Zartman and Delgado (eds) *L'Etat.* . . . On the Kenyatta state, see M. Schatzberg (ed.) *The Political Economy of Kenya* (New York, 1987); C. Gertzel, *ibid.*; J. Barkan and J. Okumu (eds) *Politics and Public Policy in Kenya and Tanzania* (New York, 1970).

18. For a recent interpretation of the African state based roughly on this idea, see J.-F. Bayart, *L'Etat en Afrique* (Paris, 1989).

19. R. Crook, 'Patrimonialism, Administrative Effectiveness and Economic Development in Côte d'Ivoire', *African Affairs* (April 1989).

20. Bakary, 'Elite Transformation . . .'.

21. Amondji, *Félix Houphouët* . . .
22. C. de Miras, 'L'Entrepreneur Ivoirien ou une Bourgeoisie Privée de son Etat', in Fauré and Medard (eds) *Etat et Bourgeoisie* . . ., pp. 181–239.
23. Bakary, 'Elite Transformation . . .'.
24. T. Callaghy, 'Politics and Vision in Africa: the Interplay of Domination, Equality and Liberty', in P. Chabal (ed.) *Political Domination in Africa* (Cambridge, 1986).
25. There are some observations of the phenomenon in Nigeria (J. Ibrahim).
26. J.-L. Amselle, 'Introduction', in J.-L. Amselle and E. M'Bokolo (eds) *Au Coeur de l'Ethnie* (Paris, 1985).
27. C. Leys, *Underdevelopment in Kenya: The Political Economy of Neo-Colonialism 1964–1971* (London, 1975). In 1978 C. Leys revised his positions.
28. G. Kitching, 'Politics, Methods and Evidence in the Kenyan Debate', in H. Bernstein and B. Campbell (eds) *Contradictions in Accumulation in Africa* (London, 1985).
29. G. Hyden, 'Capital Accumulation Resources, Distribution and Governance in Kenya: the Role of the Economy of Affection', in Schatzberg (ed.) *The Political Economy* . . .
30. Cohen, *Urban Policy* . . .
31. See Amondji, *Félix Houphouët* . . .; L. Gbagbo, *Côte d'Ivoire: pour une Alternative Démocratique* (Paris, 1983); Front Populaire Ivoirien, *Propositions pour Gouverner la Côte d'Ivoire* (Paris, 1987), for the point of view of the opposition. On the permanence of Houphouët's popularity, in spite of the present crisis, see C. Moutout, 'Qui Croit Encore au Miracle Ivoirien?', *Le Monde Diplomatique* (December 1988).
32. Bakary, 'Elite Transformation . . .'
33. Cohen, *Urban Policy* . . .
34. Bourmaud, *Histoire Politique* . . .
35. Barkan and Okumu, *Politics and Public Policy* . . .
36. Bourmaud, *Histoire Politique* . . .
37. J. Karimi and P. Ochieng, *The Kenyatta Succession* (Nairobi, 1980).
38. B. Contamin and Y. A. Fauré, *La Restructuration des Entreprises Publiques en Côte d'Ivoire*, forthcoming.
39. L. Gouffern, 'Les Limites d'un Modèle? A propos d'Etat et Bourgeoisie en Côte d'Ivoire', *Politique Africaine* (May 1982).
40. Bakary, 'Elite Transformation . . .'.
41. Y. N'Goran, *Le Ministre de la Fonction Publique et la Mission de la Réforme Administrative en Côte d'Ivoire* (thèse Driot, Université de Bordeaux 1, 1989).
42. Contamin and Fauré, *Le Restructuration* . . .
43. Bakary, 'Elite Transformation . . .'.
44. *Ibid.*
45. *Ibid.*
46. Y. N'Goran, personal communication.
47. Bourmaud, *Histoire Politique* . . ., p. 215, and his 'Elections Semi Compétitives et Autoritarisme: la Crise de la Régulation Politique au Kenya', *Revue Française de Science Politique* (April 1985); J. Ngoba, 'Les Municipalités Urbaines au Kenya: Une Crise sans Issue', *Cités Africaines – African Cities*, (Autumn 1985).

48. Houphouët-Boigny finally had to lower the prices of cocoa paid to the farmers.
49. G. Dauch and D. Martin, *L'Héritage de Kenyatta: La Transition Politique au Kenya* (Paris, 1985); P. Anyang Nyongo, 'Succession et Héritage Politique, le Président, l'Etat et le Capital après la Mort de Jomo Kenyatta', *Politique Africaine* (September 1981).
50. GEMA was a Kikuyu economic grouping with close ties to the Kenyatta family.
51. D. Throup, 'The Construction and Destruction of the Kenyatta State', in Schatzberg (ed.) *The Political Economy* . . ., pp. 34–74.
52. J.-F. Medard, 'Charles Njonjo, un "Big Man" au Kenya', in Terray (ed.) *L'Etat Contemporain* . . .
53. He was not an important Kikuyu leader and has been replaced since.
54. Bourmaud, *Histoire Politique* . . ., p. 189.
55. See among others the affair of the magazine *Beyond*.
56. Crook, 'Patrimonialism, Administrative Effectiveness . . .'.
57. Crook refers mainly to R. Sandbrook, *The Politics of African Stagnation* (Cambridge, 1985).
58. On the concepts of patrimonialism and neo-patrimonialism, see J.-F. Medard, 'The Underdeveloped State in Tropical Africa: Political Clientelism or Neo-Patrimonialism?', in C. Clapham (ed.) *Private Patronage and Public Power: Political Clientelism in the Modern State* (London, 1982), and 'La Spécificité du Pouvoir en Afrique', *Pouvoirs* (April 1983).
59. With the exception of certain East African states.
60. M. Sahlins, 'Poor Man, Rich Man, Big Man, Chief: Political Types in Melanesia and Polynesia', S. Schmidt, *et al.* (eds) *Friends, Followers and Factions* (Berkeley, Calif., 1977) pp. 220–31.

CHAPTER TEN

State, Society and Political Institutions in Côte d'Ivoire and Ghana

Richard Crook

Côte d'Ivoire and Ghana are adjacent states on the West African coast, one an ex-British colony, the other an ex-French colony. They are, at least superficially, similar in geographic, economic and sociological terms. Yet their post-independence political and economic histories have diverged quite markedly, providing the occasion for a continuing debate on the causes of these contrasting outcomes.[1] Côte d'Ivoire's spectacular growth rates in the 1960s and 1970s, fuelled by foreign investment and the expansion of cocoa and coffee exports, were said to prove the superiority of opening up the economy to the disciplines of the international market; Ghana's economic decline, to the point where the state had lost control of its currency and agricultural exports dropped to levels below those of the 1920s, was held up as a warning against state-led protected industrialisation.[2] Now that Côte d'Ivoire, as the world's largest cocoa producer, is facing the worst economic crisis in its entire history as a result of falling commodity prices and the burden of 1970s foreign debts, the debate as to whether reliance on primary exports leads inevitably to structural failure and political collapse is still topical.[3]

The purpose of this chapter is, however, to argue that the really significant differences between Ghana and Côte d'Ivoire lie, not in the realms of economic policy but in the areas of state–society relations and state capacity. With the exception of the Convention People's Party's (CPP) brief experiment with rapid state-led industrialisation 1960–6 (which apparently owed more to Rostow and Hirschman than to Karl Marx),[4] Ghana has continued throughout its post-independence history to be as dependent on its cocoa export economy as Côte d'Ivoire; but it has been less successful at *managing* that economy both in the macro and micro senses. And it is no accident that the principal political contrast between the two countries is in their respective records of political stability.

Côte d'Ivoire has been ruled not just by the same regime but by the same small leadership group associated with Houphouët-Boigny since 1952, when the French colonial administration decided to coopt Houphouët's party (the PDCI) as their local successors. Although the regime has both destroyed or coopted opposition where necessary and slowly admitted younger generations it is virtually a geronto-cracy, now displaying dangerous *immobilisme* as the aged president resolutely postpones all questions of the succession. Ghana, on the other hand, since the overthrow of its decolonisation regime in 1966 (the CPP had ruled from 1951, six years before independence) has experienced seven changes of regime – two elected and five military – and an even greater number of governmental changes and attempted *coups d'état*. Its current government, that of Flight-Lieutenant Jerry Rawlings, is the result of a bloody upheaval of 'other ranks' and junior officers within the Armed Forces, supported initially by populist and radical civilian groups. It has survived at least six coup attempts since 1982, partly through Rawlings's ability to deal ruth-lessly with the Army, and partly because the World Bank and the International Monetary Fund (IMF) have provided enough cash to fund life-saving improvements in the economy. Its future remains precarious.[5]

My principal focus, then, is to try to explain through comparison Côte d'Ivoire's stability and Ghana's endemic instability, and to establish the consequences of instability/stability for the state's effec-tiveness in the implementation of an economic strategy. At the root of these differing histories are differences between Ivorian and Ghana-ian societies, and the processes of political elite and state formation in each country. It will be argued that the most powerful explanation of the different outcomes is to be found in the different kinds of interactions which have occurred between state and civil society. These differences may be briefly described as differences in the relative 'balance' or 'proportion' between state and civil society which char-acterise each country. Such an hypothesis assumes, of course, that 'state' and 'civil society' can be validly conceived as separate categories capable of interacting with and balancing each other, and therefore assumes a certain definition of the term civil society, particularly as it relates to the African context.

Bayart has already provided much useful discussion of this topic, although he tends, as does John Dunn, to the conclusion that civil society in Africa is mainly significant 'by its absence'. This conclusion derives from a definition which is simultaneously broad – all of the 'social space' outside of the state – but narrowly qualified by the requirement that civil society is self-consciously 'in opposition' to the state, that is it forms a social whole with its own 'organisational principle'.[6] Given the richness and ambiguity of the concept, deriving from the number of metamorphoses it has undergone from Locke through to Hegel, Marx and Gramsci,[7] it would seem preferable to follow Poggi in giving it a precise historical definition: civil society in this chapter will refer to all those self-conscious associations and institutions representing private interest groups and local, class, religious and intellectual 'publics' which tend to emerge with the rise of a market economy.[8] It thus encompasses but is not confined (as in Marx's use) to the social relations of particular forms of production and exchange. These institutional and associational forms in fact mediate between the state and individuals *qua* economic actors, and thus have political significance. The realm of the state begins at the points where the state enforces, upholds or represses particular relationships within civil society.

Despite Bayart's doubts about the applicability of the concept in Africa, during the colonial period social groups analogous to those of early bourgeois Europe did emerge, subject of course to the differences deriving from indigenous societies and the particular form of the market relations which developed. Here it is perhaps sufficient to note the growth of ethnic associations (products of local community consciousness as well as of urban migration), improvement societies and youth associations, free churches, schools, farmers' and traders' organisations, professional groupings and eventually political parties and trade unions. All these were signs of the differentiation of social and economic life which occurred during the colonial period and of the consequent conscious organisation of local communities (local political elites) and of cultural ('national') and class groupings. Where Bayart is perfectly correct is in emphasising the heterogeneity of emerging civil society or rather societies in most African states, a factor which explains to some extent their weakness in the face of the state.[9] It also highlights what will be the major theme of the ensuing discussion, namely the concept of varying degrees of 'balance' between state and civil society, as measured by both the degree of interpenetration and by the relative power of the one to limit or define the other. Thus in Ghana a relatively strong state has been balanced by an equally strong yet highly fractured civil society, control of which has been difficult to establish; in Côte d'Ivoire, what began as a weakly established post-colonial state was able ultimately to overwhelm and dominate an even weaker and underdeveloped civil society.

STATE AND CIVIL SOCIETY

The geographic and socio-economic similarities between Côte d'Ivoire and Ghana are well known and need only be described briefly here. Their economies are both dominated by peasant cultivation of perennial tree crops (cocoa and coffee) for export. They have never known landlord, feudal or large-scale plantation systems of production of any significance, although various forms of sharecropper and wage labour have been used by rich peasants. The location of these crops in the southern forest zones together with the historical influences of colonialism and international trade have produced in both countries a pattern of uneven development such that the majority of the population, the largest urban centres and largest shares of national income are concentrated in the south. The northern savannah has on the whole remained an impoverished labour reservoir although both states have attempted regional development policies – Côte d'Ivoire's new cotton industry being the most successful.[10] At the time of independence per capita income was fairly similar, although Ghana had always been the larger, more developed economy, with a longer history of established colonial rule and overseas trade, and mineral wealth in the form of gold.[11]

The most important dimension of similarity between the two countries, however, is to be found in their political economy, whose basic structure was set during the colonial period. As bureaucratic states ruling over peasant societies using a fundamentally untransformed technology and mode of production (extensive use of land, labour rather than capital intensive), both can be characterised as 'neomercantilist' in their relation to society and the world market.[12] These states exist by monopolising the surpluses from peasant exports or other primary production and by offering economic rents to those who wish to participate either in the import-export trade, or foreign businesses investing in protected domestic or agri-business enterprises. In the absence of industrial production geared to world markets (as found in the NICs of Asia) it is the state which sets the opportunities for profit in a trading economy, and which needs itself to have effective means for controlling peasant production and exports. As with many other tropical African states, such a system has reinforced the centrality of the state and the political elite as a source of accumulation and of patronage politics; whether either state was fully appropriated by a patrimonial elite is a question for further discussion.

Assuming this basic similarity, the first and most fundamental difference between the two countries can be established. In Côte d'Ivoire the state has maintained effective mechanisms for controlling, taxing and yet also encouraging the expansion of the peasant export and trading economies. Revenues were thus buoyant, foreign confidence maintained and the elite prospered. In Ghana on the other hand the state has experienced a cumulative failure in its ability to control an economy which was itself shrinking – even during the period of booming commodity prices in the 1970s. This failure was crucially reflected in loss of control over its currency and international borders, and the decline of its revenue bases in export crops and foreign investment. One reason why the current regime in Ghana is credited with success by international agencies is, of course, that it is beginning to rebuild the 'colonial' export economy and hence its revenue base. For an explanation of how such differences emerged one must look at both objective features of their civil societies, and at the history of elite formation and state–society interactions since the mid-colonial period.

First, Côte d'Ivoire has always been more sparsely populated with fewer concentrations of population than Ghana. Although larger in land area (322,463 sq. km to Ghana's 238,539) Côte d'Ivoire had a population of only 2.06 million in 1948 compared to Ghana's 4.1 million. More telling than this, only 7 per cent of this small population lived in settlements of over 2,000 people compared to 25.6 per cent in Ghana.[13] Côte d'Ivoire was like a vast, virtually empty forest. By 1960 the contrast was even greater, in spite of the growth of Abidjan and other urban centres. By then, 60 per cent of Ghana's 6.7 million people lived in the 'densely settled' southern forest zone at average densities of 77.2 per sq. km. In this zone too were located 78 out of the 94 towns with populations of over 5,000, an overall urbanisation rate of 23.1 per cent.[14] Although by 1965 Côte d'Ivoire had a similar urbanisation rate (24.5 per cent in settlements over 4,000), there was still a vast difference in spread and density.[15] Ghana's *national* population density was twenty-eight per sq. km; yet even the most densely populated southern *cercles* of Côte d'Ivoire only reached twenty-two to thirty-three per sq. km.[16] Côte d'Ivoire's 'urban explosion' since 1960 has been primarily an Abidjan and (latterly) a Bouaké affair; these two towns accounted for 45 per cent of the urban population by

1965, predicted to increase to 65 per cent by 1990.[17] The demographer's definition of 'urban' as settlements of over 4,000 people is also perhaps highly optimistic even today, with an urbanisation rate of 46.8 per cent out of a population of around 10 million. Côte d'Ivoire has had great difficulty in creating a viable local urban government policy.[18] Since 1980, 135 *communes* have been created in order to encourage (for the first time in the country's history) a sense of local civic responsibility and enthusiasm for local development. Yet 51 per cent of these *communes* have populations of less than 12,000 and their prospects of autonomous success are slight.[19] This historic pattern therefore persists – together with its political and social ramifications.

The scarcity of Côte d'Ivoire's population was of course not ecologically determined unless one counts the lack of any good harbours and hence the area's lack of trading contacts with the colonial powers. It was principally a function of its location within the political map of pre-colonial Africa. The French colonialists drew a line around an area which was in fact the meeting-point of the 'marches' or peripheries of the surrounding African powers, principally Asante and the Samory and Mossi empires. The peoples of Côte d'Ivoire were scattered groups of refugees and migrants from other core areas; the 'oldest inhabitants', the so-called Kru, were apparently, like the Celts of Britain, driven to the remotest western forests by these waves of migrants. The consequences for the growth of a civil society during the colonial period were important. Whereas in Ghana political and social identities and local political life were a legacy of the highly articulated core states and pre-existing urban centres – Asante, Dagomba, Fanti, Akim and so on – in Côte d'Ivoire there were very few state-organised identities or pre-colonial centres of power which could underpin an autonomous 'African' civic life.[20] As Chauveau and Dozon have so eloquently shown, even the standard classification of the population into its main ethnic groups – Akan, Senoufo, Mandé North and South and Krou – was the invention of colonial ethnography, and 'ethnic politics' based on these identities a product as in so many other African states of colonial migrations. None corresponded to pre-colonial political entities, except the petty Akan kingdoms of the south-east, former Asante tributaries.[21]

The objective differences in the number, strength and degree of political self-consciousness of local communities in each country were partly a product of two further important features of the colonial period. First, the early growth of the cash crop economy in southern Ghana gave a major push to both population growth and the emergence of Ghana's characteristic 'agro-town/large village' society.

Although the south-eastern corner of Côte d'Ivoire – Agni country – experienced a pale imitation of this process, the contrast is most vividly expressed by the export figures for 1928; at that date, Ghana was already exporting 229,602 tonnes of cocoa, while Côte d'Ivoire exported only 16,515 tonnes of cocoa and 239 tonnes of coffee.[22] The 'cocoa frontier' continued to expand throughout southern Ghana for the next thirty or forty years, assuming its most dynamic form in mid- and western Ashanti in the 1950s. Côte d'Ivoire's coffee boom did not start until the 1950s, in the south-central area, and cocoa took off in the same area spreading westwards into the forest during the boom of the 1960s and 1970s.

Second, the British colonial policy of Indirect Rule had major long-term political and social consequences which were not part of the Ivorian experience. By Indirect Rule I mean, not just the vague notion of 'preserving traditional chieftaincy'; I refer to the whole complex of legal and institutional forms which were introduced by the British: Native Authorities and Native Treasuries, the representation of chiefs in official bodies, and a dual legal system in which Native Courts administered 'customary' law. This was as important in the north and the non-cocoa areas as it was in the south. Of particular significance, however, was the impact on land law, since the decision to recognise judicially concepts of 'community' ownership was intimately connected with both the political claims of the chieftaincy and the development of the cocoa economy. Migration and the extension of cultivation into 'unused' land was at the core of this development – as it was later in Côte d'Ivoire – but in Ghana the end result was that, on the whole, throughout a long history of conflict and local litigations, the legally expressed claims of indigenes and chiefs came out on top. Paradoxically, however (as I have argued elsewhere), British enforcement of 'customary' land law prevented the emergence of a true landlord class. The rich peasant class which emerged was not exclusively chiefly, and land itself did not become a class or an ethnic issue. Instead, the interests of cocoa farmers came to be represented by an 'agro-commercial' class more concerned with marketing than land.[23]

In Côte d'Ivoire, on the other hand, French colonial policy not only failed to create a neo-traditional elite in colonial society (which is not to deny that some *chefs de canton* were able to use their privileges to amass some personal wealth and power), but also failed to legalise – and moralise – the land regime which emerged almost spontaneously and without administrative intervention in the early years of the cocoa industry in Agni country. There was never any equivalent of the 1897–1912 Lands Bill agitations in Côte d'Ivoire! It was not until the coffee and cocoa booms and their associated migrations had got well started that mutterings of discontent began to be heard about indigenes' land rights – and similar arguments put forward about 'community ownership' as were heard from the Gold Coast chiefs in the 1920s. But for the indigenes it was too late; much of the Agni land had been virtually given away and the political and economic context of Côte d'Ivoire in the 1960s was quite different.[24] Here was a government which quite deliberately fuelled a land 'free-for-all' and the gold-rush mentality that went with it. The government's official land policy was *'la terre appartient à celui qui la cultive'*, a policy which particularly favoured the interests of mainly Baoulé migrants in the 'Wild West' Ivorian cocoa frontier, and ignored the claims of both the older Agni areas and the indigenes of the west.[25] The political connection not just with the general interests of the state in maximising revenue, but also with the more particular interests of the Baoulé 'inner core' elite dating from the origins of the regime in the 1950s, has not gone unnoticed. Indeed some scholars have claimed that the 'anarchy' of land relations was systematically used by the state administration, when settling the constant local disputes, in favour of migrants and to encourage an unrestrained commercialisation of peasant agriculture.[26] Both the land issue and the classic processes of uneven development produced an ethnic stratification which was not a notable feature of Ghanaian cocoa politics – although Ghana too attracted many foreign migrant labourers.

The rich peasant/small town society of southern Ghana which emerged during the colonial period was, therefore, rooted in local communities with highly elaborated political, moral and legal institutions and identities. The vigour of local political life and the degree of participation which developed, even before the party conflicts of the decolonisation period, have been recorded by numerous local studies. It is only when the party, associational or class groupings and neo-traditional mobilisations of the 1950s and 1960s are added to this legacy that some idea of the self-consciousness and strength of Ghanaian civil society can be grasped. In Côte d'Ivoire there were very many fewer of these local communities; those that did exist, far from being politically and legally 'moralised', were systematically crushed by colonial policy. The land free-for-all of the 1960s, with its anarchic and sometimes violent conflicts, was possible only against societies too weak to resist. It is difficult to imagine a similar process having occurred in Ghana.

POLITICAL ELITES AND STATE FORMATION

Côte d'Ivoire

The general underdevelopment of local communities and the weak constitution of civil society in Côte d'Ivoire was compounded and reinforced during the 1950s with the rise of an African successor elite. This was a crucial period in the formation of patterns of interaction between the nascent post-colonial state and society. Much has been written about the so-called 'planter bourgeoisie' which was said to be the basis of Houphouët-Boigny's early election victories and his subsequent rise to power.[27] It is true that his fight to obtain labour supplies for the large coffee planters of the Syndicat Agricole Africain (SAA, who were disgruntled by the forced labour made available to the small number of white planters) gave him a particular power base, which was also predominantly from the central (Baoulé) region and the ethnic associations of Abidjan.[28] But even in the very limited elections of the late 1940s and early 1950s – an electorate of one out of seven of the adult population in 1952 – his electoral machine was both broader and shallower than this. The original leadership group, as Zolberg pointed out in 1964, was predominantly from the tiny *evolué* elite – junior civil servants, teachers, pharmacists – Houphouët's classmates from the Ecole William Ponty in Dakar.[29]

Like Houphouët, many of them had commercial farms; but once having made their accommodation with the French in 1951, the logic of state-centred accumulation of power and wealth set in – and with it a process of *de*participation and stasis. No PDCI congress was held between 1949 and 1959, the crucial years of power consolidation; the original leadership clique stayed in power, intermarrying and creating their own elite family corporations. Neither local party democracy nor formal local government or community politics were developed.[30] The party's election victory in 1957 – the first under universal suffrage – was a product of elite power broking (including the whites in the colony) and local party machines run by centrally appointed secretaries. The trajectory of the centralised, highly policed French prefectoral administration continued uninterrupted. The opposition which emerged, predominantly from areas threatened by the coffee and cocoa expansion, or the 'original' cocoa elites of the south-east, was fairly easily crushed or coopted on terms set by the PDCI.

The early possession and use of state power by this group had more to do with their survival in office until independence than any popular 'peasant' base. The smoothness of this capture was also aided by the lack of mobilisation or representation of associational groups or other institutions within the state. An Ivorian bureaucracy, for instance, hardly existed. In 1957 there was not a single African in an executive position in the civil service. Even in the lower grades of white-collar employment, foreign Africans (Dahomeyans, Senegalese, Togolese) dominated; one-third of all clerical recruits in 1954 were foreign Africans.[31] The inevitable Ivorian protests against both whites and foreign Africans were crushed by the PDCI government. A junior civil servants strike in 1959 organised by the nascent Ivorian union movement led to wholesale sackings. While it was convenient for the regime to continue using European administrators (in 1965 80 per cent of managerial cadres in the civil service were expatriates, a figure which still stood at 48 per cent in 1973),[32] discontent could be managed by getting rid of foreign Africans and admitting a slow trickle of Ivorians. Thus an indigenous civil service did not emerge until after independence, and then it was very much a creature of the regime, recruited and controlled by the political elite.

Neither trade unions nor the bureaucracy presented any autonomous challenge to the PDCI in the 1950s. The same could be said for business elites, farmers and, after the crises of 1959–63, the educated middle classes and the university. Like the civil service, an Ivorian business class hardly existed. Nor has the PDCI regime shown until recently any interest in a policy for 'national capitalism'. Nearly thirty years after independence, foreign, particularly French, firms dominate the manufacturing, financial and agri-business private sectors; Ivorianisation of private managerial cadres still has a long way to go (only 32 per cent of top management and 62 per cent of '*cadres supérieurs*' in 1984).[33] In the small and medium sector – taxis, transport, shopkeeping, up-country crop buying – one need only note that there are around 100,000 Lebanese in Côte d'Ivoire, the largest Lebanese community in the world outside the Lebanon.[34] Ivorian business is very much a dependent of state patronage, either in the crop trading field or through the para-public sector which boomed so dramatically in the 1970s.[35]

The regime's connection with cash crop farming interests through the SAA was of a very particular kind. Unlike Ghana, farmers had never been mobilised in the 'mass movements' associated with the pre-war cocoa hold-ups in that country. Ethnic stratification and the migration/land issues, as indicated earlier, also meant that a united organisation comparable to the Ghana Farmers Congress of the 1940s never emerged in Côte d'Ivoire, even though in class terms the leadership of the GFC was, like that of the SAA, a similar blend of large planter and cocoa broking interests. In Ghana the farmers' organisation gave conditional support to the nationalist movement which after the break with the CPP over the marketing issue was the basis for an equally autonomous focus of opposition.[36] In Côte d'Ivoire the SAA coffee planters elite was not at loggerheads with the state in the 1940s and 1950s over the general issue of marketing; on the contrary, it was busy arranging a special deal with the French to give special prices and protected quotas in the French domestic market to the coffee produced during the 1950s expansion.[37] It is difficult to disentangle in this deal the interests of the elite as holders of state power from their interests in the coffee industry.

While the price deal did obviously benefit all farmers (and cemented the policy commitment of the political elite to export crop expansion), the special interests of the elite were soon manifested in the 'open door' policy on immigration which produced the extraordinary flood of foreign migrants into the rural areas in the 1960s; again while plentiful labour supplies benefited larger farmers, not all migrants intended to be – or remain – labourers. The pressure of both foreign and internal migrations, together with the free land policy, produced fragmentation in the farming community along ethnic and regional lines.[38] The political representation of farming interests offered by the SAA/PDCI axis was therefore always very partial; but representation and eventually opposition outside its framework took an ethnic/regional form, and was thus easily marginalised or crushed.

Finally, an organised educated/professional middle-class interest hardly existed in the 1950s, outside the very small group already incorporated into the PDCI. There was no university, and the small number of students in higher education (about 850 by 1960) were mainly in France or Senegal.[39] School enrolment of the 5 to 19 age group even by 1965 was only 29 per cent (compared to Ghana's 55 per cent) and was even more highly skewed regionally, being almost exclusively southern.[40] The founding of the University of Abidjan in 1960 led initially (and typically) to a large influx of foreign students; of the 1,900 students enrolled in 1965, only one-third were Ivorians! Nevertheless it was from 'radical' students that Houphouët experienced his first real challenges in the late 1950s, leading to the formation of the *Jeunesse RDA de la Côte d'Ivoire* in 1958, the PDCI's youth wing which was very quickly destroyed in the plot upheavals of 1963.[41] The weakness of the students and intellectuals was that they had no real local base. They were mainly 'returnees' looking for jobs in a very small market where the deliberately slow replacement of expatriates was the government's principal controlling mechanism.

Since independence the education system has expanded massively at the lower levels – the government spends more than any in Africa – but its products are still treated with extreme caution, and not without reason. Even though the majority of secondary school teachers were French until the early 1980s (now reduced to about 30 per cent)[42] the teaching unions and university students have regularly provided some of the rare ripples in the smooth surface of political conformity maintained by the regime.[43] But such dissent has never been allowed to persist; the lesson of the *Jeunesse* affair remained firmly imprinted on Houphouët's mind, and the original weakness of this group in social terms has been maintained politically through ruthless control of the job market and manipulation of the 'foreigner' factor. Whenever resentments against whites or foreign Africans build up, the government can buy popularity by generously mitigating the effects of its own policies. It is no accident that the recent slow-down in economic expansion has led to a rapid speed-up of Ivorianisation.[44] Only when that process is fully completed will the regime have to look for an alternative safety valve – and hope meanwhile for a recovery of the cocoa market!

Overall therefore the political elite which took power under French colonial tutelage in 1952 was able to build an Ivorian state very much on its own terms. The weakness and the lack of mobilisation of civil society both in local community and associational and class dimensions was such that the state was relatively free to choose what to incorporate and what to ignore or crush. Such contestations as did emerge did not permeate the state or seriously challenge elite unity and strength. The externality of the colonial state was reproduced but, unlike in Ghana, the lack of any agreed identity or legitimacy for the state hardly mattered. In spite of the view of some scholars that the Ivorian state represents the '*baoulisation*' of society,[45] the Ivorian governing class has always been notoriously unconcerned about what it means to be an Ivorian; official propaganda peddles a rather feeble 'folk-lore' image of a pluralistic nation of village farming communities each with its own 'customs'. This rather unconvincing effort conceals not tribal dominance but the emergence of a powerful, centralised 'Abidjan' elite rooted in the state and its mercantile dependents. The cultural identity of this elite – increasingly multi-ethnic in origin although still southern Akan dominated – is unashamedly modern, French and *nouveau riche* or wealth-seeking.

The autonomy of the state owes much, therefore, to the legacy of the decolonisation period and to the economic and political links established with France in the 1950s. But that is by no means the whole story. What happened after independence was even more extraordinary. While the weakness of indigenous society was perpetuated through continuing departicipation, the state grew out of all proportion to that society using foreign factors of production.

The number of foreigners in Côte d'Ivoire is not just a useful addition to the labour supply, to be celebrated by liberal economists; it is central to one's understanding of the regime. The Ivorian state has created a kind of regional 'colony in reverse'. The territory has been offered as a market and an 'empty land' for migrants to 'make their fortune'; the development of the territory for cocoa and coffee exports, agribusiness and local manufacturing would not have been possible without foreign labour from the West African region and Europe, foreign capital, and the substantial internal migrations. The importance of French and Lebanese business, and expatriate managerial cadres in the private and public sectors has already been mentioned. Here, the state's maintenance of the French-backed CFA currency has been crucial. In the urban and rural unskilled sectors the foreign labour attracted by the 'open door' and the cocoa rush was equally important. In 1973, 25 per cent of the total population was foreign (30 per cent, if children born to foreigners were included); even in 1985, with the onset of the crisis, it was still 20 per cent.[46] But these figures do not convey the full significance of the immigrants. As over half the total population are children, immigrants form a much higher proportion of the work-force; *41 per cent of those aged between 15 and 60 in 1980!*[47] Foreign Africans accounted for 57 per cent of all jobs in the urban 'informal and artisan' sector in 1976, and 42 per cent in the overall 'unskilled modern sector'.[48] In the primary sector, they accounted for a staggering 72.7 per cent of all paid jobs in 1971 – reflecting the fact that Ivorian farmers are either 'self-employed' – or employers.[49] Even as a proportion of total population the figure reaches 50 per cent in some southern districts, and over 30 per cent in the new cocoa area.[50]

Using these foreign factors of production, the Ivorian state facilitated – indeed participated in through its own investments – the successful economic boom of the 1960s and 1970s; it also used the wealth so created to expand itself enormously yet without any integration with or obligation to the social basis of that wealth. The greater part of 'Ivorian' society is outside the boundaries of the Ivorian political community. State expansion, apart from creating channels of patronage whose attractions were irresistible, created an administrative and security machine which is out of all proportion to the small size and weakness of what remains of an indigenous civil society. The distance between the state and the peasant villager or urban labourer, both in cultural and power terms, is much greater now than in colonial times. Control mechanisms are formidable, participation (notwithstanding recent attempts at reform) virtually nil. In this highly policed society, challenge from autonomous community or associational groupings is unlikely, and the rewards of cooperation overwhelming. The Abidjan state has therefore built itself without needing to worry about integrating social conflicts which could reproduce themselves within the political arena. The real conflicts over land and labour present in the agrarian economy have not been represented politically by ethnic 'barons'; Houphouët-Boigny's famed skill at ethnic balancing has in fact been more of a token cooptation of educated elites and technocrats. Anybody seen as a real challenge with a potential following is excluded. The likeliest sources of elite disunity are internal – personal or familial factions, generational or institutional conflicts including the fully integrated Armed Forces.[51]

The Ivorian state machine which, it is argued, has maintained effective control over this 'colonial' economy, is very obviously the creature of the political elite whose economic policies have produced the resources for its expansion. Elite consensus and coherence together with management of the Ivorianisation of a highly foreign dominated administrative and managerial sector have maintained strong forms of accountability in the administration. This is because political controls can be combined with an ostensibly technocratic and meritocratic ideology. The restricted output of highly educated manpower has meant that the very possession of the requisite educational qualifications is evidence of elite membership (like the 'Oxbridge' origins of the English ruling class).[52] Within these basic educational parameters, the pace of Ivorianisation and of expansion have enabled the regime to manipulate (until recently) a relative fit between the number of candidates and jobs. This permits the preservation of meritocratic criteria while 'political' criteria can be used in the more subtle allocation of different types of jobs and postings. An explanation of this system in terms of 'personal rule' or the 'charisma' of Houphouët-Boigny is redundant; the power, the autonomy, the wealth and the unity of the political elite, and the lack of alternatives where even the wealthier foreign sector is intimately linked to the state, give a convincing enough account of the loyalty and effectiveness of the administration. Indeed if it were more purely 'personal', how could the state have escaped the destructive and chaotic corruption of Mobutu's Zaïre?[53]

Ghana

In comparing the formation of political elites and the post-independence state in Ghana during the same period, the contrasts could not be more striking. Not only was the basic constitution of civil society stronger and more autonomous, but also the 1950s saw a growth in participation, and in associational and class formation which gave a political structuring to society that has determined all subsequent conflicts. These conflicts have been consistently reflected within the realm of the state, which itself possessed a more highly articulated machinery.

The Convention People's Party initially put together in 1949 a national coalition of farmers' associations, trade unions, small businessmen, white-collar workers and community-based 'youth associations' (some of which would be called ethnic in Côte d'Ivoire). The prior mobilisation of the rural areas over the cocoa 'swollen shoot' disease and the price/marketing issues, and the mobilisation of the urban masses through the Boycott Committees (organised to protest against European business) had already been intense.[54] When the cocoa farmers broke with the CPP after its election victory in 1951 and its subsequent decision to follow the colonial line on a marketing system for the cocoa exports, the CPP did not shrink to being just an elite with state power. Nor, in spite of the emergence of regionalist parties in the north and among the Ewe irredentists on the Togo border, could it be called an ethnically organised or interested party. Throughout the 1950s, fighting two democratic general elections and innumerable local elections in the new local government systems designed by colonial reformers to 'modernise' Indirect Rule, the CPP established itself as the representative of some well-identified general interests.

First, in the already well-established arenas of local politics the CPP was not just another local faction; it was the party of centralism and the state against the party of local autonomy, chiefly rule and all the legal, tenurial and economic structures associated with the colonial defence of 'traditional' culture.[55] A large proportion of the CPP's cadres, those who became leading officials in the 1960s, had come through this 'school' of local politics.[56] In the post-independence centralisation process, the CPP managed to integrate and coopt these locally based elites – the only organisation in Ghana's political history to have achieved this, then or subsequently. But the opposition to the CPP was equally well entrenched. After 1954 the Ashanti national identity was mobilised in defence of the neo-traditional and estab-

227

lished business classes not just in Ashanti but throughout Ghana. The regional dimension was explicity expressed in the demand for a 'federal' constitution, and just as fiercely attacked by the CPP, which was attempting to articulate an ethnically neutral, secular and popular nationalism. The conflict was therefore *national* and split communities in Ashanti as elsewhere; but the politicisation of pre-colonial state and ethnic identities remained a permanent potentiality for conflict. (The northern regional interest turned out to be the weakest and most easily coopted at the elite level.)[57]

Second, the CPP represented a populism of the 'petty bourgeois'; its ideology of raising up the 'common man' and the black man (in Nkrumah's Garveyite rhetoric) appealed to the less well-educated clerks, brokers and small businessmen of Ghanaian society as well as of course to the working class (until the latter broke with the regime after independence).[58] Ghana's professional middle classes, its established businessmen and senior civil servants were generally hostile and supported the opposition. Although large foreign companies have continued to operate in Ghana (mining, trading, local manufacture and services) since independence, an indigenous business class has grown outside the state.[59]

The demands of the 'popular' classes were easily translated, once the CPP had state power, into demands for the expansion of bureaucratic employment and the urban economy. The statist and centralising logic of the state was of course already powerfully present as it was in Côte d'Ivoire. But it was the CPP's constituency which sought social mobility through state employment that gave it a politically irresistible push. The conflict with the farmers over the state's decision to monopolise the cocoa marketing system through the mechanism of the Cocoa Marketing Board and the United Ghana Farmers Council set a fateful seal on the new state's attitude to the cocoa economy. The surpluses accumulated from cocoa exports were to be used for state-financed development and bureaucratic expansion – exactly as in Côte d'Ivoire.[60] But in Ghana the industry was regarded as a convenient milch cow whose historic fate was to be transcended by a state-led industrialisation, *not* encouraged to further expansion. This policy, later dubbed socialist by Nkrumah, fitted conveniently not only the interests and statist aspirations of the CPP's militant supporters, but also accorded with their perception of the cocoa farmers as an opposition. The most dynamic area of the cocoa economy in the 1950s was Ashanti; but whereas the Baoulé coffee farmers in Côte d'Ivoire were enjoying the patronage of the French taxpayer and the colonial state, the Ashanti cocoa farmers were regarded by the CPP in much the same light as Mrs Thatcher regarded the British coal-mining industry in the 1980s.

At the level of state institutions the CPP state also experienced early contestation. The Ghanaian civil service was large and (compared to Côte d'Ivoire) well established at the time of independence. The administrative grades of the civil service were 80 per cent Africanised by 1960;[61] the service had already developed an institutional identity, and was connected socially with the educated elite and the university intelligentsia. The CPP regime eventually came into increasing conflict with the civil service and was moving from oblique attacks and the creation of parallel institutions to an outright politicisation just before its overthrow. The immediate impact of the CPP period on the civil service was increasingly poor morale, bad discipline and internal conflict;[62] the long-term result, as regime succeeded regime, was an increasing failure of accountability and retreat into formalism and self-serving behaviour. Unstable or permanently shifting patterns of attempted politicisation also took their toll on the autonomy and effectiveness of the service, its worst moment being perhaps the 'purge' of the Busia regime in 1970. But equally bad was the experience under military rule of neglect alternating with wild demands, and the constantly creeping spread of corruption and cronyism. Yet through it all the public service continued to expand and survive as an institution, while suffering the results of permanent contestation within the state. Unlike the Ivorian civil service, which was kept disciplined by the extreme nature of both the rewards and sanctions controlled by the political elite, and rarely questioned its subordination, the original strength of the Ghanaian service made it an object of contestation, so that it was permeated both by the pulls of resistance and cooperation as well as the conflicts of political factions and interests. Like the Army, it was an institution riven with ethnic rivalries caused by the passage of recruitment cohorts.

The educated middle classes in Ghana also possessed an early political significance. The University of Ghana, founded in 1951, quickly became one of Africa's leading institutions and a world leader in African studies pioneered by a committed group of expatriates and Ghanaians in the 1950s. Its values were set by the 'Oxbridge' conceptions of its classicist first Principal, and by the late 1950s and early 1960s it was producing a stream of well-educated graduates. Together with the expansion of the primary base and (unlike Côte d'Ivoire) the secondary system, the result was the creation of a relatively large (by African standards) professional and lower-middle class. By the mid-1960s the size and complexity of the output from Ghana's three universities and its teacher training colleges was such that the 'middle classes' could not in any sense be encompassed – or catered to – by the state. Unlike the Ivorian scene, the public sector could not absorb the products of the higher and secondary system, and *Africanisation was virtually complete.*[63] White-collar jobs required constant state expansion – and the economy to support that expansion.

The political salience and articulateness of this class has been a constant feature of Ghanaian politics. The university intelligentsia in particular asserted its institutional and ideological independence from the state in conflict with the CPP regime in the early 1960s. Lawyers and the legal profession have also played an especially important role in political and economic life both as politicians and advocates for chiefly land disputes and within Ghana's highly developed state judicial system. The high point for these groups was probably the Busia regime of 1969–72; but they were the groups to suffer the most markedly – and protest most vigorously – with the collapse of the monetary system and the public and trading economy under the Acheampong military government of 1972–8.[64] Under the Rawlings government, at least in its 'radical' phase, the British-style legal system has suffered the most damaging – possibly fatal – attacks on its professionalism and independence.

Thus not only was the nascent Ghanaian state opposed from the beginning by farmers, the neo-traditional elites, professional, edu-cated and business classes and the forces of 'localism' and regionalism; these forces were encouraged through electoral politics both local and national to become nationally organised and articulated. Even though the CPP regime managed to incorporate or repress these groups (and the trade unions) between 1960 and 1966, the state was fully per-meated and contested by these social interests – particularly the local communities – as its subsequent history has demonstrated. Further periods of competitive party politics between 1969–72 and 1979–82 revealed the legacy of this period of intense politicisation and mobilisation – as did the conflicts which the military regimes have experienced. Although the trajectory of statist, bureaucratic expansion and dominance has continued with only minor interruptions, the pendulum has continued to swing between localism and centralism, professional and business classes against populism, cocoa farmers against the state bureaucracy.

The first Army regime, the NLC (1966–9), was probably the first to indulge in ethnic politics perhaps because of the prominent role of 'minority' officers from the Ewe and Ga. But this was itself a reflection of the nature of the Army as an institution, one of the few in Ghanaian life in which ethnicity had always been systematically and self-consciously manipulated.[65] The seizure of the state by the Army therefore brought into state institutions a new type of contestation – one never acknowledged by the CPP, but which it accused its opponents of peddling – which had further corrosive effects on subsequent regimes. The NLC itself eventually prepared the ground for a hand-over to the CPP's opposition – the business and professional classes and neo-traditional elites. But the Busia regime was also troubled by accusations of 'Akan tribalism', although the 'Akan' label – which is a language grouping – had never been used before in Ghanaian politics and had no pre-colonial referent. The regime in fact incorporated virtually all elements including the north; it was only the 'Ewe' sensitivity set up by the preceding military regime and the attempt to stigmatise Busia's ex-CPP opponents in the elections with the tribal label which set up this rather theoretical opposition.

The succeeding military regime – the NRC – unfortunately created a deepening whirlpool of ethnic and personal factionalism within the Army, the full violence of which was revealed only in the first Rawlings upheaval of 1979. While most accounts of this mutiny of soldiers and NCOs emphasise the 'radical' attack on corruption, one should not forget the important role played by northern and Ewe resentments.[66] The ethnic politics of the Acheampong regime were a symptom, perhaps, of what Chazan has described as the virtual privatisation of political channels as the officer corps turned in on itself, losing contact with and control over the machinery of state – and over the hundreds of officers given administrative jobs. Yet, at the same time as the state machine was drifting, the government publicly espoused the CPP's statist tradition in economic policy and presided over the biggest expansions in the bureaucracy and the most extreme exploitation and corrupt mishandling of the cocoa economy the country has ever known. It was no accident therefore that the ethnic factionalism was cross-cut publicly by opposition from the old 'anti-CPP' social forces.

The elected PNP government which followed the first Rawlings coup incorporated once again many of the old CPP elements, at least in organisational terms, but the social forces which had once underpinned the CPP's populist rhetoric – the urban masses and lower-middle classes – were in fact excluded and unrepresented. The PNP, in spite of its attempt to live off the Nkrumah myths, was a fake. Unlike the CPP it had no capacity to integrate either the community-based politics or the mobilised associations and class forces of Ghanaian society. Nor could it cope with the post-CPP legacy of ethnic mobilisation; and crucially it showed absolutely no capacity to re-establish control over the cocoa economy – or even how first to revive it, since it could see no alternative to the flawed bureaucratic instruments at its disposal.

The PNP's replacement – the second Rawlings government – at first looked even weaker. The PNDC has been firmly enmeshed, and has fought for its survival, within the murky and violent world of a disintegrating Army, in which the authority of the officer corps has been smashed,[67] and ethnic and personal cliques have fought among themselves. Rawlings's 'Ewe' troops within the Army have until now ensured him victory, as evidenced by Rawlings's success in killing or demobilising most of his opponents, particularly northern soldiers. (He has succeeded in reducing the Army from around 12,000 to only 5,000 men.)[68] In relation to civil society the regime appears to have no organised base since it broke with the radical student and intellectual movements and the urban workers after the failure of the 'spontaneous' Workers' and People's Defence Committees. Even more ominously, Rawlings's inner clique is publicly known to be an Ewe and familial group.[69] The ideological stance of the regime is even more confusing; in some senses the heir to a CPP-style populism, it has in practice shifted state policy firmly towards favouring the encouragement of cocoa exports and a better deal for farmers.

Ghanaian regimes have thus come full circle; beginning with the CPP's fatal attempt to bureaucratise the expropriation of the cocoa export surpluses, an attempt which failed through the CPP's lack of control over its bureaucratic creation, the cocoa farmers have suffered the most comprehensively through all regimes. Since the late 1970s they have appeared almost as demobilised as an Ivorian local electorate. It is perhaps significant that their first champion in many years, Jerry Rawlings, has also recently implemented a plan for democracy which consists of elections at local level to district councils[70] – an exact repetition of the colonial reformers' assertion in the late 1940s that truly representative democracy could grow only at the local level. A hopeful interpretation of these moves is that the Ghanaian state is attempting at last to re-establish relations with elements of civil society long neglected or hostile; and to reduce the degree of contestation within the state to the point where discipline and accountability can be rebuilt.

The particular formation of the Ghanaian state during the 1950s and its mode of interaction with society since independence have together produced an unstable series of political elites, each failing to grapple with and integrate the conflicts arising from a highly mobilised and fractured civil society. In other polities, the develop-ment of civil society and of a state rooted in that society is normally regarded as healthy. Why has it been so destructive in Ghana? The explanation offered here is that during the decolonisation process the state failed to create an uncontested source of either power or legitimacy. As in Côte d'Ivoire, the CPP reproduced the externality of the colonial state, an externality rooted in bureaucratic extraction from a peasant society with no organic connection to the state through landlord or agrarian classes. But the CPP, because of its 'statist' political constituency, not only failed to establish a legitimate and effective relationship with the peasant economy, but also attacked the powerfully developed albeit pluralistic sources of legiti-macy in local society.

Its attempt to build a secular nationalist elite might have succeeded given time, power and resources. But unlike the Ivorian elite, it did not have the autonomy, power and wealth which came from that elite's ability to pursue a strategy of 'internal colonialism' and to act virtually independently of civil society. The CPP state was too strongly contested right from the start; it *mattered* that the character and representativeness of the Ghanaian state was not agreed, and that one of the regime's most fundamental interests, the peasant economy, was alienated and excluded.[71] The political economy of cocoa in Ghana was quite different from that of Côte d'Ivoire; unlike the weak and scattered Ivorian communities, unable to resist the flood of migration and land-grabbing which was the hidden and potentially subversive cost of the cocoa and coffee boom, the cocoa-based communities of Ghana could resist a state policy regarded as inimical, and the boom of the 1950s did not split them so dramatically into losers and winners. Although leadership had passed from the older eastern region cocoa areas, the Ashanti controlled their own boom in the new areas.

From the CPP's initial political and economic failures, embodied most vividly in the corrupt inefficiency of the Cocoa Marketing Board and its monopoly purchasing and political organisation, the United Ghana Farmers Council, no subsequent regime seemed able to escape.[72] The state machinery continued to expand, ever more out of control and unaccountable as the grip of succeeding political elites loosened and conflict within the state and with civil society intensified. The cocoa marketing story continued to be at the core of this failure, together with failures in infrastructural support and agricultural extension and lack of control over state agencies responsible for implementation.[73]

The lack of discipline and accountability in the Ghanaian state can therefore be attributed to the continuing contestation within the state arising from the lack of elite consensus and strength and from the continuing ability of civil society to oppose and resist. Inevitably the process was cumulative; each swing of the wheel of fortune reduced the power of the next group to seize the state.

It is worth putting the situation of the current regime in Ghana into this historical context. The ideology of the 'Rawlings revolution' initially stressed precisely this need for 'accountability' and 'participation' in Ghanaian public life; this was to be the purpose of the new Workers' and Peoples' Defence Committees. Yet, in assuming that the committees could emerge 'spontaneously' through self-selection, the leadership showed itself astonishingly ignorant of the structure of local and national politics in Ghana – and of the materialist perspective underlying populist rhetoric. No 'spontaneous' local committees could arise which were not either emergent from the well-established local political and social structures discussed above, or, if opposed to them, supported by a national organisation and/or the government's own administrative networks. The PNDC had no such national political organisation, and the field administrators were unlikely to help or support the PDCs against the local establishment unless they were reasonably confident in the survival of the regime and could be relied upon to carry out the policy.

The PNDC in fact had no means of articulating itself, either politically or administratively, into the countryside. The outcome was entirely predictable. The PDCs were regarded simply as hooligans extorting and running rackets in scarce imported goods where they could get the support of the local soldiery; or challenging the authority of the Army, the police and the civil service (and hence the regime's fragile bases) when successfully operating as WDCs. In Ashanti, local power structures simply crushed the PDCs even before Rawlings made his own decision to do the same.[74] The current policy is based on a return to a classic military/bureaucratic alliance and the restoration of military and administrative discipline (through fear and coercion), together with an attempt to gain official purchase on the structures of local democracy. These policy changes are entirely explicable in terms of the object lesson which Rawlings received in the realties of Ghanaian state–society relations. Yet, as Medard suggests in the analogous case of Kenya (see Chapter 9) where there are already highly politicised local elites, such a strategy may be resisted – or adapted to local interests.

STATE, SOCIETY AND INSTITUTIONAL EFFICACY

In attempting to explain the contrasting histories of stability and instability in Ghana and Côte d'Ivoire, it has been argued that important differences existed in both the relative weakness and strength of civil society and in the type of interaction which occurred between state and society during the crucial formative period of each post-colonial state. The end result was, in Côte d'Ivoire, a strong state which overpowers, indeed is out of all proportion to civil society, but which is able to maintain a strongly disciplined state machine capable of maintaining the conditions for extraction of revenue from the peasant and mercantile economy. The Ivorian state has been virtually autonomous; a unified elite was able to use foreign factors of production to create its resource base, and foreign personnel to give itself continuing control over administration (through restricted recruitment) and over the private sector.

In Ghana, instability reflected the much greater strength and articulation of civil society and the inability of successive political elites to control or integrate the permanent contestation either within the state or over the acceptance of the state by different interests. The consequence of this instability was a growing lack of effectiveness, due to a lack of accountability and control over the state machine. This failure led in turn to an inability to maintain the conditions for continued extraction from the peasant and mercantile economies, and hence to the collapse of the state's own revenue base.

The core of the difference is demonstrated in each case in the history of the crop marketing systems. In Côte d'Ivoire its efficiency does not reside in one institution but in the whole range of state institutions dealing with the countryside: the *Caisse de Stabilisation*, the prefectoral field administration, the ministries providing infra-structural inputs and the state agricultural extension agencies such as SATMACI. Contrary to what is often asserted, the *Caisse* system is not 'efficient' because it is based on private traders working within an official price structure. The system in Côte d'Ivoire is a classic piece of mercantilism, in that it is designed to *guarantee* a profit to crop exporters regardless of the world price. (The state takes a profit if the world price is above the officially imputed CIF price; but it *reimburses* the traders if it falls below this – hence the current financial crisis of the state!)[75] To be given a state licence to be a crop buyer and exporter is to be given a licence to make money. This privilege is held by around thirty agencies (some French, others Ivorian) each with a quota. But because profit depends on maximum actual purchasing,

235

farmers benefit from competition between the thousands of up-country agents of the big commercial houses. The state regulates the grant of trading licences right down to the *sous-préfecture* level and control is strict. The system is thus built around the interests of the traders, but farmers benefit because they get the official price throughout the country and actually get paid in cash (until the current crisis).[76]

Obviously the *Caisse* is at the core both of the state's revenue surpluses and of the patronage system. Although Fauré has referred to the system as 'patrimonial', it is doubtful whether the particular role of the *Caisse* should be taken as proof that there is appropriation and privatisation of state resources by office-holders throughout the state apparatus. On the contrary, as Fauré shows, Houphouët-Boigny has demonstrated a ruthless ability to 'call in', control or close down the patronage machine as in the case of the parastatal corporations when their excesses seemed to threaten accountability and discipline throughout the rest of the state.

The continuing departicipation of Ivorian society and the externality of this powerful state is on the other hand vividly demonstrated by the operations of the prefectoral system and the current attempt at *communalisation* and *responsabilisation* of local administration – and tax-gathering.[77] It is truly ironic that, thirty years after independence, a high-level administrative trainee at the Ivorian ENA could write in relation to this policy: '*l'Ivoirien peut faire maintenant son apprentissage de citoyen*'. Control within the administration and over society are still the dominant realities of the Ivorian state.

In Ghana the history of the crop marketing system provides a telling contrast. Apart from a brief interlude in the Busia regime when private up-country purchasing was tried (and failed) the marketing board (CMB) has consistently relied on buying and exporting all the crop itself using its own monopoly or near monopoly agency. The Acheampong regime went further even than the CPP and ordered the CMB to finance and operate a massive expansion of state cocoa plantations.[78] Throughout, the farmers have suffered abuses resulting from corruption and inefficiency such as delayed payment (up to nine months by the end of the 1970s) or non-payment. Meanwhile at a time when the world prices were booming and the farmers were getting only 15 per cent of those prices, the number of employees of the CMB and its agencies had swelled to 74,357, compared to the UGFC's 13,000 during the CPP period.[79] It is only under Rawlings that any changes have looked likely, with the sacking of 28,000 employees and plans for privatisation.[80]

What remains at the heart of the problem, however, whatever

system is adopted, is whether the Ghanaian state can develop the administrative honesty and efficiency to make it work and restore the conditions for successful agriculture and trade to function. The comparison with Côte d'Ivoire shows that the critical factor is accountability to a strongly established political elite. Given Ghana's turbulent political history, this may seem an unrealistic prospect. On the other hand, the strength and mobilisation of Ghanaian civil society could, if better harnessed and integrated, provide a stronger basis for a participative and civic order than in Côte d'Ivoire. A sense of community still exists in Ghana and this is an invaluable potential.

NOTES

1. See P. Foster and A. Zolberg, *Ghana and the Ivory Coast: Perspectives on Modernization* (Chicago, Ill., 1971); J. Woronoff, 'Ivory Coast: The Value of Development' and A.G. Rondos, 'Ivory Coast: The Price of Development', *Africa Report* (24 April 1979); C. Young, *Ideology and Development in Africa* (New Haven, Conn., 1982).
2. S. Amin, *Le Développement du Capitalisme en Côte d'Ivoire* (Paris, 1967); E. Eshag and P. J. Richards, 'Comparison of Economic Developments in Ghana and the Ivory Coast since 1960', *Bulletin of the Oxford University Institute of Statistics* (November 1967); World Bank, *Accelerated Development in Sub-Saharan Africa* (Washington, DC, 1981).
3. N. Ridler, 'Comparative Advantage as a Developmental Model – the Ivory Coast', *Journal of Modern African Studies* (Sept. 1985); Y. A. Fauré, 'Côte d'Ivoire: Une Crise et son Analyse', Conference on West African States, SOAS, Centre for African Studies (June 1987).
4. T. Killick, *Development Economics in Action* (London, 1978) p. 21.
5. See B. Agyeman-Duah, 'Ghana 1982–6: The Politics of the PNDC', *Journal of Modern African Studies* (Dec., 1987); D. Ray, *Ghana: Politics, Economics and Society* (London, 1986); N. Chazan, 'Politics and the State in Ghana' and R. Jeffries, 'The Political Economy of Personal Rule in Ghana', Conference on West African States, SOAS, Centre for African Studies (June 1987); J. Haynes, 'Rawlings and the Politics of Development Policy in Ghana 1979–86', Ph.D. thesis, Staffordshire Polytechnic (1988).
6. J.-F. Bayart, 'Civil Society in Africa', in P. Chabal (ed.) *Political Domination in Africa* (Cambridge, 1986) pp. 111–12, 118–19.
7. See R. Scruton, *A Dictionary of Political Thought* (London, 1982) pp. 66, 438; K. Marx, *The German Ideology* (London, 1965) p. 48; J. Urry, *The Anatomy of Capitalist Societies* (London, 1981) p. 18.
8. G. Poggi, *The Development of the Modern State* (London, 1978) pp. 77 and 81.
9. Bayart, 'Civil Society . . .', pp. 117–18.
10. L. Mytelka, 'Foreign Business and Economic Development', in I. W. Zartman and C. Delgado (eds) *The Political Economy of the Ivory Coast* (New York, 1984).

11. A. Zolberg, *One Party Government in the Ivory Coast* (Princeton, NJ, 1964) p. 159.
12. See G. Caire, 'Dependence, Independence and Interdependence in Economic Relations', in W. H. Morris-Jones and C. Fischer (eds) *Decolonisation and After* (London, 1980) p. 138; C. G. Rosberg and T. M. Callaghy (eds) *Socialism in Sub-Saharan Africa* (Berkeley, Calif., 1979) p. 126 for a discussion of this concept.
13. Zolberg, *One Party Government*, p. 40; W. Birmingham, I. Neustadt and E.N. Omaboe, *A Study of Contemporary Ghana*, vol. 2 (London, 1966) p. 132.
14. Birmingham *et al.*, *ibid.*, p. 135.
15. B. A. den Tuinder, *Ivory Coast: The Challenge of Success* (Baltimore, Md, and London, 1978) p. 308.
16. République de Côte d'Ivoire (RCI), Ministère de l'Agriculture, *Annuaire Retrospectif de Statistiques Agricoles et Forestières, 1900–1983*, vol. 1, pp. 108–9.
17. den Tuinder, *Challenge of Success*, p. 308; RCI, *Plan Quinquennial de Developpement 1981–85* (Abidjan, 1983) p. 589.
18. RCI, Ministère de l'Economie et de Finances, *La Côte d'Ivoire en Chiffres 1986–7* (Abidjan, 1988).
19. 70 per cent less than 20,000; RCI *Direction et Contrôle des Grands Travaux, Project de Développement Municipale, Tome 2: Elements de Diagnostic* (Abidjan, 1986) p. 21.
20. See R. Stryker, 'Political and Administrative Linkage in the Ivory Coast', in Foster and Zolberg, *Ghana and the Ivory Coast*, p. 76.
21. J. P. Chauveau and J. P. Dozon, 'Au Coeur des Ethnies Ivoiriennes . . . l'Etat', in E. Terray, *L'Etat Contemporain en Afrique* (Paris, 1987).
22. RCI, *Statistiques Agricoles*; G. B. Kay, *The Political Economy of Colonialism in Ghana* (Cambridge, 1972) p. 336.
23. R. Crook, 'Decolonization, the State and Chieftaincy in the Gold Coast', *African Affairs* (January 1986).
24. Chauveau and Dozon, 'Au Coeur des Ethnies . . .'. See also 'Colonisations, Economie de Plantation et Société Civile en Côte d'Ivoire', *Cahiers d'ORSTOM, ser. Sci. Hum.* (21 January 1985).
25. *Ibid.*
26. P. Ruf, 'Politiques et Encadrement Agricole; Partage des Tâches en Côte d'Ivoire' (Communication au Seminaire d'Economie et de Sociologie Rurales du CIRAD, September 1985); M. Lesourd, 'La Forêt, la Machette, et le Billet de Banque', *Cahiers d'ORSTOM, ser Sci. Hum.* (24 January 1988).
27. See Zolberg, *One Party Government*; Mytelka, 'Foreign Business . . .'; Y. A. Fauré and J.-F. Medard, *Etat et Bourgeoisie en Côte d'Ivoire* (Paris, 1982); B. Campbell, 'Ivory Coast', in J. Dunn (ed.) *West African States* (Cambridge, 1978).
28. Zolberg, *ibid.*, pp. 67–8.
29. *Ibid.*
30. They were in fact positively discouraged; see M. Cohen, 'Urban Policy and Development Strategy', in Zartman, *Political Economy*, p. 64.
31. Zolberg, *One Party Government*. pp. 101 and 246.
32. R. Clignet and P. Foster, 'Convergence and Divergence in Educational

Development in Ghana and the Ivory Coast', in Foster and Zolberg, *Ghana and the Ivory Coast*, p. 287; RCI, Ministère de la Fonction Publique, *Regards sur la Fonction Publique, 1975*.

33. RCI, Ministère du Travail et de l'Ivoirisation, *Le Secteur Privé et Semi-public en Côte d'Ivoire: Principaux Resultats 1984*.
34. *La Côte d'Ivoire en Chiffres 1986–7*, p. 19.
35. See Fauré, '. . . Une Crise et Son Analyse'.
36. See B. Beckman, *Organising the Farmers: Cocoa Politics and National Development in Ghana* (Uppsala, 1976).
37. Zolberg, *One Party Government*, p. 167.
38. Chauveau and Dozon, 'Au Coeur des Ethnies . . .'
39. den Tuinder, *Challenge of Success*, p. 279.
40. Clignet and Foster, 'Convergence and Divergence . . .', p. 273.
41. Zolberg and Foster, *Ghana and the Ivory Coast*, p. 16.
42. Ministère du Travail, *Le Secteur Privé . . .*, p. 89.
43. See for instance the recent government conflict with the teachers' union which resulted in the imprisonment of teachers' leaders and the imposition of government nominees and union officials: G. Bourke, 'An Autocratic Democrat', *West Africa* (1–7 May 1989).
44. N. Yao and I. F. Lébry, '14,5 Milliards d'Economie Grâce à la Réduction des Experts', *Fraternité Matin* (30 November 1987); Ambassade de France, *La Coopération Franco-Ivoirienne 1987* (Abidjan, 1988).
45. Chauveau and Dozon, 'Au Coeur des Ethnies . . .'.
46. den Tuinder, *Challenge of Success*, p. 124; INADES-documentation, *Etude des Consequences Sociale de la Politique de Développement en Côte d'Ivoire* (Abidjan, 1986) mimeo, p. 10.
47. Calculated from data provided in *Plan Quinquennial 1981–85*, p. 590.
48. *Ibid.*, p. 63.
49. den Tuinder, *Challenge . . .*, p. 130.
50. INADES, *Etudes . . .*, p. 9.
51. Senior military officers have been given Cabinet posts in recent years and are to be found in larger numbers in the Prefectoral service. As the rise and fall of Lamine Fadika (Minister of the Navy) between 1974 and 1987 shows, it is better to have young ambitious officers in the Cabinet as it enables the political leadership to smell trouble very quickly!
52. den Tuinder, *Challenge . . .*, p. 279; Clignert and Foster, 'Convergence and Divergence . . .', p. 275.
53. In Zaïre state offices *are* given out as 'prebends' by Mobutu and his familial ruling group, and hence systematic plunder, anarchy and inefficiency are endemic in the state machine; in Côte d'Ivoire, while the political and commercial elites undoubtedly benefit from patronage (as in the parastatal corporations and the crop trading system), there is little evidence to show from my recent observation of various ministries (including the prefectoral service) that the Ivorian bureaucracy has been 'patrimonialised' in the strict sense of this term. Many bureaucrats and technocrats, including ex-prefects, have been formally coopted into the political elite but this can be compared to the very similar career trajectories of bureaucrats in French politics. See R. Crook, 'Patrimonialism, Administrative Effectiveness and Economic Development in Côte d'Ivoire', *African Affairs* (April 1989) for a discussion of this topic. See

C. Young and T. Turner, *The Rise and Decline of the Zaïrian State* (Madison, Wis., 1985); T. M. Callaghy, *The State–Society Struggle: Zaïre in Comparative Perspective* (New York, 1984).

54. See D. Austin, *Politics in Ghana 1946–60* (London, 1964) for a general account of this period, and R. Crook, 'Decolonization . . .' for an analysis of the agrarian factor.

55. R. Crook, 'Legitimacy, Authority and the Transfer of Power in Ghana', *Political Studies* (Dec., 1987) p. 568.

56. R. Crook, 'Bureaucracy and Politics in Ghana: a Comparative Perspective', in P. Lyon and J. Manor (eds) *Transfer and Transformation: Political Institutions in the New Commonwealth* (Leicester, 1983).

57. See P. Ladouceur, *Chiefs and Politicians: The Politics of Regionalism in Northern Ghana* (London, 1979).

58. Crook, 'Legitimacy, Authority . . .'; R. Rathbone, 'Businessmen in Politics: Party Struggle in Ghana 1949–57', *Journal of Development Studies* (April 1973); R. Jeffries, *Class, Power and Ideology in Ghana: The Railwaymen of Sekondi* (Cambridge, 1978).

59. P. Kennedy, *African Capitalism: The Struggle for Ascendancy* (Cambridge, 1988).

60. R. Crook, 'Farmers and the State', in D. Rimmer (ed.) *Rural Transformation in Tropical Africa* (London, 1988) p. 129.

61. B. Amonoo, *Ghana 1957–66: The Politics of Institutional Dualism* (London, 1981) p. 33.

62. *Ibid.*, p. 61; Killick, *Development Economics*, p. 338.

63. Clignet and Foster, 'Convergence and Divergence . . .', p. 287.

64. See N. Chazan, *An Anatomy of Ghanaian Politics: Managing Political Recession 1969–82* (Boulder, Colo., 1983); R. Price, 'Neo-Colonialism and Ghana's Economic Decline', *Canadian Journal of African Studies* (1, 1984); R. Jeffries, 'Rawlings and the Political Economy of Underdevelopment in Ghana', *African Affairs* (July 1982).

65. See S. Baynham, *The Military and Politics in Nkrumah's Ghana* (Boulder, Colo., 1986) and 'Divide et Impera: Civilian Control of the Military in Ghana's Second and Third Republics', *Journal of Modern African Studies* (Dec., 1985).

66. Baynham, 'Divide et Impera . . .'; Haynes, 'Rawlings and the Politics of Development . . .', pp. 101 and 122–8.

67. Baynham, *ibid.*

68. Haynes, 'Rawlings . . .', p. 363; also Ray, *Ghana* . . .; Chazan, 'Politics and the State . . .'.

69. Haynes, 'Rawlings . . .', p. 392. The key figure in the regime is Rawlings's personal mentor and friend over many years, Kojo Tsikata, head of the security apparatus.

70. See *West Africa*, 'Ghana' Special Issue (11 January 1988); B. Ankomah, 'Elections Extraordinary', *New African* (December 1988).

71. The Kenyan state, as Médard shows in Chapter 9 in this volume, is beginning to experience the same identity problems deriving from an inability officially to admit the historically dominant role of the Kikuyu, while being unable officially to exlude them either.

72. Beckman, *Organising the Farmers*.

73. Killick, *Development Economics*, p. 191.

74. R. Jeffries, 'Personal Rule . . .'; Haynes, 'Rawlings . . .', p. 161. If the government had decided to support the PDCs, a repressive apparatus would no doubt have emerged; it is noteworthy that Rawlings's original idea for a weekend 'National Cadre School' for the PDCs focused on 'weapons training'. Luckily for the ordinary citizens of Ghana, Rawlings's personal experience of meeting the members of the PDCs in the flesh convinced him that it would be best to cancel the whole idea! (Haynes, p. 179).

75. See H. S. Marcussen, 'The Ivory Coast Facing the Economic Crisis', in J. Carlsson (ed.) *Recession in Africa* (Uppsala, 1983) p. 7; G. Delaporte, 'La CSSPPA; Vingt Années au Service du Planteur et de l'Etat', *Marchés Tropicaux* (9 April 1976); F. R. Mahieu, 'Stabilisation des Prix de Produits Agricoles d'Exploitation et Financement du Développement; l'Expérience de la CSSPPA en Côte d'Ivoire' (Abidjan, 1984).

76. The ability of the system to underwrite both traders' profits and state financial demands even in a period of falling prices was finally ended in 1987–8, caught in the scissors of further price falls and Houphouët's determination not to drop the producer price. Neither the *Caisse* nor the banks were able to fund the advances needed to buy the 1988 crop; hence, in a replay of the 1950s, the French government has helped to 'arrange' a private purchase of a substantial portion of the Ivorian crop at 'Houphouët's price'. Even though this is unlikely to solve the problem of the world price, it will help the finances of the *Caisse*! This was followed in 1989 with a halving of the producer price for cocoa. K. Whiteman, 'Bitter Chocolate', *West Africa* (12–18 June 1989); 'Quand l'Elysée se Passionne pour le Cacao', *Le Canard enchaîné* (10 May 1989).

77. Official justification for the policy may be found in *Plan Quinquennial 1981–85*, p. 752, where it is linked with deconcentration of central ministries and the creation of extra rural *sous-préfectures*. The major thrust of both the new communes and the *sous-préfectures* is in fact to try to get local communities to pay for their own 'development', a financial and political necessity in the period of '*la crise*'. Indeed local areas are now being told that they must raise the cost of having their own new *sous-préfet*! There is also open official acknowledgement of the difficulty of getting the peasants to pay their new communal taxes. See *Fraternité Matin* (19 November 1988); *Fraternité Matin, Spécial Indépendance, An 28*, 'Communes: un Pari sue l'Avenir' (7 December 1988).

78. J. Kraus, 'The Political Economy of Agrarian Regression in Ghana', in S. K. Commins, M. Lofchie and R. Payne (eds) *Africa's Agrarian Crisis* (Boulder, Colo., 1986).

79. Haynes, 'Rawlings . . .', p. 238; Beckman, *Organising the Farmers*, p. 133.

80. 'Ghana', in *Africa South of the Sahara, 1987* (London, 1988).

CHAPTER ELEVEN
State, Society and Political Institutions in Revolutionary Ethiopia
Christopher Clapham

Though evidently sharing many features of the common Third World experience, Ethiopia is distinguished from virtually all other African states (though not from a number of Asian ones) by a pattern of state formation and a consequent dynamic of political change which are overwhelmingly indigenous rather than colonial in origin. It is further distinguished from most (though again not all) Third World states by its commitment since the 1974 revolution to a Marxist-Leninist political trajectory which, especially since the creation of the Workers' Party of Ethiopia (WPE) in 1984, has led to the creation of formal political institutions consciously derived from Soviet models. One obvious concern in discussing Ethiopia must therefore be for the relevance and applicability of such models to the current circumstances of the Third World. This is an exercise from which some useful conclusions can be drawn. Yet generalisation must be approached with caution. Ethiopian socialism (no less than Soviet, Chinese or Cuban socialisms) is marked by distinctive features which must be ascribed to its local setting. With that in mind, I shall look first at the bases of Ethiopian statehood, then at the process of revolutionary transformation which has led to the creation of the present institutional structure, and finally at the problems faced by this structure in responding to the all too evident crisis of the Ethiopian state and economy.

ORIGINS OF STATE AND REVOLUTION

Ethiopia is virtually unique in Africa in possessing a tradition of the state which long predates the colonial era. While most African

societies (including, of course, several peoples subsequently incorporated into Ethiopia) were governed through political systems based
on a mythology of descent from a common ancestor (and describable,
despite the enormous variety of political arrangements to which this
gave rise, as 'tribal'), Ethiopia has long been governed through a
hierarchical political structure based ultimately on the control of
territory. For many centuries this hierarchy was headed by an
emperor whose membership of a specific 'Solomonic' dynasty was
regarded as of critical importance. But the survival of the state after
the dynasty's collapse, and most significantly its revival and expansion
from the reign of Tewodros (1855–68) onwards, demonstrate that
this state was no mere dynastic creation, but was, rather, deeply
rooted in the social and economic structures of the people who
comprised it. Uniquely in sub-Saharan Africa, moreover, it was a
literate society, with its own written language through which the
historical tradition of statehood could be transmitted.

Nor, still more remarkably, was it an ethnic state. The key role of
Amhara culture in the Ethiopian political system, including the use of
Amharic as the language of government and the special status (until
the revolution) of the Ethiopian Orthodox Church, has led many
observers to view Ethiopia as a state created and maintained by the
simple imposition of 'Amhara domination' over subordinate (or
internally colonised) peoples. It is a picture that resistance movements
directed against the central government have been understandably
eager to emphasise. But it is true only in a limited sense. Ethiopia has
(like the United States) a dominant culture, to which anyone
ambitious for a place in the state apparatus, and especially for national
political power, must to some degree assimilate. This culture likewise
reflects the historically pre-eminent position of a particular group,
which gains considerable advantages not only from its familiarity
with the language of government, but also from personal contacts,
cultural identities and other affinities with the political system. But
the system is not ethnically exclusive. It has invariably included non-
Amharic speakers, the most significant of whom in historical terms,
the Tigrinya speakers of the northern plateau, can claim to be the
founders of the state itself; and positions of the highest political power
have been open to individuals of any group who have been prepared
to associate themselves with the central government.[1]

This ethnic non-exclusiveness has been essential to the survival of
the Ethiopian state, particularly as it has expanded to incorporate new
peoples since the later nineteenth century, and as the centres of
political and economic power have shifted steadily southwards. The

price it has paid – and it has been a very heavy one – has been the progressive marginalisation of peoples, especially in Eritrea and Tigray, who would once have viewed themselves as part of the historically dominant core. This has proved much more of a problem for the revolutionary regime than the management of other peoples – Oromo, Sidama, Wollamo, Kaffa, even Afar and Somali – who were incorporated into the Ethiopian state a century or less ago.

This Ethiopian state has shared the interests of states everywhere. As a hierarchy of control, manned by officials who maintain themselves by extracting a surplus from the directly productive areas of the economy, it has an interest in retaining (and if possible expanding) its territory; in extending its degree of effective control over the people within its frontiers; and in maintaining the external political and economic linkages which are essential both to surplus extraction (which in Ethiopia, as in other parts of Africa, depends to a large extent on state control of external trade), and to importing the manufactured goods (notably armaments) which are needed for central control and elite satisfaction. The modernising emperors who ruled Ethiopia from 1855 to 1974, nonetheless, could not fully achieve their state-creating goals, any more than French kings or Russian tsars could achieve theirs, because of the inherent limitations placed on them by the nature of the political structures through which they had to rule. The imperial regime failed because it could establish neither the political nor the economic and military/administrative conditions required for state transformation.

The most important failure was political. John Markakis has correctly identified the exclusion from the state of new professional elites geared to government employment as the key to the formation of separatist movements throughout the Horn of Africa, including notably those in Eritrea, Ogaden and Southern Sudan;[2] but the same applies to those who launched the 1974 revolution in Addis Ababa itself. Though the imperial regime provided employment for well-educated young men (the leading positions, even so, being largely reserved for those who had connections with the court), it had no mechanism at all for meeting their political aspirations, of the kind that was furnished by the anti-colonial nationalist movements in other parts of Africa. The absence of political parties likewise deprived the regime of any effective mechanism through which it could link the government in Addis Ababa to the vast mass of the population, especially in the countryside. This failure was most obvious in Eritrea, not least because Eritrea already had a party structure of a kind that existed nowhere else in Ethiopia, having been politically mobilised first by Italian colonialism, and then by the conflicts over the political future of the territory after the Second World War. But exactly the same gap existed throughout the country, and was shown up by incidents such as the Wako rebellion in Bale,[3] or the revolt over the agricultural income tax in Gojjam.[4] The absence of political linkages, and the restriction of government to a small coterie closely centred on the court in Addis Ababa, in turn reduced the state's effectiveness as a developmental or distributive agency – a failure most sharply illustrated by its incapacity to react to the 1973–4 famine in Wollo.

These combined failures provide the classic conditions for revolution, especially in decaying agrarian monarchies faced by the challenge of modern state formation; Ethiopia found itself in this respect, as in many others, in the mainstream of revolutionary political change. There are, however, two very different ways in which such change can be brought about.[5] On the one hand, it may be possible for the old regime, undermined by its loss of political legitimacy and effectiveness, to be overthrown by an uprising in the national capital, and displaced by a government of the revolutionary intelligentsia, which then puts through the measures such as land reform which are needed to extend the new system to the countryside; this is the experience of France and Russia, and in a variant form of Iran. Alternatively if the existing regime is capable of retaining control over the centre, the revolutionary elites may start by organising the peasantry, and through guerrilla warfare establish control over the countryside from which they can surround and capture the capital; this is, of course, the experience of China, echoed in Vietnam, Kampuchea, Cuba and Nicaragua. The major tragedy of revolutionary Ethiopia has been that it has experienced both of them simultaneously.

Accordingly I would regard both the present Ethiopian government, which gained power through the first of these mechanisms, and insurgent movements such as the EPLF (Eritrean People's Liberation Front) and TPLF (Tigrayan People's Liberation Front), which are seeking to gain power through the second, as different and opposed elements of the same revolution. This is a viewpoint which would be strongly contested by both sides, each of which seeks to present itself as the sole authentic representative of revolutionary change. But not only do both the Ethiopian government and its opponents spring from the same initial conditions; they likewise share the same ideology, the same basic goals, and many of the same policies and organisational techniques. The key goal, in each case, is the creation of a hierarchical, efficient and centrally directed state – a

Jacobin or Leninist ideal, in which popular participation is welcomed only in so far as it can be harnessed to organised central power.

THE LENINIST MODEL

Ethiopia has since 1974, and especially since the creation of the Workers' Party of Ethiopia (WPE) in 1984, made the most sustained attempt by any African state to create a Marxist-Leninist structure of government along broadly Soviet lines. This enterprise has often been criticised, from the left no less (in fact, generally more) than from the right, as the brutal imposition of an autocratic military dictatorship, using a largely meretricious Marxist rhetoric – a charge summed up in John Markakis's widely cited phrase, 'garrison socialism'.[6] Much of this criticism is justified. The Ethiopian regime does indeed have a substantial military element in its top leadership, and has readily resorted to force as a response to the chronic economic and political problems which it has faced – and which its own rigidly centralist attitude has often exacerbated. But it is not enough to use this as a pretext for dismissing the Ethiopian experience as a serious attempt to apply 'socialist' solutions to the peculiarly intractable problems facing African states. It may be more helpful, indeed, to regard socialism (in its Leninist form) as a doctrine specially apposite to state consolidation in the Third World, which may be expected to appeal to elites whose primary goal is the creation of a centralised and disciplined structure of political control. This is of course a goal which the military, as the most hierarchically organised section of the state bureaucracy, may be expected to share. The problems of revolutionary state consolidation in Ethiopia, along with many of its achievements, must be ascribed at least in part to the Leninist model itself.

That military rulers do not more often use Leninism as a tool for state formation may be due, not so much to the unacceptability of the goal, as to the difficulty of reconciling this means of achieving it with the military's existing interests and alliances. Military regimes which depend on Western (and especially American) support readily regard 'communism' as the arch-enemy. They may be engaged in warfare against guerrilla opposition movements which draw their inspiration from Marx, and look to anti-communism as an ideological prop to their own nationalist mission. The officer corps often have strong links with social classes whose interests are the first to be threatened by a Leninist ideology which seeks to centralise economic power in the hands of the state. And a Leninist party structure undermines the institutional autonomy of the military itself, which must be subordinated to the control of the party apparatus in a way which undercuts the military command.

All of these obstacles stood in the way of a Leninist military regime in Ethiopia. The Ethiopian military's long-standing dependence on the United States was reinforced, at the time the revolution broke out in 1974, by heavy Soviet support for Ethiopia's main regional rival, the Somali Republic. The insurgency in Eritrea, supported by radical Arab states with Cuban assistance and the indirect backing of the Soviet Union, was articulating an increasingly Marxist rationale for its struggle for separate independence. The army, whose members had been regularly rewarded over the previous century with grants of land in the conquered territories of the south and west, had an evident interest in maintaining the highly exploitative relations of production which this system of land tenure created.

In the hands of the revolutionary regime, Leninism none the less provided a means to consolidate and extend the power of the state, while divorcing it from the bankrupt formula of absolute monarchy which had previously been used to sustain it. Though the outcome of the revolution was at one level the result of bloody power struggles between contending groups and individuals, it also represented, at the level of consciousness, an effective synthesis between a historical tradition of the state which was most strongly entrenched in the military, and a means to implement a conception of centralised state power which could be viewed through the prism of Marxism-Leninism as rational, progressive and above all scientific. The extraordinary determination with which the Ethiopian military regime and its Marxist civilian allies sought to create an institutional structure based on broadly Soviet models was thus derived, not merely from an immediate need for Soviet military aid, but from a '*longue durée*' of political evolution which Ethiopia shared with no other state in Africa. To this end, the military reversed its superpower alliance (exposing itself in the process to the Somali invasion of 1977–8), took over the ideology associated with its secessionist enemies, pushed through a series of far-reaching reforms which destroyed the economic base of the aristocratic and landholding classes, and created a Leninist vanguard party which is rather more than a mere front for the maintenance of military dictatorship. Though the regime's overriding goal is, as under Haile Selassie, the maintenance and extension of a centralised Ethiopian state, the revolutionary transformation of

247

the means to achieve this goal deserves rather greater recognition than it has usually received.

This transformation consisted in three interlocking elements, through which the new regime sought to create the intermediary institutions between central political power and the social and economic base which had been so evidently inadequate under its predecessor: first, the establishment of a new structure of institutional control; second, the drastic reorganisation of the economic basis of state power; and third, a selective widening of political representation. All of these ends were systematically and (for the most part) sincerely pursued, and contributed to the vast extension of state power and effectiveness which has taken place since the revolution. All likewise contained flaws which help to explain the current crisis of the Ethiopian state.

INSTITUTIONAL TRANSFORMATION

The revolutionary regime could, as already noted, draw on the powerful tradition of statehood which had enabled the central Ethiopian highlands to sustain a recognisable political structure over a period of some 2,000 years, and preserve Ethiopia's independence through the colonial scramble for the continent. The revolution resulted in the transformation of a previously largely personal set of relationships, within a characteristically feudal structure of deference and subordination, into institutional relationships of much greater complexity and effectiveness. But the new regime did not have to cope with the problem of creating either the state itself, or the attitudes to authority which sustained it.

The key base-level institutions of revolutionary Ethiopia are the peasants' associations and the urban dwellers' associations (or *kebelles*), which were both established as agencies of local self-administration, replacing mechanisms for rural and urban control which had been destroyed by the great revolutionary reforms of 1975. The rural land reform, which abolished all private land ownership and the private hire of agricultural labour, could be implemented only through an organisation which allocated land within a given area (notionally of 800 hectares, but in practice very variable) among the peasant families which farmed it. The urban land reform, which abolished privately rented housing, likewise required an organisation to allocate housing and collect rents on a communal basis.

These two institutions have now become so firmly established that their disappearance is inconceivable, regardless of what further upheavals Ethiopia may yet have to suffer. They were given from the start a wide range of administrative functions in addition to the basic ones for which they were established, and these have steadily been added to, as each new government programme calls on them for its local level implementation. Every urban house is numbered and registered. The *kebelle* provides (and can, as a punishment, take away) the ration cards which families in major towns need to buy their allocation of subsidised food. It has its own administrative headquarters, its judicial tribunal, its shop, and its women's and youth organisations. It provides the structure through which to run aid projects and literacy campaigns, to get out the crowd for obligatory demonstrations, and to enforce the military conscription. Its armed guards police the streets at night, enforce the curfew and help to make Ethiopian cities remarkably free from violent crime.

The peasants' association provides a similar range of services, with additional responsibilities imposed by the requirements of control over the rural economy. Its most important function is to allocate the basic economic resource, land, among its member families. It may also select families in eroded highland areas for resettlement in the south and west, and serves as the basic unit for the villagisation programme, under which scattered homesteads are being concentrated in villages laid out on a uniform grid – a process which brings peasants much more directly under the control of their associations. And while *kebelles* supervise the distribution of food to their inhabitants, peasants' associations have had the much less popular task of extracting quotas of grain from farmers at government-controlled prices.

While pre-revolutionary landlords and local governors had a position which depended to a large extent on their personal status, the role of *kebelle* and peasants' association chairmen is much more directly created by state power. They are therefore more easily displaced, and more amenable to incorporation into an administrative hierarchy. Initially they had a good deal of autonomy, but since the end of the terror in 1978 they have become government agents under an electoral veneer. *Kebelles* are grouped into 'highers' (or *keftenyas*) and, in the largest cities, zones. Peasants' associations come under the regional administrative hierarchy. These hierarchies are in turn being progressively permeated by party (rather than state) officials. A similar process of centralisation and party penetration has taken place in other mass organisations such as the trade unions and the women's and youth associations. Participation by women in leadership positions is almost entirely restricted to the women's associations, and to posts in the party structure concerned with women's affairs.

The second major institutional structure is the party, established under the guise of the Commission for Organising the Party of the Working People of Ethiopia (COPWE) from late 1979, and formally launched as the Workers' Party of Ethiopia (WPE) in September 1984. A vanguard party constructed on strictly Leninist lines, this is straightforwardly directed from the top. Ritual references to the 'broad masses' barely disguise a political structure which is run by and in the interests of classes dependent on state employment. Government figures attest to the small proportion of party members, and still less of party leaders, who are either peasants or workers. But although emphatically a party of the state apparatus, it is not simply a party of the military. The Political Bureau includes several influential survivors of the group of civilian Marxist intellectuals who were prominent in the early years of the revolution, and as one moves down the party hierarchy, the proportion of military appointeees steadily diminishes. Of the thirty regional party first secretaries announced late in 1988, for example, eighteen were former soldiers, while the great majority of the hundred or so provincial first secretaries are civilians. Most of these are former petty functionaries of the kind who take local level leadership positions in political parties throughout the continent, including schoolteachers, other technical agents of state administration such as health and agricultural employees, and some officials who have crossed the dividing line from the ordinary bureaucracy. Most of them found their way into active politics (some at a very early age) during the upheavals of the mid-1970s.

Party officials take the lead at every level in local administration. Political power in rural Africa is nothing if not visible. Who has the biggest office? Who gives the orders? Who demonstrates deference to whom? In Ethiopia, all of these signs point to the supremacy of the party, even when the provincial first secretary is a former teacher, and the provincial administrator (his counterpart in the state administration) is an ex-army officer. And though the real commitment of party officials to Marxist-Leninist dogma is something that they may well keep to themselves, they certainly have gone through an extensive programme of ideological and organisation training, either in the USSR and Eastern Europe, or in the ideological schools in Ethiopia itself. The total membership of the party was about 30,000 late in 1985, rather less than 0.1 per cent of the total national population, though it has since grown to probably about 80,000 members. Ordinary party members have been expected to take a leading role in implementing government policies such as agricultural resettlement (when groups of cadres were sent to set up special party units in resettlement zones), or villagisation and the establishment of agricultural producers' cooperatives (or collective farms). Many of those whom I have seen, especially in outlying rural areas, perform these tasks with considerable dedication.

Within the military, party officials form a distinct cadre. The former military men (almost all of whom were officers) who hold high positions in the WPE leadership went into politics from 1974 onwards, and (except for the few who still hold military appointments) have long since dropped their military ranks and uniforms. Most of these were members of the Derg, though some (including several personal associates of Mengistu Haile-Maryam) have come in through other channels. Though they hold party positions, the survivors of the Derg are steadily declining in importance with each successive government re-shuffle or organisational change, even when – like Melaku Teferra, the Derg's most brutal strongman and former party first secretary in Gonder – they are not dismissed altogether. Within the armed forces, distinct career patterns separate officers in command positions from those in the party hierarchy, which has developed from the former Military Political Administration of the Armed Forces. Though leading military commanders are members of the Central Committee of the WPE, this is no more than a titular recognition of their status, and their commitment to any form of Marxist-Leninism is sometimes paper-thin. This division between career officers and party officials within the military underlay the attempted *coup d'état* of May 1989, which was led by a group of senior military commanders.

The third leg of the new institutional structure is the military and the civil bureaucracy, vastly expanded in the case of the military from some 45,000 before the revolution to probably about 300,000 from the late 1970s onwards; some estimates of its current strength go as high as half a million. Despite the Somali war of 1977–8, these are, of course, overwhelmingly committed to the demands of internal control, at which in the later 1980s they have proved decreasingly effective. With the partial demobilisation of the peasant levies raised in the late 1970s, numbers have been kept up from the mid-1980s by a regular though selective process of conscription, which has proved increasingly difficult to enforce following successive disasters in the north.

The civilian bureaucracy has also expanded considerably. The only authoratitive figures that I have been able to find show an increase from 109,322 to 167,860 between 1977–8 and 1982–3 in the number of civilian employees financed from the central government budget, an annual growth rate of some 9.5 per cent. Even though civil service salaries have remained unchanged (despite a high rate of inflation) since the revolution, this rate of increase is likely to have slowed in the later 1980s, owing to pressure on tax revenues. It excludes the large growth of employment in *kebelles* and peasants' associations, other mass organisations, and state corporations. And along with the expansion of state regulatory power, 'breaches of regulations' (together with misappropriation of public property and 'crimes against the economy') have overtaken private offences such as assault and theft as the commonest category of crime.

THE ECONOMIC BASIS OF STATE POWER

This vast expansion in the institutional structure of the state was built on a productive base of (even for an African state) quite exceptional fragility. Ethiopia was, and remains, one of the poorest states in the world – on current World Bank figures, it is by some way *the* poorest.[7] It has virtually no commercially exploitable minerals, and at the time of the revolution, when all foreign companies were nationalised without compensation, there were scarcely any companies of any importance to nationalise; the major American enterprise, for which compensation was later agreed at a mere US $5 million, was Kalamazoo Spice, a buying agency for peasant-grown herbs and spices. The level of incorporation into the global economy was one of the lowest in Africa, with some 60 per cent of published exports coming from a single crop, coffee. And that this relative economic autonomy held no evident potential for indigenous economic growth was most starkly demonstrated by the predominance of a peasant mode of production barely able to assure its own subsistence, and vulnerable (as in Wollo and Tigray in 1973/4) to catastrophic famine.

Since the revolution, the whole of the economy (apart from some areas of petty trade) has been brought under state control. Industry is managed through state corporations, and small-scale and handicraft producers have been induced (though not formally compelled) to join together as cooperatives. Though compensation has been agreed for some of the foreign enterprises nationalised in 1974–5, the former management has not returned, and no new foreign businesses have been established. Trade in the commodities most important to government, notably grain and coffee, is closely controlled, and the regime has pursued a policy of voluntary agricultural collectivisation, aided by tax and other inducements. Peasants' association chairmen, for example, can be encouraged to form collectives, and thus gain both official favour and greater control over their own members. A formal structure of command planning was introduced in September 1984 (with the aid of a team of Soviet Gosplan advisers), though its implementation has been impeded both by the impracticability of the plan itself, and by the need to divert resources to meet crises such as famine.

Under the imperial regime, the revenue base of the state was derived largely from a small group of taxes on urban income and consumption. The subsistence sector was virtually untaxable, and even taxes on coffee exports accounted for no more than 6–7 per cent of total government revenues. The revolutionary regime, however, both created and required a vastly greater capacity for surplus extraction, expressed in a rise in government tax revenues from 779.8 million birr in 1973–4 to 1,996.6 million in 1982–3. Much of this increase came from the expropriation of the assets of the former economically dominant classes which after the revolution accrued to the state. By 1982–3, nearly 20 per cent of total government revenues came from 'profits, interest and rent', or in other words from nationalised businesses and urban houses. Direct taxes on trade also rose sharply, and the percentage of coffee export values retained by the producer dropped from an average of 62.3 per cent in 1960–74 to only 41.3 per cent in 1978–84. By far the greater part of the increase in government revenues came immediately after the revolution, in the form of a once-and-for-all rise in extractive capacity; thereafter, the rate of increase tailed off sharply, along with the economy from which the revenues were drawn. Although central government income from the subsistence sector remained at much the same low level (about 5 per cent of total revenues) after the revolution as before, actual exactions from the peasantry were increased by a variety of local demands and special levies, and also by the imposition of quotas for grain which peasants (especially in surplus-producing areas) were required to sell at official prices to government buying agencies. The efficiency of the government's extraction apparatus was indicated by its ability to collect a high proportion of the taxes due even from badly famine-affected regions.[8]

All that this amounted to, however, was the expropriation of an increasing proportion of a diminishing surplus. The underlying level of per capita grain production declined steadily during the later 1970s and the 1980s, independently of the considerable fluctuations due to weather conditions and other local factors. So did the level of coffee and other export crop production (with the possible exception of the narcotic *chat*, which was exported largely to the Arabian peninsula), and stringent controls on internal trade and local consumption were needed to extract enough coffee from the domestic economy to meet Ethiopia's export quota under the International Coffee Agreement. Internal customs posts (a feature of Ethiopia's political economy before 1935) have been reintroduced to control trade in coffee, grain and contraband imported goods, and in the process to demonstrate the level of physical control which the government needs to police the economy. These revenues were used overwhelmingly for consumption purposes, and especially to maintain the military, which by 1988 accounted (on Mengistu Haile-Maryam's admission) for about half of government expenditure and 15 per cent of gross domestic product.[9] Such funds as remained for investment were disproportionately channelled into a small number of highly capitalised enterprises, with low rates of return, including the state farms and a few showpiece industrial projects built with Eastern European assistance.

A further critical aspect of revolutionary surplus expropriation is its geographical distribution. The economy that matters is concentrated almost entirely in the centre, south and west of the country, in areas that have remained under firm government control. The major coffee-producing regions, notably Kaffa and Sidamo, are in the southwest. By far the greater part of surplus grain is grown in the three central regions of Shoa, Arsi and Gojjam, together with adjacent areas of northern Bale and Welega. *Chat* production is heavily concentrated in highland Hararge, while such industry as Ethiopia possesses is almost all in Addis Ababa, or strung out along the road and rail links south and east of the city. The areas of major insurgent activity, both in the north (Eritrea, Tigray, and northern Gonder and Wollo) and in the Ogaden, produce virtually no marketable surplus, and are also the regions most chronically short of food. The most important exception is the farming complex around Humera on the Sudanese border in north-west Gonder, where sesame seed cultivation expanded dynamically in the years immediately before the revolution. In the 1980s, however, even before Humera was lost to the government early in 1989, the state farms in the area, together with those in western Eritrea, were maintained at a substantial loss for symbolic purposes. Despite the enormous drain of resources to fight the wars in the north, the amount of direct damage that they have done to the sections of the economy required for state maintenance has therefore been surprisingly slight.

THE STRUCTURE OF REPRESENTATION

The major impetus for revolutionary transformation comes from a massive expansion of popular participation in political life. People become involved in politics to an extent, and in ways, that were previously inconceivable. This has certainly occurred in Ethiopia, even though this participation is not free or democratic in any Western liberal sense of the words. The elections to institutions such as the National Shengo (or supreme soviet) established since 1987 under the constitution of the People's Democratic Republic of Ethiopia (PDRE) are very little more than a rubber-stamping of central nominations. Even within local level institutions such as *kebelles* and peasants' associations, the leadership (though drawn from local residents) is effectively put in place by higher state or party officials. But none the less, the 'broad masses' (as they are usually termed) have been brought into politics through measures such as land reform and the abolition of private rented housing, through frequent meetings of *kebelles*, peasants' associations and other mass organisations, and through the expansion of education and literacy.

The central political problem for any revolutionary regime is to combine this increased level of participation with the requirements of state consolidation. At one level, this has been achieved in Ethiopia through the institutional structure already outlined. The draft constitution of the PDRE, for example, was discussed at meetings of *kebelles*, peasants' associations and other mass organisations throughout the country (and indeed abroad), and a number of amendments (none of which affected the basic provisions of the document) were made as a result. The most significant was the abandonment of a commitment to monogamy, in deference to Muslim wishes. At another level, that of formal state ideology, there seems to me to have been very little attempt to articulate any sophisticated application of Marxism to a society at Ethiopia's level of development. The inculcation of Marxism in schools and mass organisations is simplistic and mechanical, and constant invocation of the 'broad masses' substitutes in official rhetoric for any serious class analysis.

But by far the most critical area is the representation of ethnic or regional interests, commonly described as 'nationalities'. For the past century (precisely, since the Emperor Menilek's accession in 1889), the political and geographical centre of Ethiopia has been Shoa, a region of mixed Oromo, Amhara and other peoples, most of whose population is of Oromo origin, even though much of it is assimilated to Amhara language and culture. Many Shoans are ethnically unidentifiable. Given its ethnic heterogeneity, its geographical centrality, its dominance of the state, and its key position in the modern externally oriented economy, this Shoan core has had an evident interest in articulating a composite Ethiopian nationalism – just as, conversely, the regions to the north have developed their own peripheral nationalisms, in response to their increasing economic marginalisation and their distance from the new centres of political power. This Ethiopian nationalism has likewise – and equally understandably, in keeping with their own interests and mission – become deeply entrenched in central government institutions, and notably the armed forces.

The revolutionary leadership sought from the start, under the slogan *Ityopya tikdem* or Ethiopia First, to mobilise this composite nationalism as a source of popular unity, and to extend its appeal by removing elements of traditional political identity, such as adherence to Orthodox Christianity, which prevented it from serving as a fully national symbol. This leadership was itself drawn from a wide variety of ethnic origins. The first chairman of the Provisional Military Administrative Council, Aman Andom, was Eritrean; the second, Teferi Benti, was a Shoan Oromo; Mengistu Haile-Maryam is generally regarded as of Wollamo origin, from Sidamo in the south; the former second-ranking member of the Derg and subsequent vice-president, Fisseha Desta, is from Tigray; the third-ranking member and prime minister, Fikre-Selassie Wogderes, is a Shoan of indeterminate ethnicity from a largely Oromo area. Given this range of origins, as well as the regime's willingness to overthrow the previous structure of domination indicated by land reform, there is no reason to regard its commitment to an undifferentiated Ethiopian nationalism as merely the cover for 'Amhara domination' which it is frequently portrayed as by its opponents.

This nationalist commitment was allied to a Jacobin emphasis on centralisation. Apart from a brief period early in the revolution, when the Derg (under the influence of its then civilian ally, Meison) appointed governors of local origin to the major southern regions, its concern was almost exclusively with central control. Where, as in much of southern Ethiopia, the revolution brought evident benefits to the mass of the population by abolishing the previously exploitative structure of landholding, this centralisation was broadly acceptable, and enabled many areas of the country to be much more effectively incorporated into a national political structure than ever before. Where, as in Gonder or Tigray, land reform had little to offer a peasantry which already largely controlled its own means of prouction, and traditions of local autonomy were well entrenched, centralisation was catastrophically counterproductive. Regional representatives of the Derg, reacting repressively to what they saw as 'narrow nationalism', regional chauvinism, peasant backwardness or outright counter-revolutionary activity, succeeded only in driving large areas of the country into the arms of the opposition.

It is here worth emphasising the striking discrepancy between the charges of ethnic domination often brought against the Ethiopian central government, and the actual distribution of effective regional opposition to the regime. The areas of effective opposition – highland Eritrea, Tigray, northern Wollo and Gonder – are for the most part Orthodox Christian regions, inhabited by Tigrinya and even Amharic-speaking peoples, which have been closely associated with the Ethiopian state since the earliest times; their people have been readily recruited to central government institutions (though in appreciably smaller numbers than the Shoans), and they have suffered little evident economic exploitation. The recently conquered regions of the south and west, on the other hand, have been culturally far less closely attuned to the dominant group, have been subject to a vastly greater level of economic exploitation, and have been virtually excluded from central government office; yet attempts by Oromo and other opposition movements to mobilise ethnic identities against the central government have achieved nothing remotely approaching the success of the opposition movements in the north. It is economic marginalisation, not ethnic discrimination, that accounts for the 'national question' in modern Ethiopia.

Despite the high level of regional opposition, there is no reason to suppose that the regime has abandoned its centralist priorities. The constitution of the PDRE introduced in 1987, though it makes provision for 'autonomous regions' in addition to ordinary administrative regions, at the same time makes clear that Ethiopia is a unitary state, and both the powers and the boundaries of the regions can at any time be changed by the National Shengo in Addis Ababa. The WPE is likewise a unitary organisation, guided by the principles of democratic centralism, to which local party organs are subservient. I am not aware of any pronouncement by Mengistu Haile-Maryam, or anyone else in the top party leadership, indicating that local autonomy or the identities of individual nationalities are to be valued in themselves, rather than forced on the leadership in response to conditions that it cannot control.

None the less, the central government has been obliged to make at least some formal concessions to demands for regional autonomy. From early in the revolution, the regime started broadcasting in other languages than Amharic; and from 1979 the national literacy campaign was conducted in fifteen 'nationality languages', even though its main function was to make people literate in Amharic. With the introduction of the PDRE, a formal structure of local government was created, which entailed an almost complete redrawing of the regional boundaries which had existed (with minor modifications) since the early 1940s. These boundaries were drawn up by a think-tank manned largely by academics, the Institute for the Study of Ethiopian Nationalities, which did its work with considerable sophistication. The areas inhabited by different peoples were carefully demarcated, and used (in conjunction with other criteria, such as transport networks) to create a set of thirty regions which corresponded as accurately as possible to the mosaic of Ethiopian nationalities.

These changes had an evident political rationale as well, in that by offering local peoples their own region, they could provide a counterweight to the demands of the various separatist movements. The Afar, a nomadic people scattered across the Red Sea plain, were offered an autonomous region drawn from Afar-inhabited areas of Eritrea, Tigray and Wollo, thus denying the claims of the EPLF to an Eritrean state which followed the old Italian colonial boundaries. The remainder of Eritrea, which was accorded the status of an autonomous region with special powers, was subdivided into three subordinate administrative regions which broadly corresponded to the needs of ethnic representation, political allegiance, and strategic control. But the fact that these boundaries were redrawn late in 1988, in response to requests from a delegation claiming to represent the Muslim-dominated ELF, shows how the new regional structure could be altered at will from the centre. The Somali-inhabited areas were divided into different regions corresponding to the Issa clan (which has maintained a peaceful *modus vivendi* with the Ethiopian government), the Isaq clans (which generally support the anti-Siyad SNM), and the Darod clans (which have most strongly supported the incorporation of the Somali-inhabited areas of Ethiopia into the Somali Republic). Peripheral peoples such as the Boran in the south, and the Anuak and Nuer in the Gambela salient on the Sudanese border, also gained regions of their own. The whole exercise indicated a political sensitivity such as the Ethiopian government has very rarely shown; if Ethiopia under any regime is to have a structure of local government which roughly corresponds to its ethnic diversity, this demarcation has as good a chance of providing it as any.

The problems lie in its implementation. Before the long process of reorganising local government had even started, it was postponed following the military disaster at Afabet in March 1988, while the government concentrated all its resources on stabilising the position in Eritrea – an apt commentary on the subordination of long-term planning to desperate crisis management, which echoed the coincidence between the announcement of the Ten-Year Plan and the famine crisis in September 1984. The names of the WPE first secretaries in the new regions were announced late in 1988, and indicated the contrasting priorities of representation and control. In some regions, such as the Afar autonomous region and Gambela, the new first secretaries were local men with previously very junior status in the party; neither was even an alternate member of the Central Committee. In regions such as Eritrea, Tigray and Ogaden, they were drawn from the senior political cadres of the armed forces, and had virtually no local standing at all. Elsewhere there was a mixture; though several old Derg members remained, they were mostly assigned to regions with which they had some connection, while the number of civilians was increased. Had the new structure been introduced much earlier in the revolution, and at a time when there was general acquiescence with the basic goals of the regime, there would have been at least a chance that it might have provided an acceptable balance between the demands of national unity and the recognition of regional diversity. Coming so late in the day, from a regime with an intense commitment to central control, its prospects are much more uncertain, even outside areas such as Tigray and Eritrea where simple lack of government control prevents its implementation.

In Ethiopia, as in France, the Soviet Union, and the People's Republic of China, revolution has served as a means of centralising state power on the foundation provided by a decaying monarchy. The Ethiopian revolution has failed to live up to the example of those earlier revolutions, not because it has been too ruthlessly autocratic, but because (in a sense) it has proved unable to be autocratic enough. Despite an intense concern for political organisation, and a massive expansion in the apparatus of state power, it has been unable to surmount the limitations imposed, first, by the extremely fragile and undeveloped economy on which the state is perched and, second, by regional resistance movements which have become increasingly effective as the weaknesses of the central state have been exposed.

Much that the revolution has achieved has now been established beyond any serious possibility of reversal. Ethiopia has a highly effective structure of rural and urban government, and an equitable system of landholding. The educational system has been greatly expanded, and literacy vastly increased. Many of the reforms introduced by the central government have been adopted by the regional opposition movements in Eritrea and Tigray, which – trying to construct a similar political apparatus on a similar social base, and confronting much the same problems of military survival and decaying peasant agriculture – often resemble the regime which they oppose.

The regime's most basic failure, however, has been to see state power as the answer to all its problems. It has regarded the imposition of a centralised state and party structure as the solution to the problem of national unity, almost regardless of regional diversities which demand, at the very least, substantial opportunities for local autonomy. It has regarded a centrally directed economy as the only answer to the problem of development, almost regardless likewise of the demonstratable inefficiencies of state direction, especially in agriculture. The demands of revolutionary state consolidation have in turn required the construction of a greatly expanded state apparatus on an economic base which is increasingly obviously unable to support it.

Whereas in much of sub-Saharan Africa, there has been a real problem of how to create effective political power, in Ethiopia the problem of power has thus been one, not of how to create power, but rather of what can be done with it. It has been widely assumed in the Third World (and not just in Ethiopia) that the key to 'development' is the organisational capacity of the state. From this viewpoint, the essential task is to forge the state as an effective power tool, characterised by hierarchy, discipline, honesty and efficiency, which can then be used in order to create prosperity, welfare, national unity, or whatever other goals are sought by the national leadership. This conception of the instrumental state is particularly intense in revolutionary situations, since it appeals very strongly to revolutionary elites, who look to state power as the means to implement their policies of social and economic transformation – an attitude encapsulated in the central role of the 'plan', through which the goals of the top leadership are (in a phrase constantly on the lips of the present Ethiopian ruling elite) 'transformed into deeds'. In Ethiopia this attitude is reinforced by a long tradition of government from the top, which has scarcely been affected by a revolution whose function has been to transform the conditions of social and economic existence, rather than to replace a hierarchy by a more participatory form of government. Government in Ethiopia is a matter for experts who know what to do; the ignorant peasant, by contrast, is there to be organised, villagised, cooperativised, resettled, conscripted, taxed, or, in a word, governed.

There is no more dramatic symbol of the power of these mental constructs in shaping the way in which people live than the villages which, since 1985, have sprung up all over the Ethiopian countryside. Their identical houses laid out in ruler-straight lines, the placement of compounds, offices, even latrines, is strictly in accordance with the guidelines issued from Addis Ababa.[10] The 'rationality' of the central plan is thus made to substitute for the converse rationality of peasant agriculture, under which homesteads had previously been scattered according to the dictates of shelter, drainage, or proximity to resources such as fields and water.

The conjunction in Ethiopia of perhaps the most powerful indigenous state structure in Africa with probably its poorest economy, and the persistence of chronic problems of famine and civil war which appear to be well beyond the state's capacity to resolve, thus raise doubts about the appropriateness of the model of purposive state action as the motor for development which is shared, it would seem to me, by government and opposition movements alike. There are, of course, some goals which this model is well adapted to achieve, because they require the hierarchical organisation which it provides. The most obvious of these is raising an army, and the mass mobilisation of 1977–8, which (quite as much as Soviet weapons or Cuban support) defeated the Somali invasion and contained the EPLF in Eritrea, remains one of the most dramatic achievements of the central regime. That the Ethiopian army has not been more effective in Eritrea must at least in part be due to the fact that it has been fighting an Eritrean revolutionary army which is every bit as well organised as itself, and has the further incentive of fighting for survival in its own territory. At a more mundane level, both government and opposition movements can achieve a high level of effectiveness in tasks such as literacy campaigns or relief aid distribution, which likewise depend on hierarchical organisation.

But there are two very basic problems which do not respond to management through centralised hierarchy; these, uncoincidentally, are the two main failures of revolutionary Ethiopia. The first is the problem of meeting the aspirations of groups which cannot simply be incorporated into a homogenised nationalism, whether this national-ism be Ethiopian, or indeed Eritrean. The system is remarkably good at incorporating, on terms at any rate approaching equality, anyone who wishes to be fully assimilated into it. Even the government administration in Eritrea is very largely manned by indigenous Eritreans. But a government structure based on hierarchy is corre-spondingly weak at acknowledging any separate identity for groups which wish to maintain their own distinctiveness. Exactly the same problem has handicapped the resistance movements in Eritrea. The ELF's initial insistence on a Muslim (or even Arab) dimension to Eritrean nationalism inherently restricted its appeal to Christian Eritreans. The EPLF, in extending its appeal within a Marxist framework to Eritreans of all ethnic and religious persuasions, has been reluctant to acknowledge internal ethnic or religious qualifica-tions to its own conception of a homogeneous Eritrean nationalism, and has thereby limited its capacity to gain support from groups, such as the Kunama and Afar, which have a distinct identity of their own.

The second is the problem of managing agrarian transformation, and especially of growing food. A classic deficiency of Leninist systems of government throughout the world, this would seem to stem not so much from ideological objections to rural class formation (or kulakisation) as from the needs of central surplus expropriation. The measures, such as cooperativisation and villagisation, which have been encouraged by the government ostensibly in order to promote a more efficient structure of agricultural production, in practice have as their main effect the concentration of production into a smaller number of large units which are much easier to control than scattered rural homesteads. There is no evidence at all that they actually promote more efficient production, let alone any increase in yields per hectare, and the available evidence for agricultural producers' cooperatives runs strongly in the contrary direction. The main function of cooperatives is, rather, indicated by the requirement that they sell their entire marketed output to the Agricultural Marketing Corporation at state-controlled prices. The role of the state farms in providing grain for government disposal is even more evident, as is their absorption of a very high proportion of the capital available for agricultural investment. This grain is in turn required to feed the cities and the Army. The political imperatives of averting urban unrest and maintaining the apparatus of state control, oblige the government to pay prices to peasants which provide a strong disincentive to production. Agricultural production in the parts of Tigray and Eritrea controlled by the opposition movements has been disrupted by warfare, and these areas have in any case normally had to import grain since long before the revolution; but there is little evidence to suggest that either the EPLF or the TPLF has achieved anything approaching the level of effectiveness in agricultural production that they have done in military organisation.

The key problem in each case is that the state cannot achieve its goals because success requires a devolution of decision-making, either to the local level or to the market, which challenges the Leninist model of the all-powerful party-state. In a broader sense, the intermediary institutions which the Ethiopian government has struggled so hard to create are not real intermediaries between state and people at all. They are mechanisms through which to express the superior wisdom of a government which, whether this wisdom derived from divine right or Marxism-Leninism, has had no real interest in establishing a dialogue with its own people.

The question of the level of regional or market autonomy which is compatible with a Leninist political structure is currently at issue throughout the socialist world, most dramatically in the Soviet Union itself; the Ethiopian government (under strong external pressure) has recently made some concessions on both counts, through the regional government reforms already discussed, and through the adoption of changes in agricultural marketing urged on it both by the World Bank, and by the team of Soviet Gosplan advisers attached to the Ethiopian planning office. There has, none the less, been no real sign of any willingness on the part of the Ethiopian government to relinquish the central control which constitutes the basic rationale for a Leninist political structure. It is indeed virtually inconceivable that any effective regional autonomy could be implemented while the present government headed by Mengistu Haile-Maryam remains in power; his ruthless suppression of all opposition has been such that none of the movements whose acceptance of autonomy is essential to its success would be likely to accept any role under his leadership.[11] The most recent attempt to open the way to negotiation with the separatist movements in the north, by removing Mengistu, ended in bloody failure in May 1989. The impasse thus remains. But the underlying problem is one, not of personality, but of the adequacy of the model which Mengistu has come to embody.

Ali Mazrui once wrote that 'The real danger posed by state socialism in a society with fragile institutions is not a danger of making the government too strong but the risk of making it more

263

conspicuously ineffectual.'[12] The institutions of revolutionary government in Ethiopia are not fragile, and the government is conspicuously strong, but much of Mazrui's warning is still valid. In so starkly demonstrating its own limitations, it has delivered a severe and possibly terminal blow to the idea that the creation of a powerful state and party apparatus on broadly Leninist lines offers a plausible solution to the crisis of African development.

POSTSCRIPT

During the year after this study was completed in July 1989, the crisis of the Ethiopian state rapidly intensified, as a result both of its own internal weaknesses and of developments in the international system as a whole. Domestically the government's demoralised armies, greatly weakened by the removal of many of their leading commanders after the attempted *coup d'état* of May 1989, suffered major defeats both in Eritrea and further south. The loss of the port of Massawa in February 1990 left a large Ethiopian army surrounded in the Eritrean highlands, suppliable only by air. The TPLF and its allies overran much of Wollo region from September 1989 onwards, and penetrated into Shoa. The regime made desperate efforts to plug each gap in its defences, and in June 1990 Mengistu Haile-Maryam warned of imminent national collapse.

Only to a very limited extent could this collapse be directly ascribed to events in Eastern Europe and the Soviet Union. Although the USSR signalled a desire to disengage from the Horn, and was increasingly reluctant to supply additional weapons to the Mengistu regime, it was not the lack of weapons so much as the loss of capacity to use them that made the difference on the ground. The Ethiopian economy had never disengaged from Western markets and suppliers, and was only marginally affected by the collapse of Comecon. The spectacular failure of the Leninist model in Eastern Europe, together with the Soviet Union's evident unwillingness to sustain the expensive commitments of the Brezhnev era, none the less had knock-on effects for the most explicitly Leninist state in Africa. In March 1990 Mengistu announced the formal abandonment of Marxism-Leninism, and even offered to convert the Workers' Party of Ethiopia into a Democratic Unity Party open to the regime's opponents – an offer which, unsurprisingly, was not taken up. The regime restored diplomatic relations with Israel, in an act of desperation borne of the need to find a regional ally and arms supplier, even at the cost of exacerbating relations with neighbouring Arab states.

Analogous developments took place within the insurgent movements. The EPLF, which gained much of its financial support from the Eritrean community abroad, especially in the United States, had long been adept at combining a Leninist structure of internal control with an external rhetoric appealing to liberal principles of national self-determination, but shifted (at least for external purposes) towards a more explicitly capitalist approach to economic development. The TPLF, lacking such external contacts and constraints, had as late as November 1989 touted an Albanian model of autonomous socialist development; this became muted during the first half of 1990, as its leadership became aware of the negligible appeal of such a programme, either within Ethiopia or outside.

But while the Leninist model of state consolidation and economic development in Ethiopia had for public purposes virtually disappeared, it was far less easy to see what could take its place. Unlike Eastern Europe, there was no plausible escape route into either liberal democracy or capitalist development. And though the formal ideology was abandoned, the ruling groups that espoused it still controlled both the central government and the insurgent movements, and depended on the centralised structures through which their former policies had been pursued. At one level, the failure of numerous attempts at reconciliation reflected both tactical considerations (especially on the part of the insurgent movements, which saw no incentive for negotiation at the moment of apparent military triumph), and the determination of the existing leaderships to cling to their positions of power. More basically, however, it indicated an inability to find any alternative to a model of centralised statehood which could all too evidently be seen to have failed.

NOTES

Much of this contribution draws on my book, *Transformation and Continuity in Revolutionary Ethiopia* (Cambridge, 1988) and sources noted in the book are not footnoted here.

1. If this seems disputable, it may be helpful to consider when last an ethnic Amhara held the supreme position in the Ethiopian state. Mengistu Haile-Maryam, though his origins are uncertain, is generally regarded as of Wollamo parentage (at least on his father's side), from northern Sidamo or southern Shoa. He was preceded by an Oromo, Teferi Benti

(1974–7), who in turn took over from an Eritrean, Aman Andom (1974). Nor could even Haile Selassie (1930–74) be regarded as unequivocally Amhara: he was more Oromo than anything else, with elements of Amhara and Gurage. Zawditu (1916–30) and Menilek (1989–1913) had probably the best claims to Amhara ethnicity, though again with Oromo elements, while Iyasu (1913–16) identified himself strongly with his father's Wollo Oromo people. Yohannes (1872–89) was Tigrayan. It is scarcely possible to find an unequivocally Amhara ruler of Ethiopia in the last 120 years.

2. See J. Markakis, *National and Class Conflict in the Horn of Africa* (Cambridge, 1987).
3. *Ibid.*, pp. 198 ff.
4. See P. Schwab, *Decision-Making in Ethiopia* (London, 1972) pp. 158–69; J. Markakis, *Ethiopia: Anatomy of a Traditional Polity* (Oxford, 1974) pp. 376–87.
5. See S. P. Huntington, *Political Order in Changing Societies* (New Haven, Conn., 1968) ch. 5.
6. See J. Markakis, *National and Class Conflict . . .*, chs 8–9.
7. The World Bank, *World Development Report 1989* (Washington, DC, 1989) p. 164, gives Ethiopia's GNP per capita in 1987 as \$130, compared with \$150 for the next poorest state in the world; there are also a few states for which figures are not available.
8. This point is made in an interesting paper, Adhana Haile Adhana, 'Peasant Response to Famine in Ethiopia 1975–85', International Conference on Environmental Stress and Security, Stockholm (December 1988).
9. Mengistu Haile-Maryam, Speech to the Ninth Session of the Central Committee of the WPE (7 November 1988).
10. J. M. Cohen and N. I. Isaksson, *Villagization in the Arsi Region of Ethiopia* (Uppsala, 1987), show an aerial photograph of a village, with the corresponding plan from the government guidelines; I have noted the same phenomenon while flying over Ethiopia.
11. At the time of writing, the first publicly acknowledged talks between the Ethiopian government and the EPLF are taking place; their outcome remains unclear.
12. Ali Mazrui and M. Tidy, *Nationalism and New States in Africa* (London, 1984) p. 294

CHAPTER TWELVE

Successful Economic Development and Political Change in Taiwan and South Korea

Eberhard Sandschneider

In undertaking a comparison of Taiwan and South Korea, we shift the reader's attention not only regionally to East Asia, but also thematically, since we must address a different set of questions. We are not so much occupied with problems of development and reasons for economic failure, as with problems resulting from extraordinary economic success. We focus first on why these countries developed at all; second, on why they developed in such a remarkably successful way; and third, on what the political and social results of that success are or may be.

THE CHARACTERISTICS OF ECONOMIC DEVELOPMENT IN TAIWAN AND SOUTH KOREA

The list of aspects discussed below – comparative aspects of these economic success stories – is certainly not exhaustive and is not meant to be so. My argument is that these and perhaps other features helped to achieve development, although they cannot fully explain it. As general prerequisites, however, they are of specific historical and thus also analytical importance. The multiplicity of factors at work in both countries' economic, social and political development processes are in the following survey structured along an external vs. internal dividing line.

Three major *external features* are presented here. The first is the powerful Chinese cultural impact. Historically speaking, both Taiwan and South Korea were for centuries strongly influenced politically, economically and culturally by their towering and overwhelming neighbour, China. They share, therefore, the historical legacy of a Confucian heritage, which is characterised by 'strong and economically active states, traditions of social and political hierarchy and strong national sentiments underpinned by cultural homogeneity and reinforced by external threats'.[1] All of these aspects may to a considerable extent be recognised again in today's development.

The second feature is the considerable infrastructural help provided during the period of Japanese occupation (1895–1945). Especially during the period of wartime occupation, the Japanese heavily invested in such areas as road- and railroad-building for military reasons. The products of these investments could be used in the early economic development efforts after 1945.[2]

The third feature was Western aid and technology transfer. In addition to a highly favourable international environment, substantial and continuous help from Western countries, especially the United States, contributed greatly to the growth of financial, educational, scientific and technological know-how.

As far as foreign investment and world market mechanisms are concerned, however, both systems falsify major assumptions of dependency theory. Foreign economic penetration neither led to a slow-down in economic growth, nor to heightened inequality. On the contrary, both economic growth and the process of equal income distribution were accelerated and improved by foreign capital influx.[3] And – as Liebenstein has correctly stated – there was also an implicit further advantage to Western help: 'Late starters do not have to live through the technological mistakes made by those who experimented with technologies earlier. They can, as it were, choose from the sub-set of techniques that have proven themselves.'[4] Thus, the economic latecomer status was turned into a major comparative advantage.

Among the most important *internal features*, there is first the issue of natural resources and geographical size. Both systems are characterised by limited natural resources, which should have made economic success even less probable – as was the widespread opinion during the 1950s and the early 1960s. To be sure, more resources are better than less. But Taiwan and South Korea, as well as Japan and Switzerland, have proved that successful economic development with high growth rates and high per capita income are possible with extremely limited natural resources. Furthermore, with 36,188 square kilometres for Taiwan and 98,484 sq. km for South Korea, it is quite evident that infrastructural or distributional policies are much easier, faster and cheaper to implement than for example in mainland China with its 9,561 million sq. km.

A second important internal aspect concerns population and population growth, an extremely difficult and pressing problem for all Third World countries, but again effectively and successfully managed both by Taiwan and by South Korea. Taiwan, with presently 19.14 million people and 528.8 inhabitants per square kilometre, as well as South Korea, with its 41.84 million people and 428.8 inhabitants per square kilometre, both have a comparatively restricted population size and – even more important – a controlled and balanced population growth at a rate of 1.1 per cent for Taiwan and 1.5 per cent for South Korea in 1988. By comparison, China with its roughly 1.3 billion people and a growth rate of 1.4 per cent is much worse off.[5]

Third and finally, both countries have cheap and industrious labour forces. While old values have crumbled and new ones still are considered suspect,[6] there is the declared and definite will of the people of both countries to get 'modern', which (if you talk to them) first and foremost means to get rich and if possible still richer.

These factors – and I have mentioned only the most important, both externally and internally – certainly facilitated development without being able to explain exactly why Taiwan and South Korea and not Brazil, Spain or others produced the biggest economic miracles in the second half of our century. What follows is a series of more systematic questions. What are the basic characteristics of developmental strategies in both systems? What is the interrelationship between economic development, social change and political transition? What are the lessons for successful economic development which can be learned from the Taiwan and South Korean cases?

DEVELOPMENT STRATEGY

Political regimes in divided nations usually seek to legitimise themselves by trying to be successfully different – economically and socially in the case of Taiwan and South Korea (and the Federal Republic of Germany), politically and ideologically in the People's Republic of China and North Korea (and the former German Democratic Republic).

The general explanation of economists for Taiwan's and South Korea's economic miracles has been summarised by Ian Little in terms of four key elements: 'the creation of a virtual free trade regime for exports, conservative government budgeting, high interest rates and a free labour market'.[7] True as this may be, it neglects the real

269

historical lesson from these two systems. The view presented below offers a different perspective and emphasises four distinctive aspects of success:

1 redistribution before growth cycles
2 balancing import substitution and export orientation
3 rise in educational standards
4 the transition from authoritarianism

Redistribution before Growth Cycles

Both Taiwan and South Korea followed the same path in their economic development strategies, which can be summarised as follows: relying on an export-led, open, labour- and skill-intensive growth process, they followed the 'redistribution-before-productivity-improvement sequence dynamically at each stage of the development process'.[8]

The first major step was taken in both countries with an extensive and successful land reform. These reforms initiated a dynamic process of economic change in the countryside which can be described as a four-stage model. An agrarian economy with low productivity was, after the land reform, turned into an agrarian economy with high productivity and then started to move on to a mixed agrarian/commercial economy, and finally to a mixed agrarian/commercial/industrial economy with a growing stress on the commercial/industrial sector.

However, redistribution before growth alone cannot explain the enormous economic success of Taiwan and South Korea, since other systems – such as China and Yugoslavia – also redistributed land, but could not follow up with comparable economic successes. This leads us to a second distinctive feature of their economic success.

Balancing Import Substitution and Export Orientation

In both countries – as we have already seen – there was not an abundance of natural resources. As Irma Adelman correctly observed, it was therefore

> quite apparent that an acceleration of their growth could only be based on a labour-intensive industrial process. At first, this industrialization was oriented toward import substitution, that is, toward increasing domestic production of previously imported goods. . . . In the middle to late 1960's, however, import substitution possibilities were exhausted, and

there was a shift in both countries toward export-oriented, labour-intensive development. And that effort was extremely successful both in terms of growth and in terms of distribution. Both Korea and Taiwan underwent within one generation a development process which put them in the ranks of developed countries. In that process they more than tripled the household incomes of the poorest members of their populations.[9]

From a purely economic perspective, this factor best explains how Taiwan and South Korea could develop in that rapid and successful way.

Rise in Educational Standards

Here we find a similar situation for all East Asian societies, namely the combined heritage of traditional and Confucian education principles. The classic ideal in Chinese art, literature and culture was not to create something new and progressive, but instead to imitate the old and (both technically and aesthetically) to come as close to the standards of the old masterpieces as possible. This cannot be the ideal of a modernising society.

Furthermore, these countries had to bridge the cognitive gap between what the Chinese still best characterise as '*chabuduozhuyi*' (the principle of doing something at a guess) and the educational requirements of absolute precision for our technical age within just a few years – a process for which European countries needed approximately one and a half generations in the second half of the nineteenth century.

Therefore both countries heavily invested in the educational sector, building schools, training teachers, sending students abroad, and so on. It was, however, not only a matter of high material investment in the educational sector, but also the taking over of the Japanese principle of 'innovative imitation' – where imitation derives from the classical Confucian heritage, while innovation refers to the embellishments leading to economic success – the ability to develop further and improve an imported technology. Again the improvement of educational standards both by Taiwan and South Korea is – in itself – not sufficient to serve as a satisfactory explanation of their economic success.

The Transition from Authoritarianism

Recent events in China have taught a clear lesson: human beings cannot be divided into two parts – a '*homo economicus*' who is flexible, active and full of initiative and a '*homo politicus*' who is obedient and loyal to whatever person or policy is offered to him. If you want to raise economic efficiency, you will sooner or later be forced to allow a 'marketisation of politics' as well.[10] And the virtues of a market-orientated economy are the exact opposite of those which leave dictators with an undisturbed sleep.

It has meanwhile become a well-established historical rule that economic success leads to social change, since the separation between politics and society tends to diminish in the context of economic development. Rising social tensions consequently lead to a point where simple political measures to suppress social tensions are doomed to failure. The increasing dysfunctionality of the status quo system then leads to growing political destabilisation and to the need for political change. The margin between functionality and dysfunctionality of a modernising authoritarian system is very narrow.

The major problem of both Taiwan and South Korea today seems to be that – after impressively reaching the status of NICs, 'Newly Industrialising Countries' – they are now forced to proceed to the difficult status of NDCs, 'Newly Democratising Countries'. This process is always painful and difficult and their respective paths towards political development will certainly be more thorny than any stage of economic development already behind them. The ensuing problems are dealt with below.

ECONOMIC DEVELOPMENT AND POLITICAL CHANGE

The Institutional Framework: Authoritarianism

Both Taiwan and South Korea must be characterised as authoritarian political regimes which, for the purposes of this discussion, are defined in two ways. The first, a phenomenological definition, states that an authoritarian regime or system is a

> type of political system, in which political power is monopolised by a ruling group or a ruling party that does not try to regulate every aspect of social and personal life, . . . [in which] the political monopoly is based on the principle of development towards a developed industrial mass society, . . . [in which] the pluralising factors are mainly provided by functional groups based on divergent interests of political and administrative sub-systems; . . . [and in which] the parameters of political competition slowly tend to widen, as elements of differentiation are cautiously articulated.[11]

In the second, functional definition, an authoritarian system is characterised by three distinctive features:

1 It acts as a political monopolist – not in the sense of weapons or legal monopolies, but in the sense that an institutionally exclusive leadership body is dominated by a non-competitive elite group.
2 It acts as a social controller, suppressing dysfunctional social pressures and tensions for the sake of relatively undisturbed economic development.
3 It acts as an economic catalyst, playing an active and even aggressive role in the industrialisation process by emphasising the mobilisation of finance (both domestic and foreign) and by targeting it into investments that raise productivity.[12]

While stressing the important role of 'states' in processes of successful latecomer development, a set of important caveats must also be taken into account. As Cal Clark and Jonathan Lemco correctly stated, a state's development strategy may fail due to a lack of resources or due to an inability to reach originally intended results.[13] One may add that such a strategy may also fail, despite the largely successful implementation of economically intended results, because they turn out to be highly disruptive in that they are politically and ideologically disrupted within the leadership elite. This leads us to a further caveat, namely that the pursuit of specific regime goals may undercut and even terminate a system's developmental efficiency. And finally, as the events in Beijing in the summer of 1989 have clearly demonstrated, political problems may arise from the state's inability to maintain supportive developmentalist coalitions.

Given these major caveats, a simplistic equation, 'strong states = development', is misleading at best. In other words, it is not the state but statecraft – a state's ability continuously and flexibly to undertake policies conducive to its development aims[14] – that matters in the process of successful and sustained economic development.

If compared, for example with the far less successful developmental experience of Communist China and formulated in a set of dichotomies, the major elements of Taiwan's and South Korea's statecraft become apparent. They include adherence to the principles of economic and intellectual openness instead of isolationism, political adaptation and flexibility instead of rigidity, strategic pragmatism instead of ideological purity, economic gradualism instead of revolutionary leaps, and a retreat from society instead of penetrating and dominating society. Consequently their developmental path and success may (and perhaps should) be imitated strategically, but it can certainly not be copied historically.

With our earlier definition of authoritarian systems in mind, the hypothesis suggested here is that – in the context of early and middle stages of development – an authoritarian system may be more functional for supporting the modernisation process than representative systems, because it offers a specific set of comparative advantages. As a political monopolist, it has the capacity to redistribute and to direct educational investments with lower frictions than any other type of political system. As a social controller, it has the capacity to suppress social tensions and dysfunctional frictions, while at the same time encouraging and strengthening society's efforts to achieve the ultimate aims of modernisation. As an economic catalyst, it has the capacity to seek, locate and then to direct major flows of investment into strategic economic sectors.

The question is: at what point of development do the structures of authoritarian systems change from functionality to dysfunctionality? The turning-point will be reached at the moment when systematic reactions (output) are not sufficient to divert or oppress further inputs from social groups demanding political change. Then the system, after perhaps a prolonged period of unrest, enters the state of rapid decline – as in Nicaragua under Somoza, Iran under Rheza Pahlevi, the Philippines under Marcos and presently the People's Republic of China under Deng Xiaoping.

One may distinguish seven warning signs of decline: decline in the physical health or mental capability of an individual authoritarian leader; military defeats; economic problems; deep social tensions; the public impression of widespread abuse of political power; widespread opposition and emerging loose coalitions of oppositional groups; and changing dispositions of the military.[15] One might add the emergence of a major, attractive, political alternative – be it a person, a party or a policy.

The present situation in Taiwan is characterised by a combination of rising social tensions, a fragmented opposition and a ruling party amenable to gradual political and social change. In South Korea high social tensions, widespread though also fragmented opposition, and perhaps also changes in the military's attitudes pose the challenge for present power-holders. Whereas both countries' economic success stories followed a more or less parallel plot, their political reactions to the dynamics of social change are quite different. This leads us to the final question of the specific characteristics of political change after successful economic development.

The Structure of Change

In an article on authoritarian regimes in transition, Hans Binnendijk offers a very useful distinction between four different types of transition from authoritarianism:[16] first, 'uncontrolled revolutionary collapse, in which most institutions of the old society collapse along with the autocrat'; second, 'revolutionary restructuring' which brings a restructuring of government within the institutions of the old society; third, 'revolution by *coup d'état*' where the military is the dominant political institution and military coups offer the only possibility for political change; and finally,

> managed transition, a process through which authoritarian leaders themselves see the need for a peaceful transition of government and plan for it. Their motives are varied and the process is not always fully under their control, but such transitions are generally successful.

In the present situation Taiwan clearly belongs to type four, whereas for South Korea anything between types one and three seems at least theoretically possible. If one also assumes as necessary prerequisites for a successful transition towards democracy a relatively orderly transfer of power, a supportive democratic role model, a society that can support moderate political institutions and a competent leadership, dedicated to making democracy work – again Taiwan seems to be far better off than South Korea, where the short-term political outlook appears rather dark.

METHODOLOGICAL IMPLICATIONS

Unlike the two long-standing approaches to Third World political studies – the dependency and political development schools – this analysis and comparison of the success stories of Taiwan and South Korea leads us away from too normative an approach to the problems of development. This discussion should also put us on our guard against overly simplistic analyses and generalisations. The role of the state in Asia's economic development has been summarised by Milton and Rose Friedman in the following way:

> Malaysia, Singapore, Korea, Taiwan, Hong Kong and Japan – relying extensively on private markets – are thriving . . . By contrast, India, Indonesia, and Communist China, all relying heavily on central planning, have experienced economic stagnation.[17]

This suggests that the remedy for economic underdevelopment should be quite easy: 'less developed country (LDC) governments must aim at increasing the trade ratio by opening the economy and at reducing the extent of government intervention in the market.'[18]

The historical lesson from Taiwan and South Korea is, however, not as simple as that. The critical determinants for their respective economic successes were summarised here as an integrated strategy of redistribution before growth cycles at all major stages of development, combined with a heavy stress on education, a state-induced change from import substitution to export orientation and, finally, a clear effort at a managed transition towards democracy. Unlike the Friedmans, however, we are not suggesting that this strategy should be adopted by other less developed countries.

The Taiwanese and South Korean path to economic success was accurately described by Ramon Myers: a high domestic savings rate, which financed most of the capital formation; a large number of small and medium-sized enterprises, which contributed to a remarkably even income distribution; a highly competitive and open labour market with labour productivity that more than kept pace with the increases in real wages; a very stable growth rate of GDP and a low inflation rate, except immediately after the first oil crisis; and a significant share of output by state-controlled enterprises which declined rapidly, however, with the advancement of private enterprises.[19]

The real economic lesson to be learned from Taiwan and South Korea then, in simple words, is: not to rely on policies which aim at protecting selected industries, but instead to choose a 'directed market approach' which allows for development to take place in all sectors and leads to substantial productivity and growth rates, technical diffusion, increased employment and thus to a balanced share of income and – one hopes – to greater political stability.

In political terms, this economic lesson necessarily impels us towards a more pragmatic view of authoritarianism. There is a long-running debate in the literature on the specific interrelationship between democracy and economic development, concentrating on the question of which comes first. The preceding discussion suggests the need for more complicated and more heretical thinking.

NOTES

1. G. White and R. Wade (eds) *Developmental States in East Asia*, IDS Research Reports No 16 (Brighton, 1985) p. 18.

2. A. Amsden, 'Taiwan's Economic History: a Case of Etatisme and a Challenge to Dependency Theory', *Modern China* (1979) pp. 341–80; C. Y. Lin, *Industrialization in Taiwan, 1946–1972 Trade and Import-Substitution Policies for Developing Countries* (New York, 1979) pp. 22–6; S. Ho, *Economic Development of Taiwan, 1860–1970* (New Haven, Conn., 1978).
3. R. E. Barrett and M. K. Whyte, 'Dependency Theory and Taiwan: Analysis of a Deviant Case', *American Journal of Sociology* (May 1982) pp. 1064–89; and generally S. W. Y. Kuo, G. Ranis and J. C. H. Fei, *The Taiwan Success Story: Rapid Growth with Improved Distribution in the Republic of China, 1952–1979* (Boulder, Colo., 1981).
4. H. Liebenstein, 'Issues in Development Economics: an Introduction', *Social Research* (Summer 1980) p. 207.
5. S. S. Lieberman, 'Rural Development and Fertility Transition in South Asia: the case for a Broad-based Strategy', *Social Research* (Summer 1980) pp. 305–38.
6. *Far Eastern Economic Review* (27 October 1988) p. 62.
7. White and Wade, *Developmental States . . .*, p. 23.
8. I. Adelman, 'Economic Development and Political Change in Developing Countries', *Social Research* (Summer 1980) p. 222.
9. *Ibid.*, p. 224.
10. Y. S. Wu, 'Marketization of Politics: the Taiwan Experience', *Asian Survey* (April 1989).
11. J. Domes, 'Political Differentiation in Taiwan: Group Formation within the Ruling Party and the Opposition Circles, 1979–1980', *Asian Survey* (October 1981) p. 1011.
12. J. A. Caporasa, 'The State's Role in Third World Economic Growth', *Annals of the American Academy of Political and Social Science* (January 1982) p. 105.
13. C. Clark and J. Lemco, 'The Strong State and Development: a Growing List of Caveats', *Journal of Developing Societies* (Jan.–April 1988) pp. 1–8.
14. S. Chan, 'Developing Strength from Weakness: the State in Taiwan', *Journal of Developing Societies* (Jan.–April 1988) p. 43.
15. H. Binnendijk, 'Authoritarian Regimes in Transition', *Washington Quarterly* (Spring 1987) pp. 155–7.
16. *Ibid.*, pp. 157–9.
17. M. Friedman and R. Friedman, *Free to Choose: A Personal Statement* (New York, 1980) p. 57.
18. White and Wade, *The Developmental State . . .*, p. 3.
19. R. Myers, 'The Economic Development of the Republic of China on Taiwan 1965–81' in L. J. Lau (ed.) *Models of Development: A Comparative Study of Economic Growth in South-Korea and Taiwan* (San Francisco, Calif., 1986).

Index